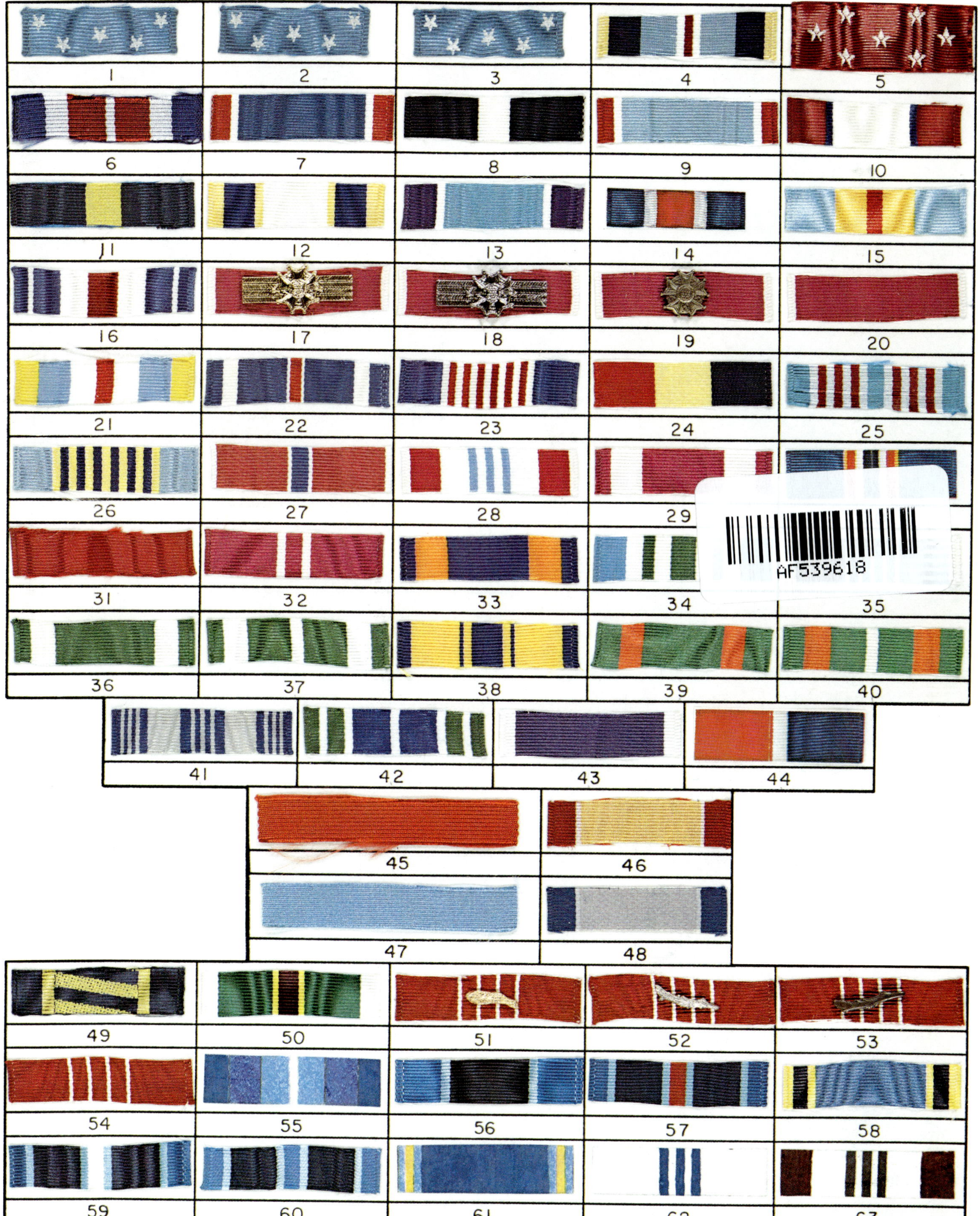

1
2
3
4
5
6
7
8
9
10
11
12
13
14
15
16
17
18
19
20
21
22
23
24
25
26
27
28
29
31
32
33
34
35
36
37
38
39
40
41
42
43
44
45
46
47
48
49
50
51
52
53
54
55
56
57
58
59
60
61
62
63

PLATE I

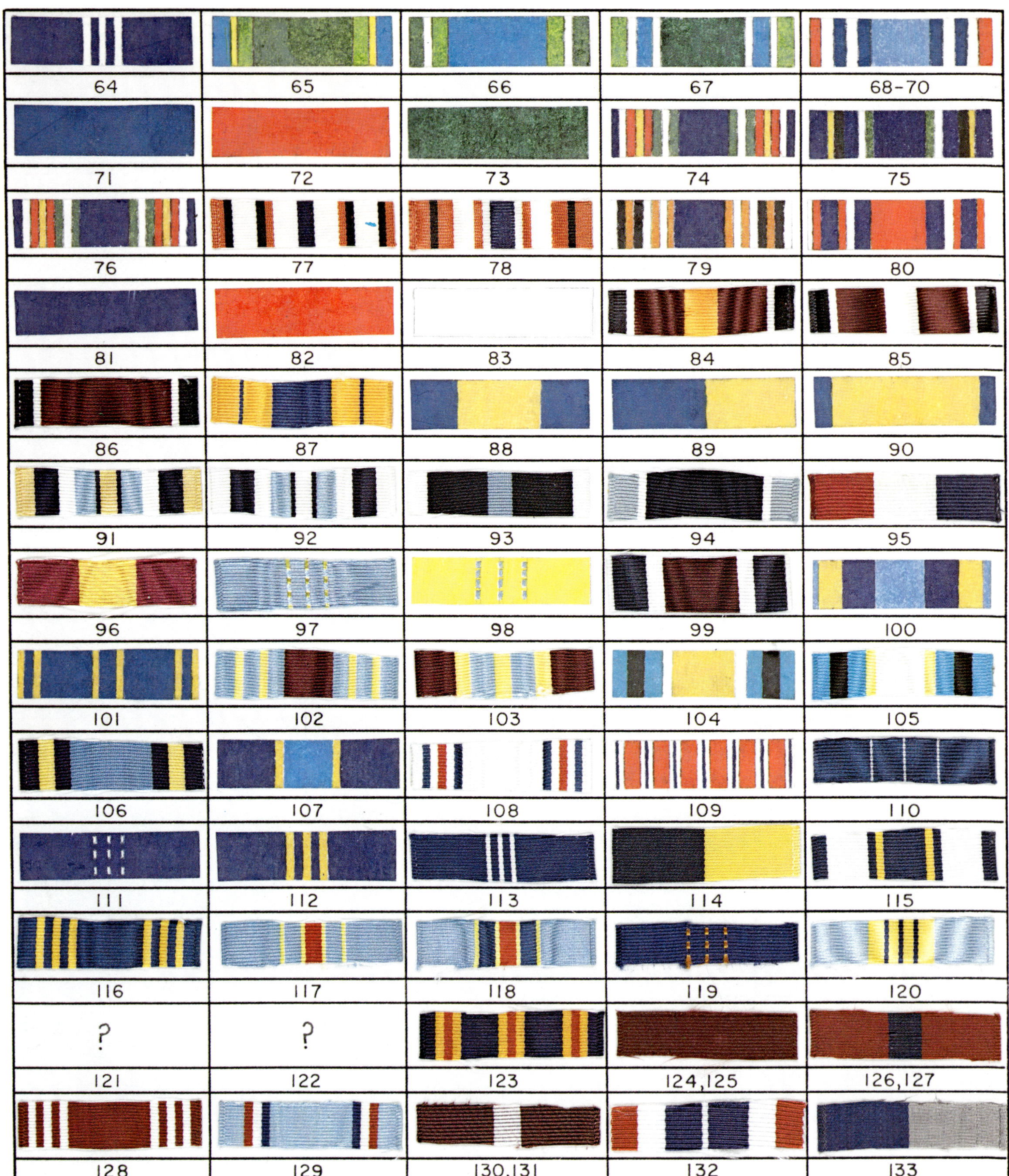
64
65
66
67
68-70
71
72
73
74
75
76
77
78
79
80
81
82
83
84
85
86
87
88
89
90
91
92
93
94
95
96
97
98
99
100
101
102
103
104
105
106
107
108
109
110
111
112
113
114
115
116
117
118
119
120
?
?
121
122
123
124,125
126,127
128
129
130,131
132
133

PLATE II

134,135
136
137
138
139
140,141
142
143
144
145,146
147
148
149,150
151
152
153,154
155
156,157
158
159,160
161,162
163,164
165
166,167
168,169
170,171
172,173
174,175
176
177
178
179
180
181
182
183
184
185
186
187
188
189
190
191
192
193
194
195
196
197
198
199
200
201
202
203,204
205
206
207
208-213
214
215
216
a 217 b
218
219
220
221
222
223

PLATE III

224
225
226
227
228
229
230
231
232
233
234
235
236
237
238
239
240
241
242
243
244
245
246
247
248
249
250
251
252
253
254
255
256
257
258
259
260
261
262
263
264
265
266
267
268
269
270
271
272
273
274
275
276
277
278
279
280
281
282
283
284
285
286
287
288
289
290
291
292
293

PLATE IV

MEDALS
MILITARY AND CIVILIAN
OF THE
UNITED STATES

MEDALS, MILITARY AND CIVILIAN of the UNITED STATES

By
David Borthick and Jack Britton

Art Work By
Cliff Cates
Ray Borthick
David Borthick

Ribbon Chart By
Daniel M. Byrne

Hardcover Edition ISBN - 0-912958-25-1
Spiralbound Edition ISBN 0-912958-26-X

Library of Congress
Catalog Card Number
83-50563

Published By

M.C.N. PRESS (Military Collectors' News Press)

P.O. Box 702073 Tulsa, Oklahoma 74170

Credits
Typesetter - Robert C. Miller, 2778 Ridgewood, Sanford, Florida 32771

****

Cover Photo

Department of the Air Force

The list of illustrations that follows does not necessarily follow order of precedence. For the correct order of precedence see: ARMY-AR 672-5-1; NAVY AND MARINE CORPS - SECNAVINST 1650.1D; AIR FORCE - AFM 35-10A; and COAST GUARD-PERS MAN (CG-207).

LIST OF ILLUSTRATIONS

DEDICATION

This book is dedicated to the men and women who have served their country and thus received the awards which this book covers.

PREFACE

This book is intended as a guide for collectors and historians. The obverse and reverse of United States decorations and medals are beautifully designed and executed, but they are difficult to photograph in such a manner as to show their fine detail. For this reason line drawings have been used rather than photos. In either case the full beauty of these medals cannot be fully appreciated until you have seen one in hand.

The information that collectors seek varies as much as their different collections; for that reason I have included as much information as possible.

There were many hands working on this project and my thanks go to all of them. But I would especially like to thank my wife, Michelle, and my brother, Ray, who have helped me in this effort.

NOTE: The drawings in this book are not to scale.

We hope this book will be of help to you, in identifying United States Medals.

INTRODUCTION

Decorations and Medals represent more than the Nation's grateful acknowledgment of fidelity. They are a constant incentive to performance of outstanding deeds. The importance of medals is now universally acknowledged, and in almost every country they are preserved with reverent care. At a glance they can take you into the past. They recall men, events, deeds, or circumstances, which have influenced the life of this young Nation. History is brought to life with the concise and faithful testimony of these silent witnesses.

A.

OBVERSE REVERSE

A. Andre Medal

AWARDED FOR: The capture of Major John Andre, a British intelligence officer. It was awarded to only three American Militiamen. This medal, was the first decoration created by Congress in 1780.
Ref. Pg. 130

B. The Kearny Medal for Officers

Awarded For: Presented to all officers who had served honorably in battle under General Kearny.

C. The Kearny Cross

Awarded For: Presented to all Non-Commissioned Officers and Privates who had distinguished themselves in battle.

B. OBVERSE C. REVERSE

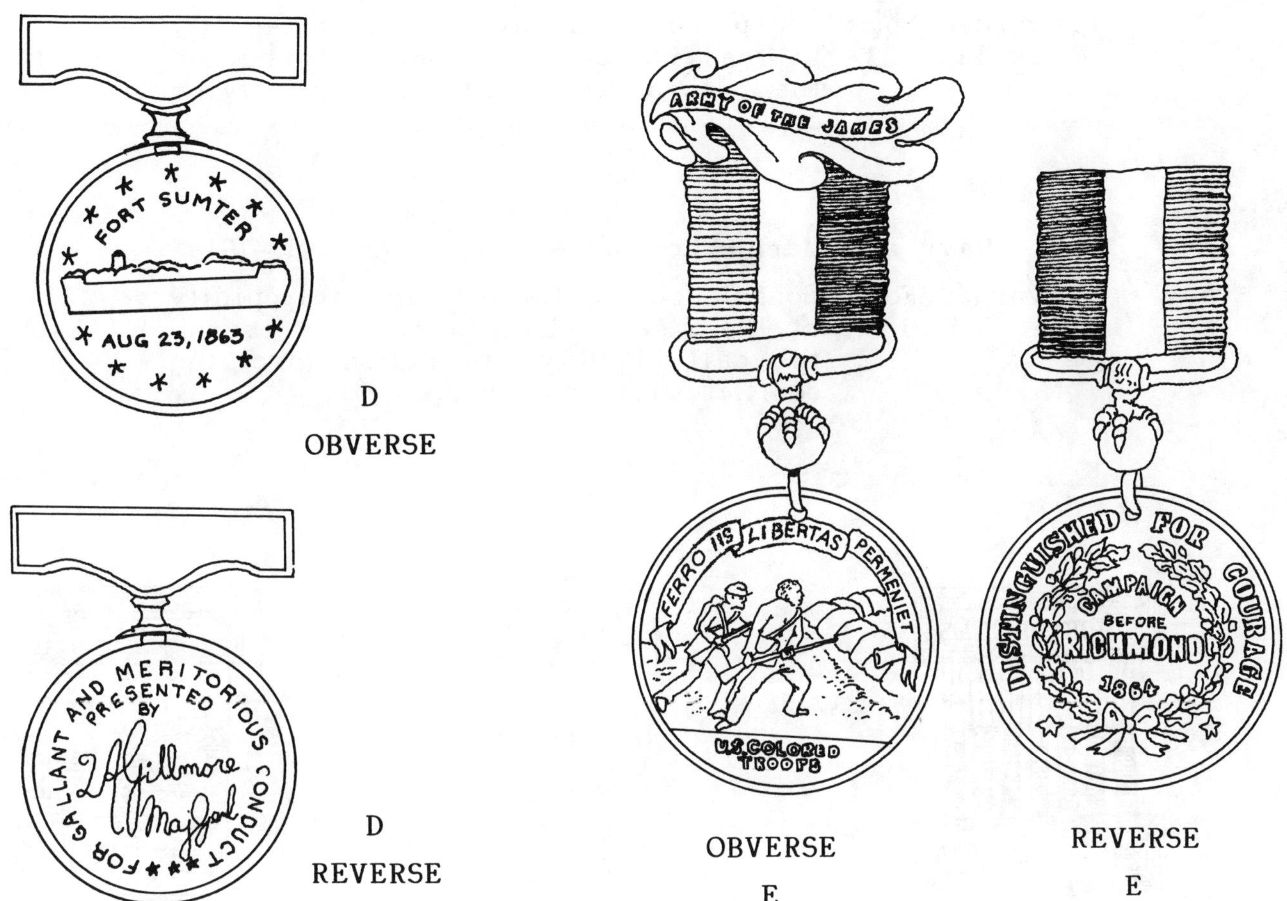

D OBVERSE

D REVERSE

OBVERSE E

REVERSE E

D. Gillmore or Fort Sumter Medal

Awarded For: Gallant and meritorious conduct during the operations before Charleston.
Ref. Pg. 131

E. Butler or Colored Troops Medal

Awarded For: Gallantry in action in the storming of New Market Heights, September 29, 1864.
Ref. Pg. 132

F. Navy and Marine Corps Medal of Honor 1861-1913

Awarded For: Conspicuous gallantry and intrepidity at the risk of life, above and beyond the call of duty, in action involving conflict with an enemy.
Ref. Pg. 133

G. Navy and Marine Corps Medal of Honor 1913-1919

Awarded For: Conspicuous gallantry and intrepidity at the risk of life, above and beyond the call of duty, in action involving conflict with an enemy.
Ref. Pg. 133

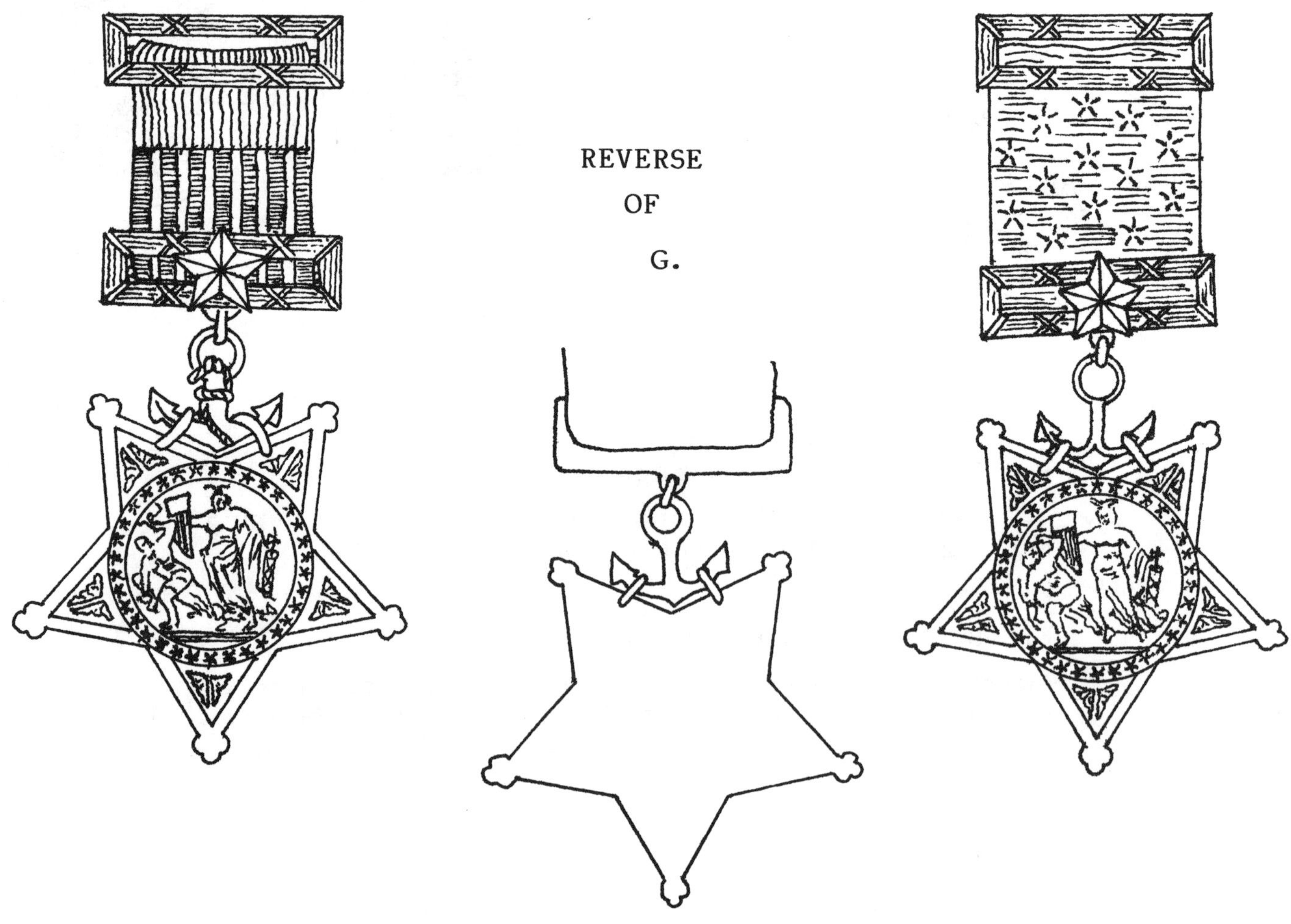

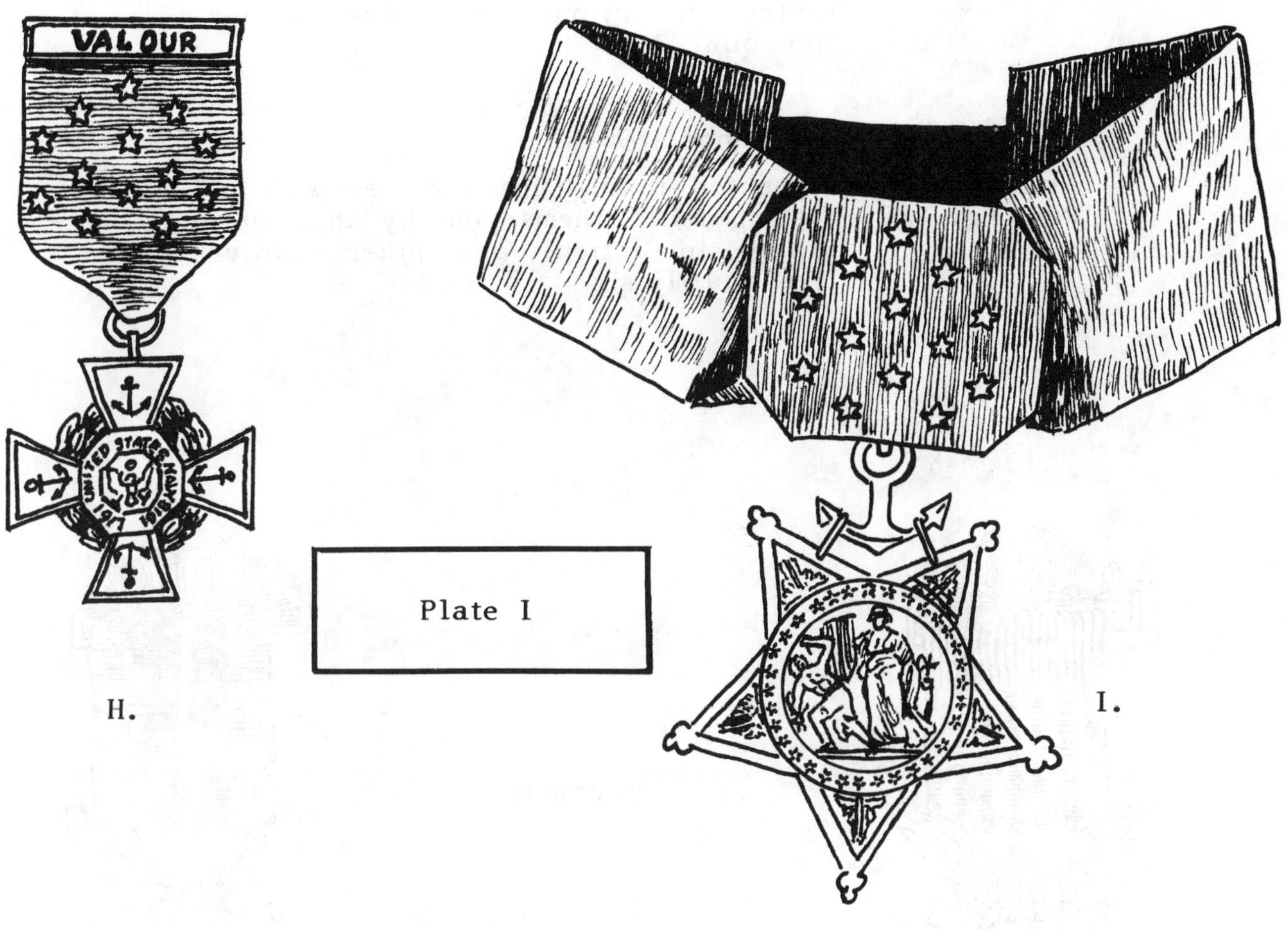

H. Medal of Honor Navy and Marine Corps 1919–1942

Awarded For: Ref. Pg. 134	Conspicuous gallantry and intrepidity at the risk of life, above and beyond the call of duty, in action involving conflict with an enemy.

I. Medal of Honor Navy and Marine Corps 1942 to Present

Awarded For: Ref. Pg. 134	Conspicuous gallantry and intrepidity at the risk of life, above and beyond the call of duty, in action involving conflict with an enemy.

I. Army Medal of Honor 1862–1896

Awarded For: Presented to officers and men who had distinguished themselves by their gallantry in action, and other soldier-like qualities.

Ref. Pg. 135

J. Army Medal of Honor 1896–1904

Awarded For: Presented to officers and men who had distinguished themselves by their gallantry in action, and other soldier-like qualities.

Ref. Pg. 135

I.

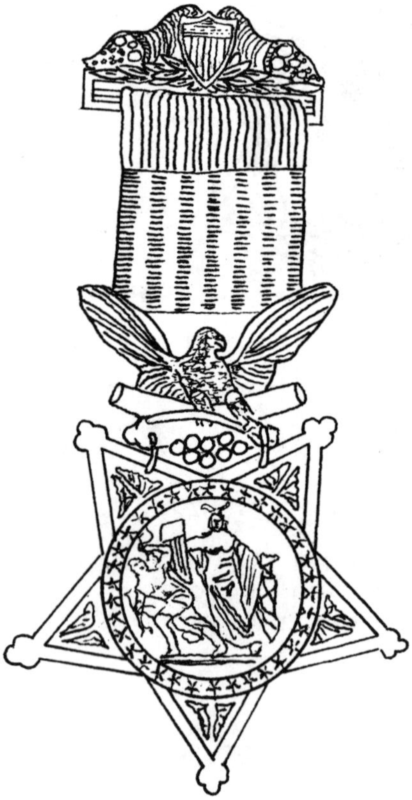

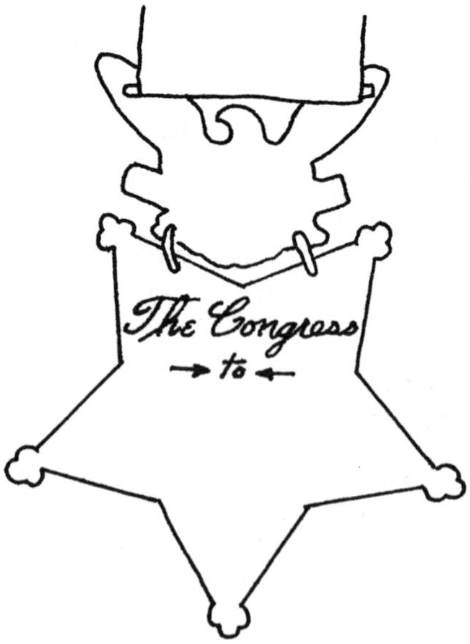

J.

REVERSE

The Congress

→ to ←

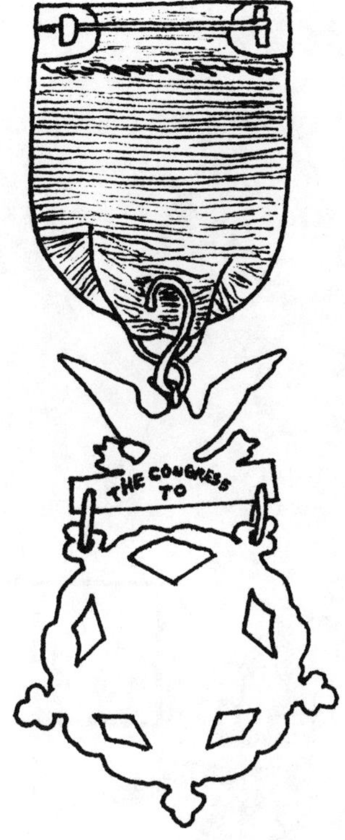

K.
OBVERSE

K.
REVERSE

K. Army Medal of Honor 1904–1945

Awarded For: Conspicuous gallantry and intrepidity at the risk of life, above and beyond the call of duty, in action involving actual conflict with an enemy.
Ref. Pg. 136

2. Army Medal of Honor 1945 to the Present

Awarded For: Ref. Pg. 136	Conspicuous gallantry and intrepidity at the risk of life, above and beyond the call of duty, in action involving actual conflict with an enemy.

Plate I

2.

Plate I

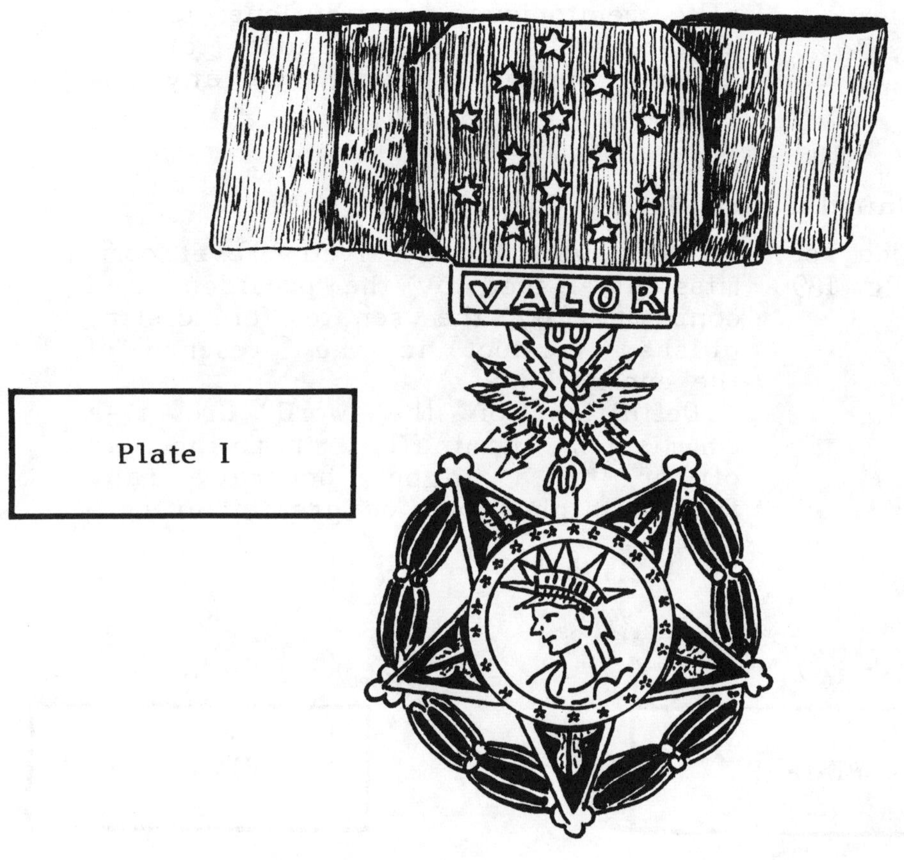

3.

3. Air Force Medal of Honor

Awarded For: Conspicuous gallantry and intrepidity at the risk of life, above and beyond the call of duty, in action involving actual conflict with an enemy.

Ref. Pg. 137

4. Congressional Space Medal of Honor

Awarded For: Performance of their duties, distinguished him or herself, by exceptionally meritorious contributions to the welfare of a mission and/or of the nation, and/or mankind, by any astronaut.

Ref. Pg. 138

5. United States Marine Corps Brevet Medal

Awarded For: Marines who had received brevet commissions issued by the president and confirmed by the senate for distinguished conduct in the presence of the enemy.

Definition of the word brevet--a commission nominally promoting an officer to a higher honorary rank without higher pay or greater authority.

Ref. Pg. 139

4.

Plate I

5.

Plate I

Plate I

6.

OBVERSE

M.

REVERSE

L.

6. Certificate of Merit, Army

Awarded For: Ref. Pg. 139	Having distinguished himself in the services of the United States in battle or peacetime for heroism involving saving life or property at the risk of ones own or for other services that the president of the United States thought were deserving of this certificate.

L. Revenue Cutter Service Cardenas Medal of Honor

Awarded For: Ref. Pg. 140	Recognition of the gallantry of the officers and men of the Hudson, who in the face of the enemy under heavy fire towed the Winslow out of range of enemy fire.

M. Bailey Medal - Discontinued

Awarded For: Ref. Pg. 140	Awarded annually to one naval apprentice with an outstanding record.

7. Army Distinguished Service Cross

Awarded For: Ref. Pg. 141	Anyone who distinguishes himself or herself by exceptionally meritorious service to the government in a duty of great responsibility, or for extraordinary heroism in connections with military operations against an armed enemy.

8. Navy Distinguished Service Cross (Navy Cross)

Awarded For: Ref. Pg. 142	While serving in any capacity with the naval service of the United States, distinguishes himself or herself by extraordinary heroism in connection with military operations against an armed enemy.

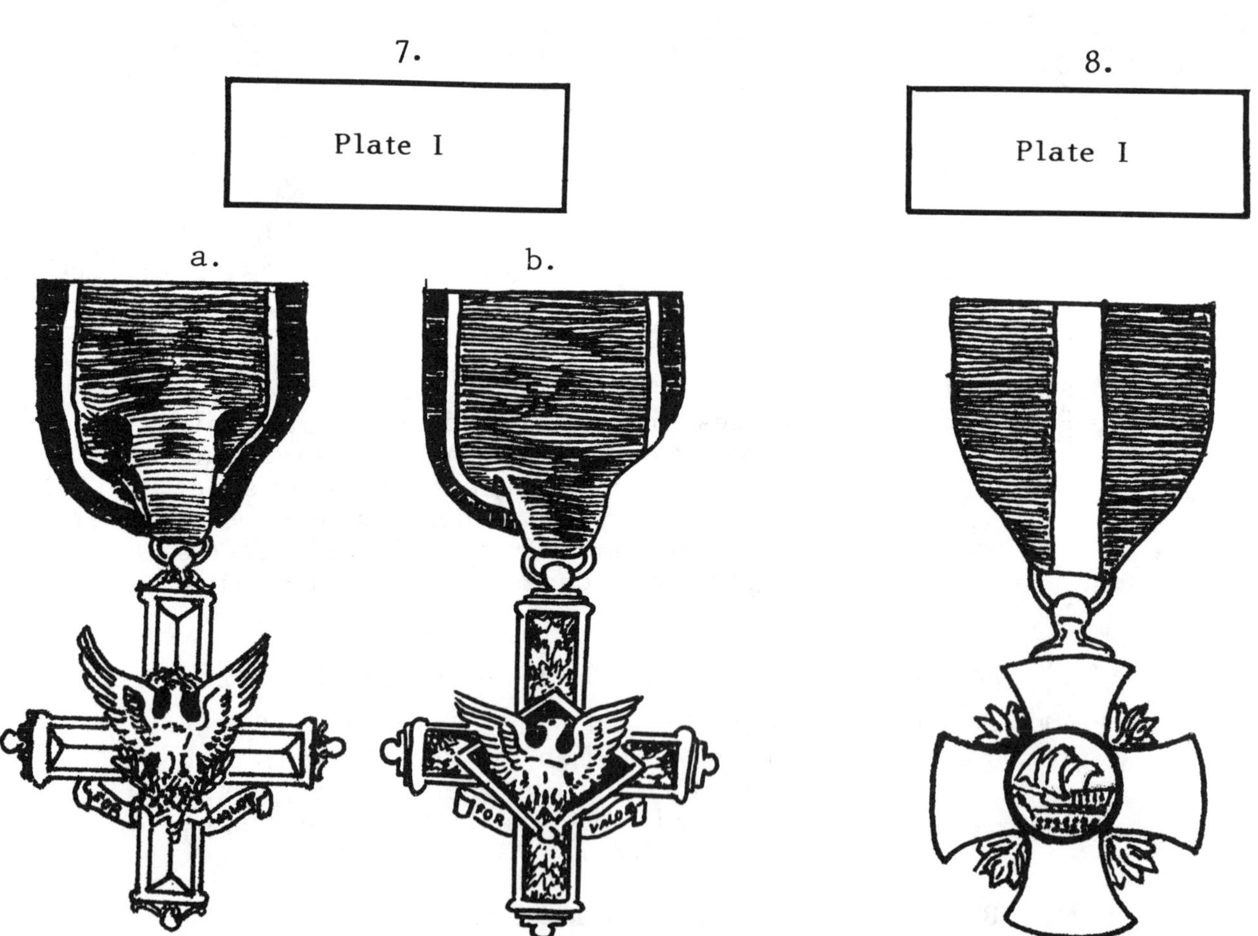

Plate I

Plate I

9.

10.

9. Air Force Distinguished Service Cross

Awarded For: Combat action only, distinguished or extraordinary heroism in connection with military operations against an armed enemy.
Ref. Pg. 142

10. Army Distinguished Service Medal

Awarded For: Exceptionally meritorious service to the government in a duty of great responsibility.
Ref. Pg. 143

11. Navy Distinguished Service Medal

Awarded For: Exceptionally meritorious service to the government in a duty of great responsibility.
Ref. Pg. 144

11.

Plate I

a.

b.

12. Air Force Distinguished Service Medal

Awarded For:	Exceptionally meritorious service to the government in a duty of great responsibility.
Ref. Pg. 145	

13. Coast Guard Distinguished Service Medal

Awarded For:	Exceptionally meritorious service to the government in a duty of great responsibility.
Ref. Pg. 145	

14. Merchant Marine Distinguished Service Medal

Awarded For:	To any person in the American Merchant Marine, who on or after September 3, 1939, has distinguished himself in the line of duty.
Ref. Pg. 146	

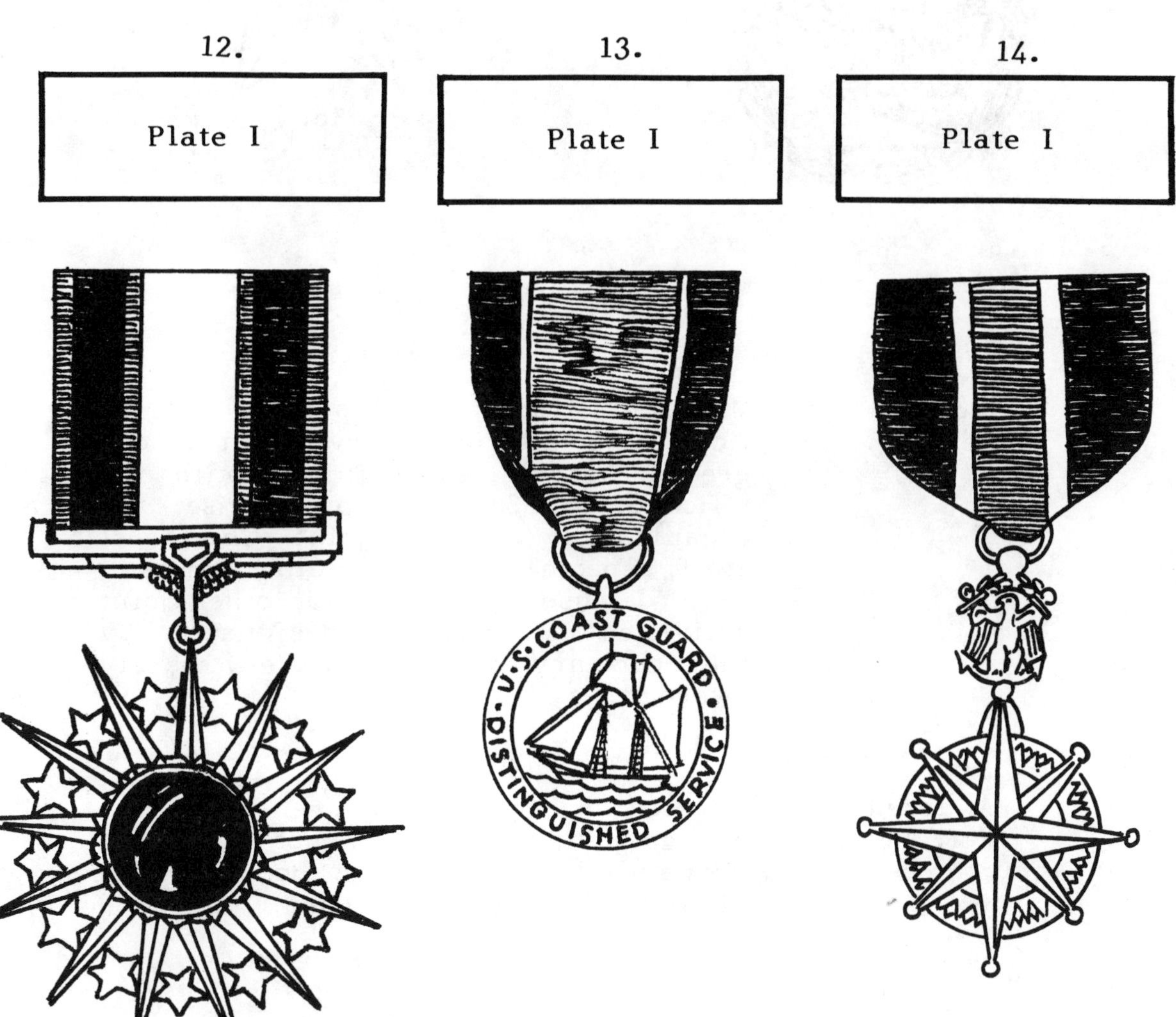

Plate I

15.

Plate I

16.

15. Defense Distinguished Service Medal

Awarded For: Military officers who perform exceptionally meritorious service in a degree of great responsibility with the office of the Secretary of Defense, the organization of the Joint Chiefs of Staff, special or outstanding command in a defense agency or for other joint activities as may be designated by the Secretary of Defense. Very rarely awarded.

Ref. Pg. 146

16. Silver Star

Awarded For: Citation of an officer or enlisted man for gallantry in action not sufficient to warrant the Medal of Honor or the Distinguished Service Cross.

Ref. Pg. 147

17. Legion of Merit, Chief Commander

Awarded For: Ref. Pg. 148	Exceptionally meritorious conduct in the performance of outstanding services. Usually awarded to heads of foreign states for service to the United States.

18. Legion of Merit, Commander

Awarded For: Ref. Pg. 149	Usually awarded to supreme commanders of foreign military who have distinguished themselves by exceptionally meritorious conduct in the performance of outstanding service to the United States.

17.

Plate I

18.

Plate I

Plate I

19.

Plate I

20.

19. Legion of Merit, Officer

Awarded For: Ref. Pg. 150	Usually awarded to foreign military officers who have distinguished themselves by exceptionally meritorious conduct in the performance of outstanding service to the United States.

20. Legion of Merit, Legionnaire

Awarded For: Ref. Pg. 151	Usually awarded to officers of the United States military who have distinguished themselves by exceptionally meritorious conduct in the performance of outstanding service to the United States.

21. Defense Superior Service Medal

Awarded For: Ref. Pg. 152	Exceptionally meritorious service in a degree of great responsibility with the office of the Secretary of Defense.

22. Distinguished Flying Cross

Awarded For: Ref. Pg. 152	After April 16, 1917, distinguishes himself or herself by heroism or extraordinary achievement while participating in an aerial flight.

23. Army Soldiers Medal

Awarded For: Ref. Pg. 153	Heroism not involving actual armed conflict with an enemy.

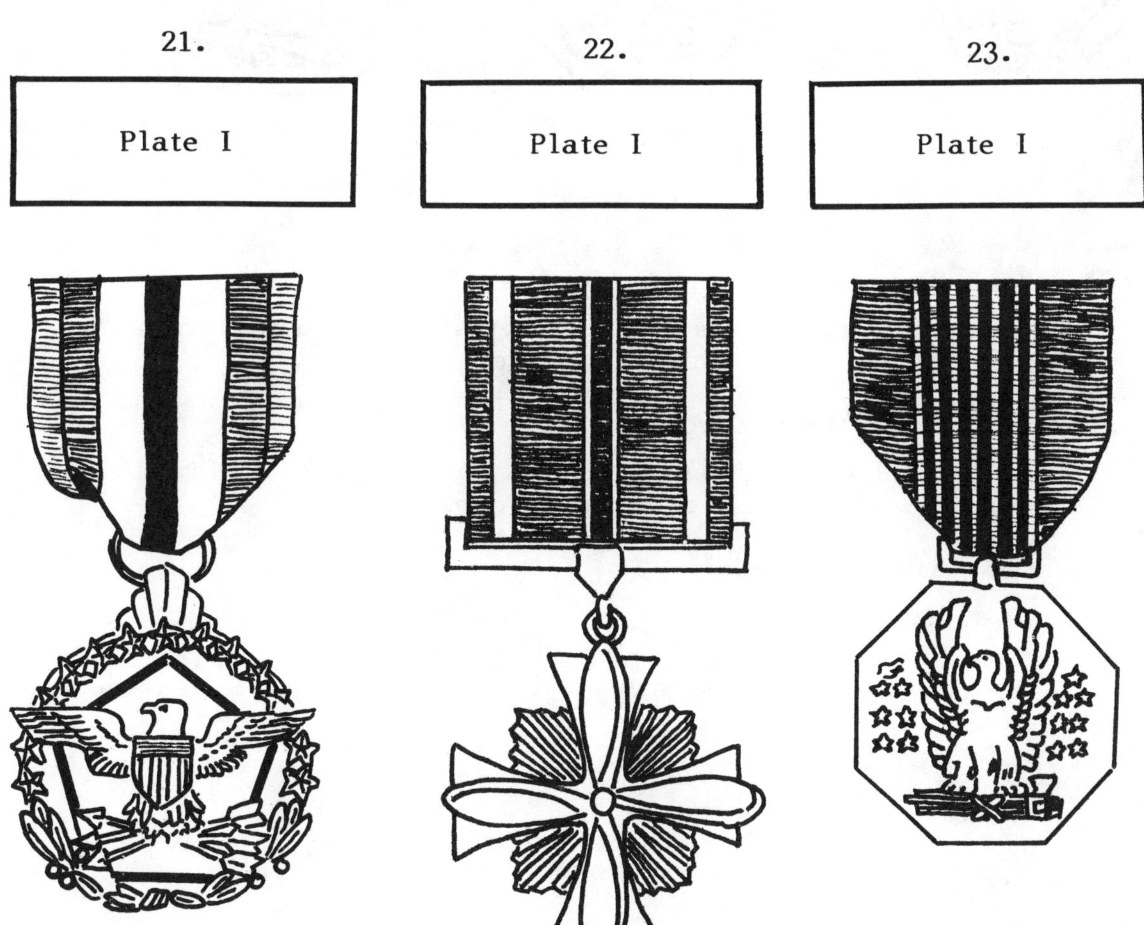

Plate I	Plate I	Plate I

24.

25.

26.

24. Navy and Marine Corps Medal

Awarded For: Heroism not involving actual armed conflict with an enemy.
Ref. Pg. 153

25. Coast Guard Medal

Awarded For: Heroism not involving actual armed conflict with an enemy.
Ref. Pg. 154

26. Airman's Medal

Awarded For: Heroism not involving actual armed conflict with an enemy.
Ref. Pg. 154

27. Bronze Star

Awarded For: Ref. Pg. 154	Any individual in the Armed Forces of the United States, who on or after December 7, 1941, shall have distinguished himself for heroic or military achievement or service not involving aerial flight.

28. Department of Defense Meritorious Service Medal

Awarded For: Ref. Pg. 155	Officers who perform exceptionally meritorious service in a degree of great responsibility with the office of Secretary of Defense, the organization of Joint Chiefs of Staff, special or outstanding command in a defense agency or for other joint activities as may be designated by the Secretary of Defense, but is not to the degree to merit a Defense Superior Service Medal.

29. Meritorious Service Medal

Awarded For: Ref. Pg. 156	Outstanding meritorious achievement or service to the United States by any member of the Armed Forces. Some portion of the completed service achievement must have been made on or after January 16, 1969.

27.

Plate I

28.

Plate I

29.

Plate I

Plate I

30.

Plate I

31.

Plate I

32.

30. Merchant Marine Meritorious Service Medal

Awarded For: Ref. Pg. 156	Meritorious conduct not of a sufficient nature to warrant the Merchant Marine Distinguished Service Medal.

31. Specially Meritorious Medal

Awarded For: Ref. Pg. 157	Recognition of officers and men for acts of specially meritorious service, other than in battle, during the war with Spain. Seldom awarded.

32. Medal for Merit

Awarded For: Ref. Pg. 157	Civilians or foreign nationals who distinguish themselves in the performance of outstanding service to the United States.

33. Air Medal

Awarded For: Ref. Pg. 158	Members of the Armed Forces, must have distinguished themselves, after September 8, 1939, by meritorious achievement in flight, that does not warrant a Distinguished Flying Cross.

34. Joint Service Commendation

Awarded For: Ref. Pg. 159	Any member of the United States Armed Forces who distinguishes himself or herself by meritorious achievement or service. The individual must be serving with either the Joint Chiefs of Staff, National Security Agency, Defense Supply, or in a joint task force control group of command.

35. Army Commendation

Awarded For: Ref. Pg. 160	Outstanding performance either in combat or non-combat and receive letters of commendation from a superior grade officer.

Plate I	Plate I	Plate I

36.

37.

38.

36. Navy Commendation Medal

Awarded For: Outstanding performance either in combat or non-combat and receive letters of commendation from a superior grade officer.
Ref. Pg. 160

37. Coast Guard Commendation Medal

Awarded For: Outstanding performance either in combat or non-combat and receive letters of commendation from a superior grade officer.
Ref. Pg. 161

38. Air Force Commendation Medal

Awarded For: Outstanding performance either in combat or non-combat and receive letters of commendation from a superior grade officer. This medal is awarded to individuals commended after March 24, 1958. Prior to this date, Air Force recipients received the Army decoration.
Ref. Pg. 161

39. Navy Achievement Medal

Awarded For: It is earned by officers for outstanding professional achievement or leadership and by enlisted men only for leadership. This medal was formerly titled the Navy Commendation for Achievement.

Ref. Pg. 162

40. Coast Guard Achievement Medal

Awarded For: Outstanding achievement and superior performance of duty by commissioned and enlisted men of the United States Coast Guard Reserve in the grade of lieutenant commander and under, on or after April 1, 1967. This medal is strictly for non-combat service.

Ref. Pg. 162

39.

Plate I

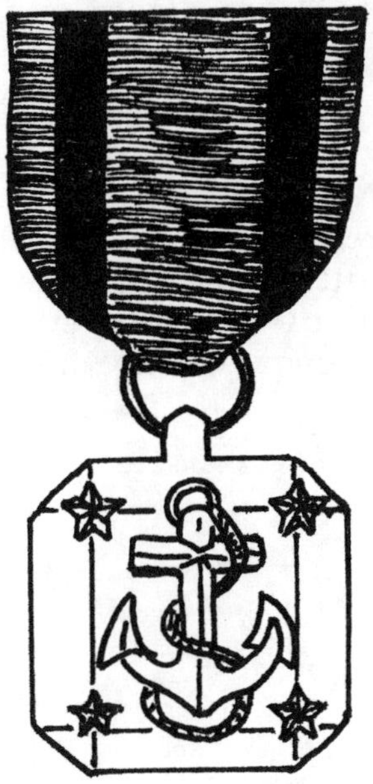

40.

Plate I

Plate I

41.

Plate I

42.

41. Air Force Achievement Medal

Awarded For: Ref. Pg. 163	Outstanding achievement and superior performance of duty by commissioned and enlisted men of the United States Air Force and Air Force Reserve in the grade of major and under.

42. Army Achievement Medal

Awarded For: Ref. Pg. 163	Outstanding achievement and superior performance of duty by commissioned and enlisted men of the United States Army and Army Reserve in the grade of major and under.

43. The Purple Heart

Awarded For:
Ref. Pg. 164

This decoration holds a very unique position in that it can be earned only by being wounded. An attendant requirement is that the wound must have been received as a direct result of enemy actions. Currently, the Purple Heart may be awarded to members of the United States Armed Forces and to civilian citizens of the United States, male or female, who, while serving with the Armed Forces, are wounded due to the result of a direct enemy action.

44. Mariners Medal, Merchant Marines

Awarded For:
Ref. Pg. 165

To any person who, while serving on any vessel in the American Merchant Marine during the war period, is wounded, suffers physical injury, or suffers through dangerous exposure as a result of an enemy of the United States.

43.

Plate I

44.

Plate I

OBVERSE

REVERSE

GOLD
MEDAL

Plate I

45. GOLD, FIRST RIBBON

Plate I

47. SILVER, FIRST
RIBBON

SILVER
MEDAL

OBVERSE

REVERSE

Plate I

46.

Plate I

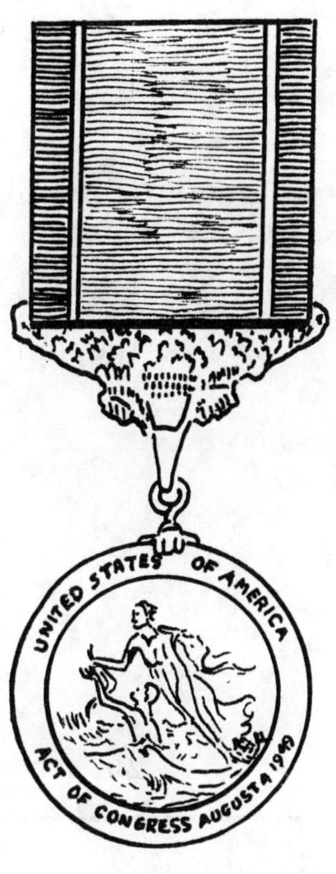

48.

46. Gold Lifesaving Medal Current Type

Awarded For: To civilians and members of the United States Armed Forces who endanger their lives in saving or attempting to save lives of others from dangers of the sea.

Ref. Pg. 166

48. Silver Lifesaving Medal Current Type

Awarded For: Under the same general conditions as the Gold Lifesaving Medal; however, it is secondary in importance and permits a lesser degree of heroism for for the award.

Ref. Pg. 167

49. National Security Medal-Obsolete

Awarded For: Any individual U.S. or foreign, military or civilian, for distinguished achievement or acts of valor on or after July 2, 1947; in the field of intelligence relating to national security.

Ref. Pg. 168

50. National Security Agency Exceptional Service Medal

Awarded For: Exceptional services to the Agency of National Security, in the interest of the United States.

Ref. Pg. 168

51.-54.

N.

Plate I	Plate I	Plate I	Plate I
51.	52.	53.	54.

51. – 54. Medal of Freedom – Obsolete

Awarded For: Ref. Pg. 169 — To any person other than a member of the Armed Forces of the United States who, after December 6, 1941, performed a meritorious act or service which aided the United States or its allies in the prosecution of a war against an armed enemy or during any period of national emergency declared by the president or the Congress furthered the interests or security of the United States or its allies during such period when the award of any other United States military decoration was not deemed appropriate.

N. Presidential Medal of Freedom

Awarded For: Ref. Pg. 170 — Those who should be honored for meritorious contributions to security or national interest of the United States, world peace, cultural, or other significant public or private endeavors. Awarded by the President of the United States at his discretion to either civilian or military Americans or foreigners. This is primarily a diplomatic order available for presentation to distinguished individuals for service to the United States that is not precisely designated.

OBVERSE O. REVERSE

O. Chaplains Medal for Heroism

Awarded For: Ref. Pg. 171	Extreme heroism and great sacrifice made by four chaplains, during World War II, when their Army transport S.S. Dorchester was torpedoed and sunk 100 miles off the coast of Greenland on February 3, 1943. The four men, Rev. George L. Fox, Rabbi Alexander D. Goode, Rev. Clark W. Bowing, and Father John R. Washington aided troops into lifeboats, and when life preservers were exhausted, they gave their own to others.

55. NASA Distinguished Service Medal Type I

Awarded For: Individuals with distinguished service who contribute to substantial progress in the United States Aeronautical and space explorations.
Ref. Pg. 172

56. NASA Distinguished Service Medal Type II

Awarded For: Individuals with distinguished service who contribute to substantial progress in the United States Aeronautical and space explorations.
Ref. Pg. 172

57. NASA Medal for Exceptional Bravery

Awarded For: Exemplary and courageous handling of an emergency in activities by individuals, regardless of personal danger, which saves lives and/or government property.
Ref. Pg. 173

55.	56.	57.
Plate I	Plate I	Plate I

Plate I

Plate I

58.

59.

58. **NASA Exceptional Service Medal**

Awarded For: Unusual services or creative ability
Ref. Pg. 173 in engineering, administrative, or space-related activities which contribute to a NASA mission.

59. **NASA Medal for Exceptional Scientific Achievement**

Awarded For: A high order of creative scientific
Ref. Pg. 174 accomplishments.

60. NASA Outstanding Leadership Medal

Awarded For: Ref. Pg. 174	Outstanding leadership which results in technological or administrative improvements for the agency.

61. NASA Medal for Distinguished Public Service

Awarded For: Ref. Pg. 175	Meritorious contributions that have aided work or scientific progress of NASA's mission by any United States citizen not employed by the United States government.

P.
OBVERSE

Q.
OBVERSE

R.
OBVERSE

S.
OBVERSE

T.
OBVERSE

REVERSE OF ALL

P. Central Intelligence Agency Distinguished Intelligence Cross, Ref. Pg. 175

Awarded For: Extraordinary heroism in the line of duty.

Q. Central Intelligence Agency Intelligence Star, Ref. Pg. 176

Awarded For: Courageous action in the line of duty.

R. Central Intelligence Agency Distinguished Intelligence Medal Ref. Pg. 176

Awarded For: Outstanding Service.

S. Central Intelligence Agency Intelligence Medal for Merit, Ref. Pg. 177

Awarded For: Meritorious Service.

T. Central Intelligence Agency Career Intelligence Medal

Awarded For: Outstanding achievement in the field
Ref. Pg. 177 of intelligence.

Plate I	Plate I	Plate II

62.

63.

64.

62. U.S. State Department Distinguished Honor Medal

Awarded For: Exceptionally outstanding service to the department or the government for achievements of marked national or international significance; for exceptionally outstanding service or leadership in administering programs which result in successful accomplishments of mission, or in major attainment of objectives, or specific accomplishment to meet unique or emergency situations; or for outstanding accomplishments over a prolonged period that involve the exercise of authority or judgement in the public interest.

Ref. Pg. 178

63. U.S. State Department Superior Honor Medal

Awarded For: Outstanding service to the department or government, service of significance where the interest of the United States are involved.

Ref. Pg. 178

64. U.S. State Department Meritorious Honor Award

Awarded For: Outstanding service in the conduct or improvement of the program or operations of the department.

Ref. Pg. 179

65. Environmental Protection Agency Exceptional Service Medal

Awarded For: One of the following; outstanding service to the mission, outstanding leadership, major contributions to scientific and technological knowledge, distinguished authorship, notable creative service, heroic action.
Ref. Pg. 179

66. Environmental Protection Agency Superior Service Medal

Awarded For: One of the following; highly meritorious service to environmental protection, the demonstration of exceptional initiative or creative ability, unusual courage or competence in an emergency related to employment, meritorious authorship, the performance of assigned task in such an outstanding manner that monetary recognition is inadequate.
Ref. Pg. 180

67. Environmental Protection Agency Commendable Service Medal

Awarded For: Highly competent performance of duties in the agency over a long period of time.
Ref. Pg. 180

65.	66.	67.
Plate II	Plate II	Plate II

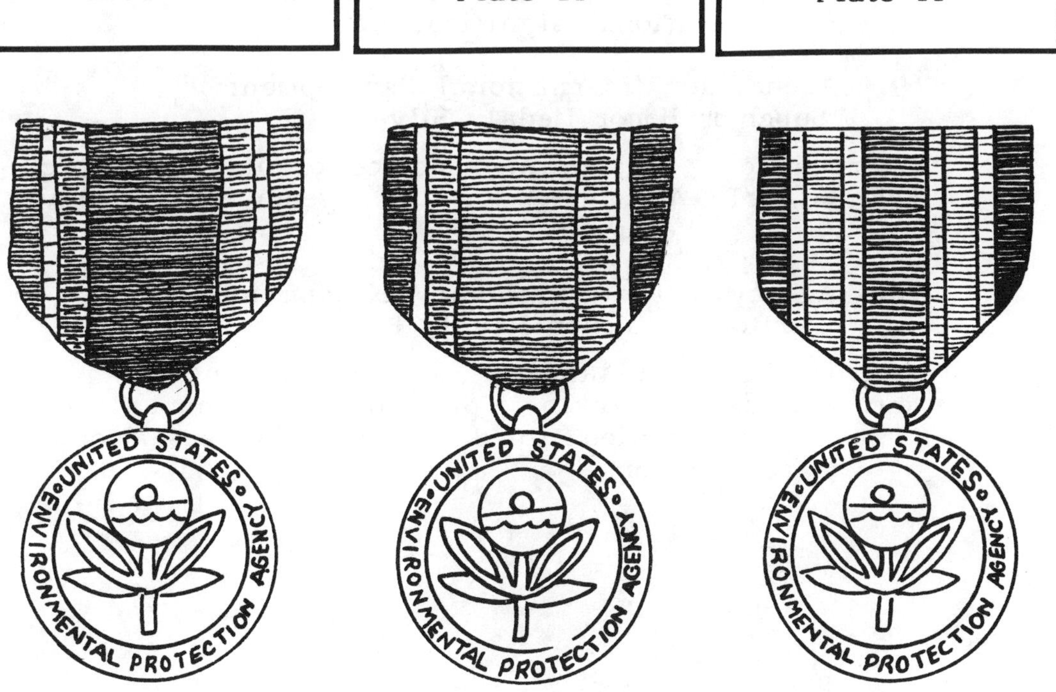

Plate II

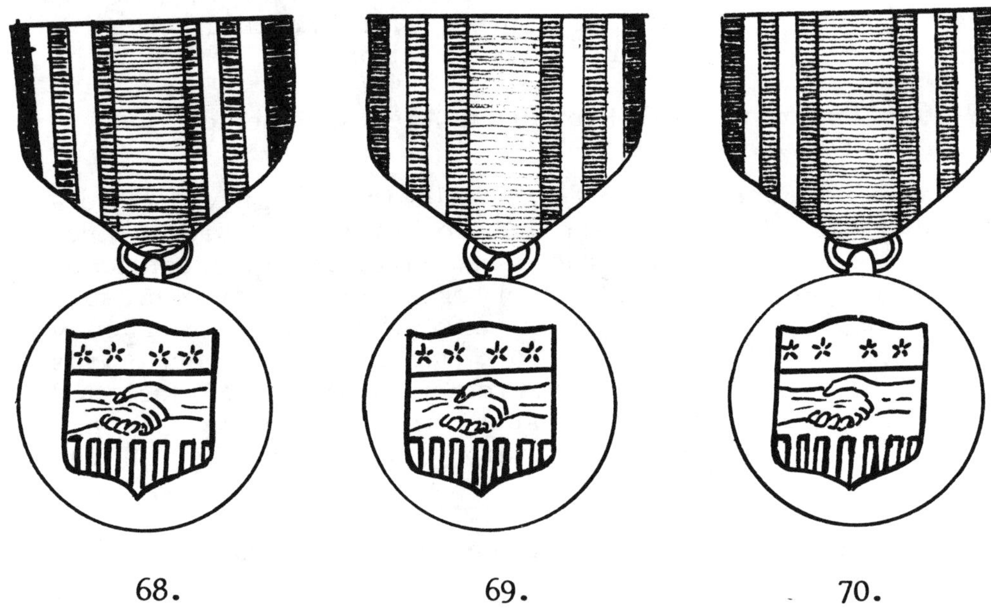

68. 69. 70.

68. Agency for International Development Distinguished Honor Medal, Gold

Awarded For: Exceptionally outstanding service to the agency or the government for achievements of national or international significance.

Ref. Pg. 181

69. Agency for International Development Superior Honor Medal, Silver

Awarded For: Outstanding service or increased productivity for the agency of the government.

Ref. Pg. 181

70. Agency for International Development Meritorious Honor Medal, Bronze

Awarded For: Outstanding service in conducting or improving programs or unusual devotion to duty under adverse conditions.

Ref. Pg. 182

71. Veterans Administration Exceptional Service Medal

Awarded For: Outstanding leadership, skill or ability in administration or for performance of duty, acts of heroism or creation of major programs benefiting the Veterans Adminstration or the government or science.
Ref. Pg. 182

72. Veterans Administration Meritorious Service Medal

Awarded For: Performance of duty in such an outstanding manner that other recognition is inadequate, for developing new work methods or for courage in emergencies.
Ref. Pg. 182

73. Veterans Administration Distinguished Career Medal

Awarded For: Employees who have earned this recognition on their retirement or on resignation, for work characterized by outstanding efficiency, integrity and dedication.
Ref. Pg. 183

71.	72.	73.
Plate II	Plate II	Plate II

Plate II

74.

Plate II

75.

Plate II

76.

74. General Accounting Office Distinguished Service Medal

Awarded For: Exceptional efficiency, usually over a period of ten years or more. Not more than five persons may receive it in any one year.
Ref. Pg. 183

75. General Accounting Office Career Development Medal

Awarded For: To recognize employees who have contributed significantly to public service. Not more than ten persons may receive it in any one year.
Ref. Pg. 184

76. General Accounting Office Meritorious Service Medal

Awarded For: Superior outstanding performance of work far above that ordinarily expected and may be received by either an individual or a group. Not more than twenty are usually conferred in one year.
Ref. Pg. 184

77. Department of Transportation Outstanding Achievement Medal

Awarded For: Outstanding leadership or other
Ref. Pg. 185 achievements as deemed appropriate.

78. Department of Transportation Meritorious Achievement Medal

Awarded For: Completing assigned duties in an outstanding manner, developing new ideas, eminent authorship, outstanding ideas or other contributions.
Ref. Pg. 185

79. Department of Transportation Medal for Valor

Awarded For: Acts of heroism involving great personal risk under unusual circumstances.
Ref. Pg. 185

80. Department of Transportation Superior Achievement Medal

Awarded For: Performance of assigned tasks in exemplary fashion, for unusual skills or for improving work methods or for inventions which result in saving of manpower, time, etc., for notable authorship, exceptional achievements, and for significant achievement in support of the department's equal opportunities program.
Ref. Pg. 186

77.	78.	79.	80.
Plate II	Plate II	Plate II	Plate II

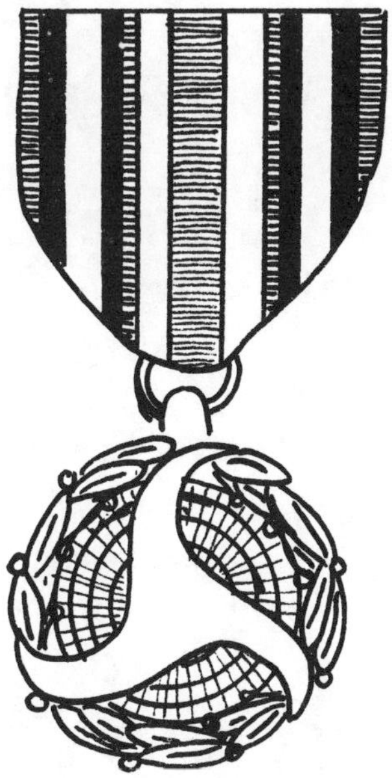

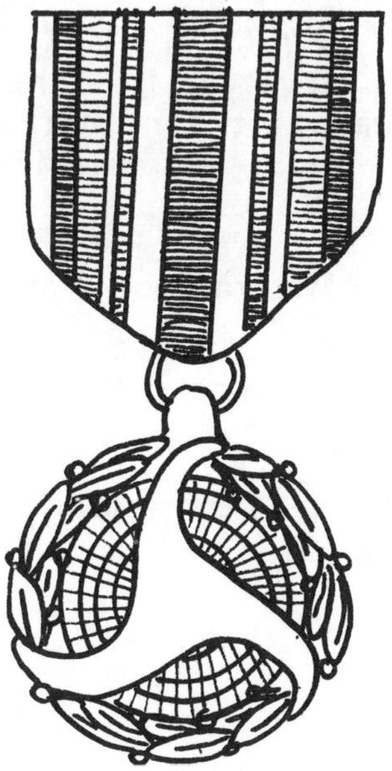

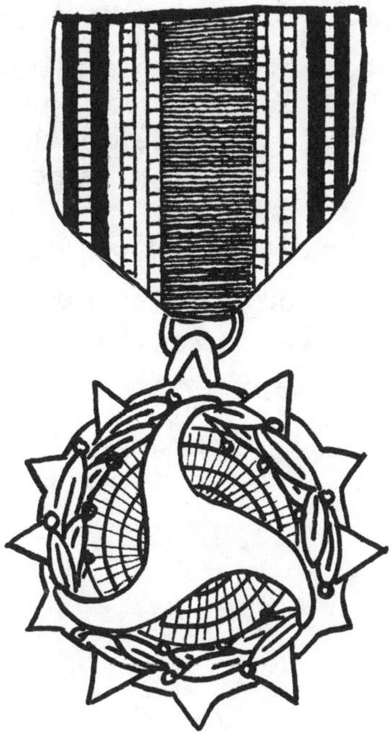

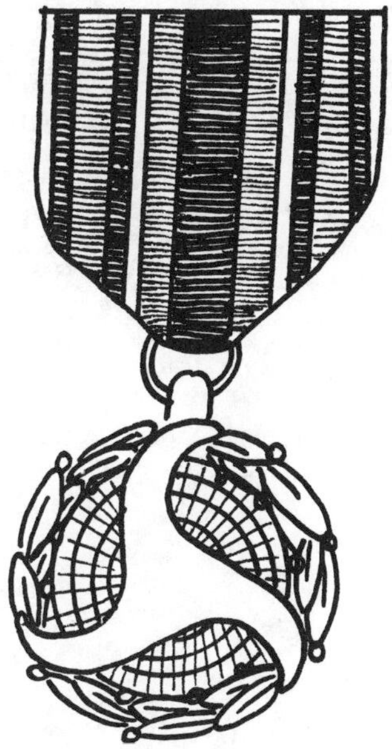

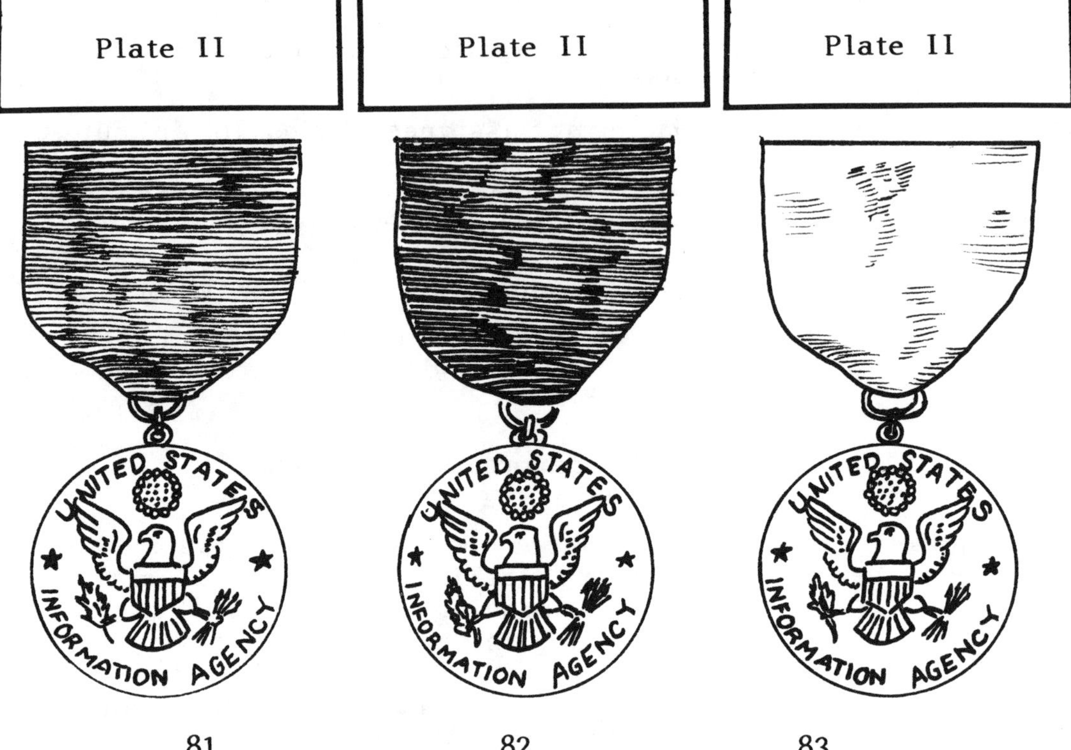

81. 82. 83.

81. U.S. Information Agency Distinguished Honor Medal

Awarded For: Ref. Pg. 186	Exceptional service in matters of marked national or international significance.

82. U.S. Information Agency Superior Honor Medal

Awarded For: Ref. Pg. 186	Outstanding service to the United States government or for furthering the mission of the U.S. Information Agency in a superior manner.

83. U.S.. Information Agency Meritorious Honor Medal

Awarded For: Ref. Pg. 187	Outstanding service to the agency in improving its products, initiating new programs or carrying out projects which surpass usual requirements. Groups as well as individuals may receive the award.

84. H.E.W. U.S. Public Health Service Distinguished Service Medal

Awarded For: Commissioned officers of the U.S. Public Health Service only, for distinguished accomplishment or for heroism in saving life or property.
Ref. Pg. 187

85. H.E.W. U.S. Public Health Service Meritorious Service Medal

Awarded For: Commissioned officers of the U.S. Public Health Service only, for important achievement, technical or professional accomplishment, or leadership.
Ref. Pg. 187

86. H.E.W. U.S. Public Health Service Commendation Medal

Awarded For: Commissioned officers of the U.S. Public Health Service only, for recognized levels of proficiency or dedication greater than expected of the average commissioned officer, sustained high performance, or unique skills.
Ref. Pg. 188

84.	85.	86.
Plate II	Plate II	Plate II

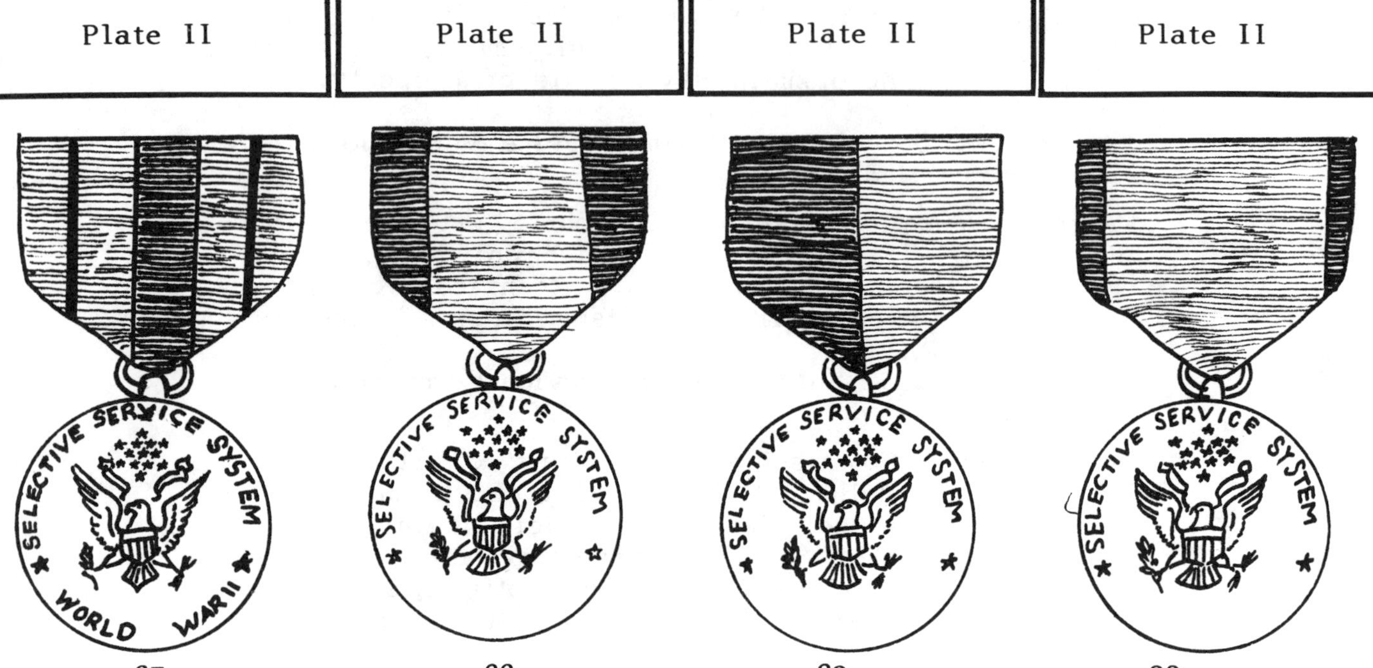

87. 88. 89. 90.

87. Selective Service Medal WWII

Awarded For: Exceptionally meritorious service or for significant achievements or inspiration to others which contributes to the goals of the Selective Service System.
Ref. Pg. 188

88. Selective Service System Distinguished Service Medal

Awarded For: Extraordinary performance or contribution to the Selective Service System Administration.
Ref. Pg. 189

89. Selective Service System Exceptional Service Medal

Awarded For: Exceptional service, and/or improvements of methods, or great acts of courage.
Ref. Pg. 189

90. Selective Service System Meritorious Service Medal

Awarded For: Exceptionally meritorious service, for significant achievements or inspiration to others which contributes to the goals of the Selective Service System.
Ref. Pg. 190

Plate II

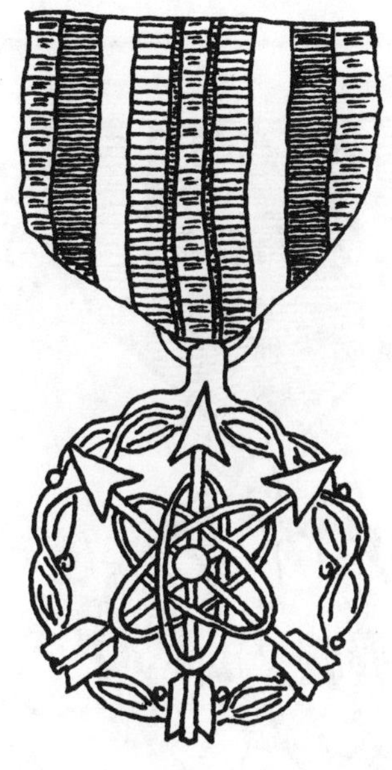

91.

Plate II

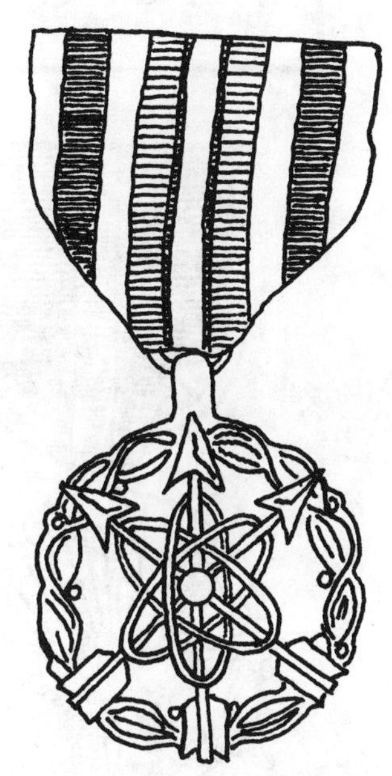

92.

91. **Defense Nuclear Agency Exceptional Service Medal**

Awarded For:
Ref. Pg. 191

92. **Defense Nuclear Agency Meritorious Service Medal**

Awarded For:
Ref. Pg. 191

93. 94.

93. Presidential Citizens Medal

Awarded For: As a personal award of the President of the United States, in recognition of exemplary deeds of service performed by any United States citizen.
Ref. Pg. 192

94. Presidential Award for Distinguished Federal Civilian Service

Awarded For: Extraordinary achievement in federal service. The award is granted annually to selected individuals whose achievements exemplify to an exceptional degree, imagination, courage, and high ability in carrying out the mission of the government.
Ref. Pg. 192

95. Air Mail Flyers Medal of Honor

Awarded For: Ref. Pg. 193	To civilian pilots for acts of outstanding bravery while carrying the mail.

96. American Typhus Commission Medal

Awarded For: Ref. Pg. 193	Meritorious service in connection with the work of the Typhus-Control Commission.

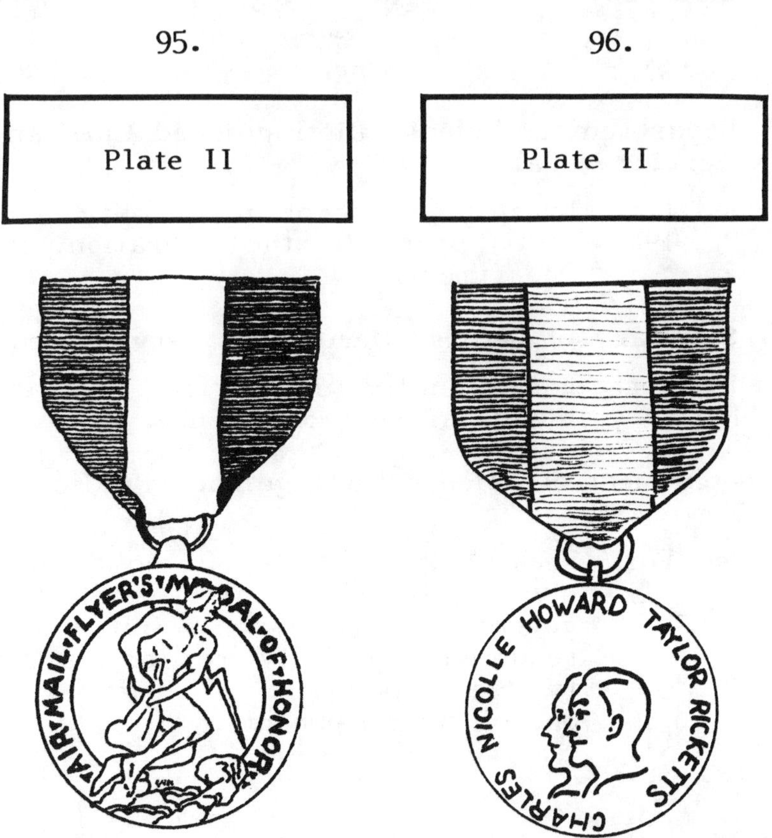

Plate II	Plate II	Plate II

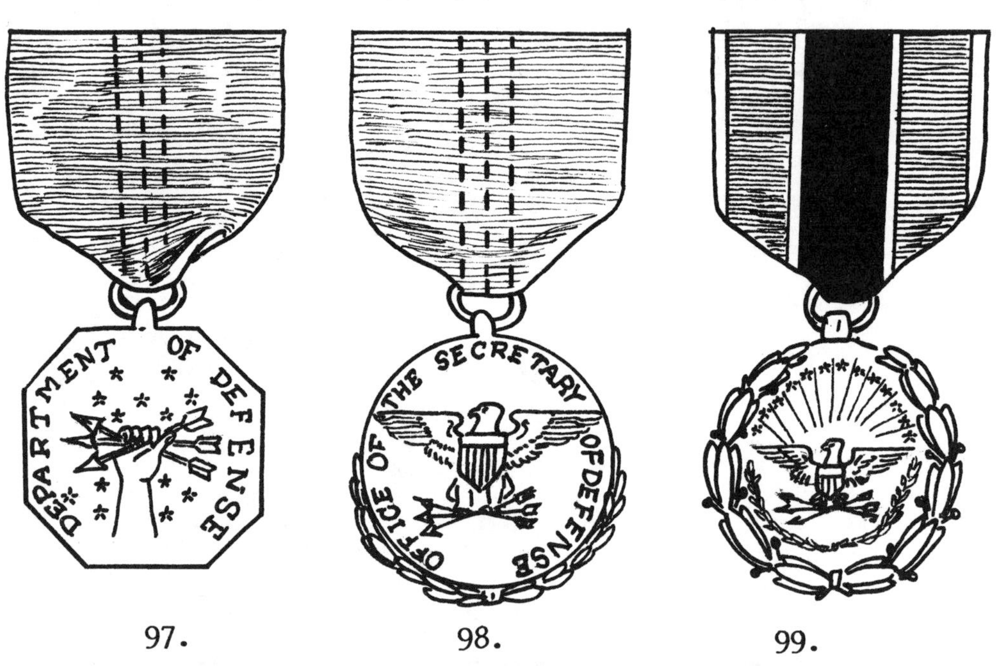

97. 98. 99.

97. Department of Defense Distinguished Civilian Service Medal

Awarded For: Exceptional devotion to duty and for contribution to the operation of the Department.
Ref. Pg. 194

98. Secretary of Defense Meritorious Service Medal

Awarded For: Exceptionally meritorious service to the Department of Defense.
Ref. Pg. 194

99. Department of Defense Distinguished Public Service Medal

Awarded For: Presented to civilians who do not derive their principal livelihood from government employment, but who have rendered especially meritorious service to the Department of Defense and/or one of its components.
Ref. Pg. 195

100. Department of Defense Civil Preparedness Agency Director's Award for Distinguished Civilian Service

Awarded For: Meritorious performance, acts or services of pre-eminent importance and value to the agency, the Department of Defense or the United States government. It can also be conferred for acts of unusual courage or competence in an agency.
Ref. Pg. 195

101. Defense Communications Agency Director's Exceptional Civilian Service Medal

Awarded For: Outstanding performance.
Ref. Pg. 196

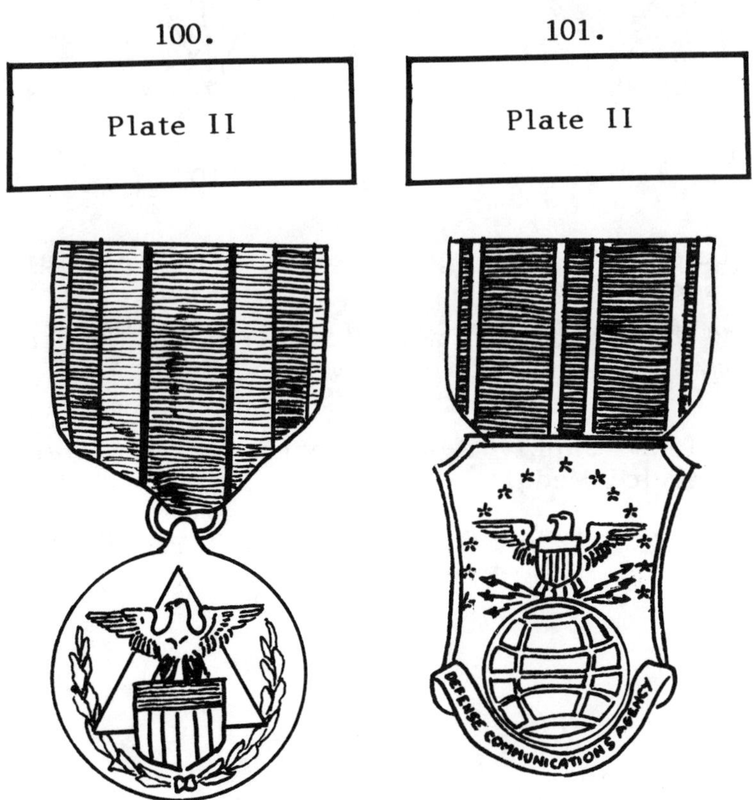

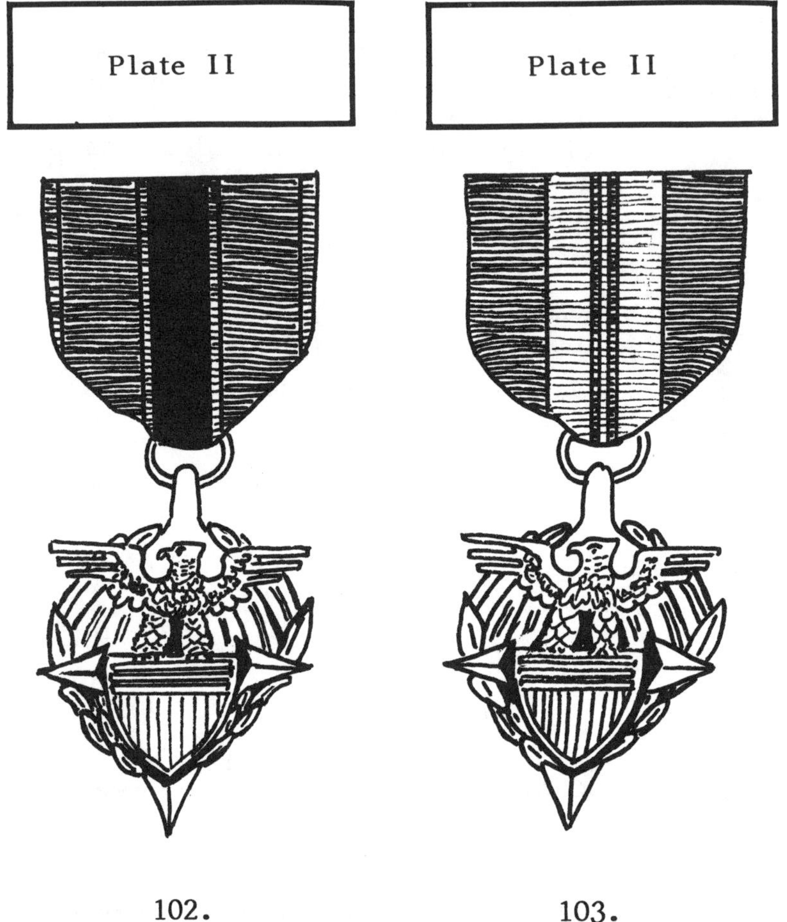

102. 103.

102. Defense Supply Agency Exceptional Civilian Service Medal

Awarded For: I have no information on the criteria
Ref. Pg. 196 the medal is awarded for.

103. Defense Supply Agency Meritorious Civilian Service Medal

Awarded For: I have no information on the criteria
Ref. Pg. 197 the medal is awarded for.

104. Defense Contract Audit Agency Distinguished Civilian Service Medal

Awarded For: I have no information on the criteria
Ref. Pg. 197 the medal is awarded for.

105. Defense Contract Audit Agency Meritorious Civilian Service Medal

Awarded For: I have no information on the criteria
Ref. Pg. 198 the medal is awarded for.

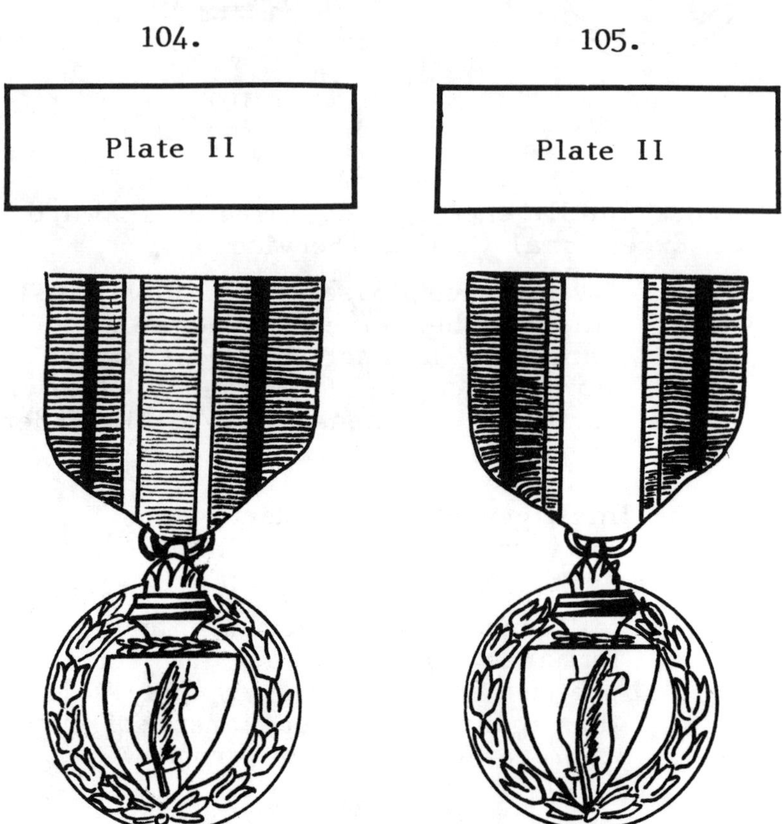

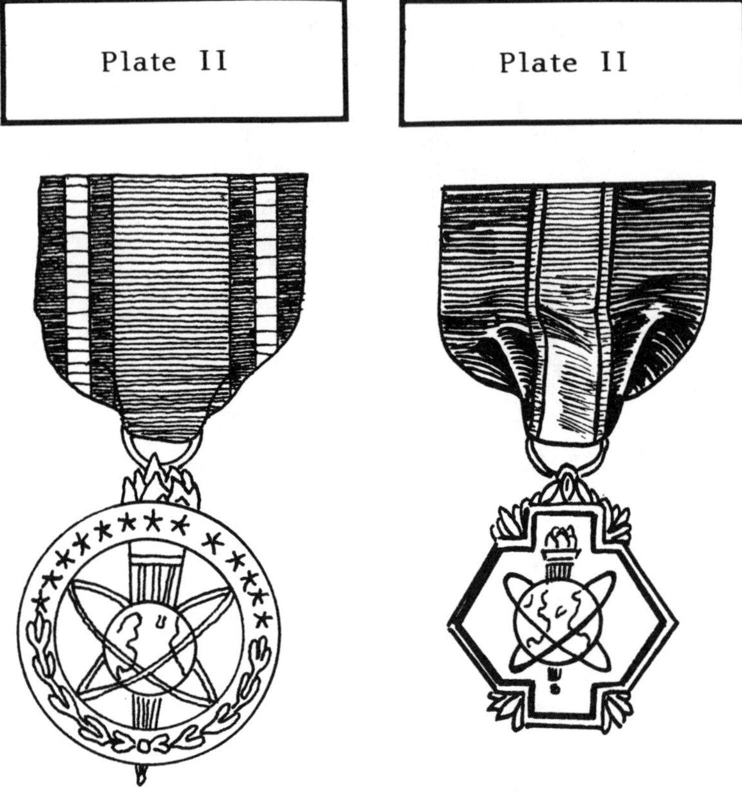

106. 107.

106. Defense Intelligence Agency Director's Award for Exceptional Civilian Service

Awarded For: Civilian employees who have distinguished themselves by notable performance or an act of great scope and significance to the agency, the Department of Defense and/or the federal government.
Ref. Pg. 198

107. Defense Intelligence Agency Meritorious Civilian Service Medal

Awarded For: Civilian employee of the Defense Intelligence Agency for meritorious performance. For an act of service of pre-eminent importance and value to the agency, the Department of Defense and/or the federal government.
Ref. Pg. 199

108. Army Distinguished Civilian Service Medal

Awarded For: To private citizens, federal government officials, and technical personnel who served the Army in an advisory capacity or as consultants. All of these must have rendered distinguished service or made a substantial contribution to the Army's mission.

Ref. Pg. 199

109. Army Outstanding Civilian Service Medal

Awarded For: To private citizens, federal government officials, and technical personnel who served the Army in an advisory capacity or as consultants. All of these must have rendered distinguished service or made a substantial contribution to the Army's mission, but not to a degree high enough to merit the Distinguished Civilian Service Medal.

Ref. Pg. 200

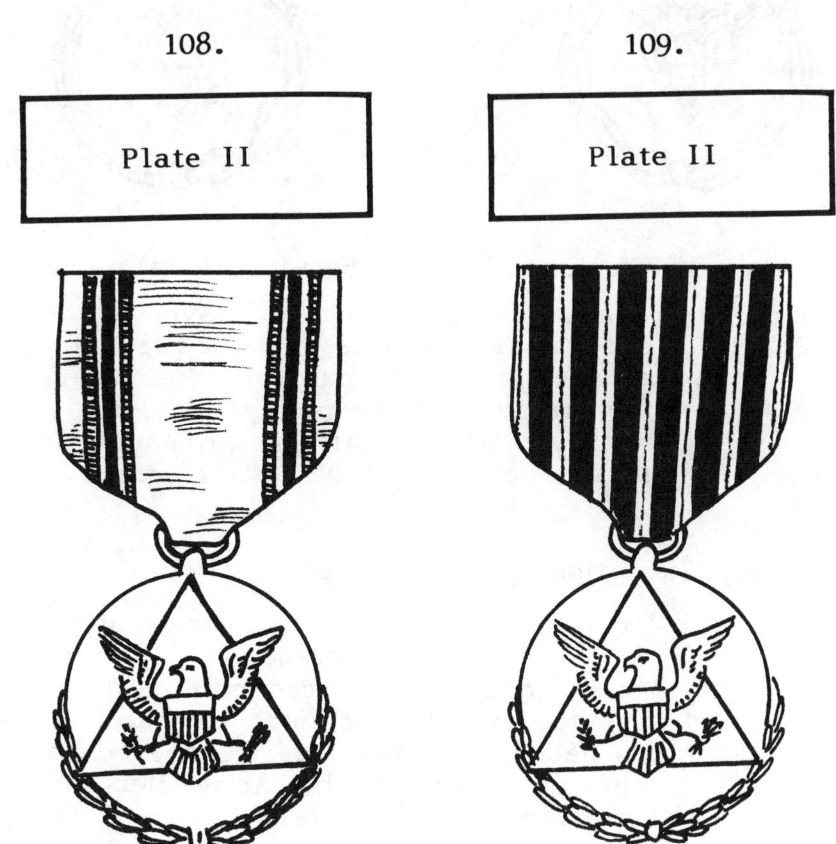

Plate II

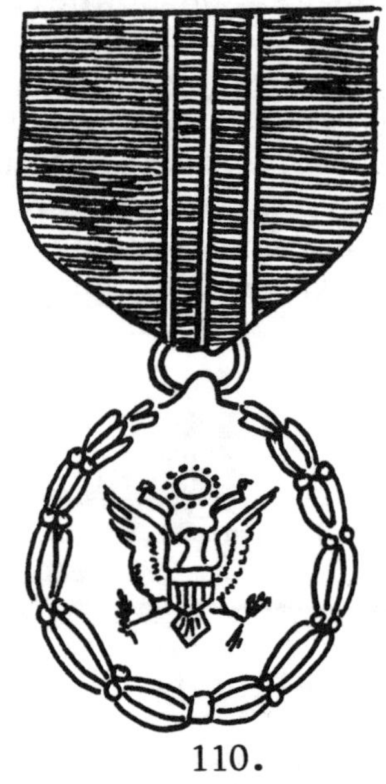

110.

111.

110. Army Meritorious Civilian Service Medal

Awarded For: Civilian employees who have rendered exceptional services to the Department of the Army. It can also be awarded for an act of heroism involving voluntary risk of life in direct benefit to the government or its personnel.

Ref. Pg. 200

111. Army Exceptional Civilian Service Medal

Awarded For: To private citizens, federal officials and technical personnel including consultants, who render outstanding service to the major command concerned, but not to a degree high enough to merit the Army Meritorious Civilian Service Medal.

Ref. Pg. 201

112. Navy Distinguished Civilian Service Medal

Awarded For: Contributions of such an extraordinary nature that recognition is deserved over that of headquarters command level. It can also be awarded for great courage in the face of danger which results in direct benefit to the government or its personnel.

Ref. Pg. 201

113. Navy Superior Civilian Service Medal

Awarded For: Superior civilian service or contributions which have resulted in exceptional benefit to the Navy.

Ref. Pg. 202

114. Navy Distinguished Public Service Medal

Awarded For: Heroic acts and significant contributions which helped to accomplish the Navy's mission.

Ref. Pg. 202

112.	113.	114.
Plate II	Plate II	Plate II

115. 116.

115. Captain Robert Dexter Conrad Medal Awarded for Distinguished Achievement in Science

Awarded For: Outstanding scientific achievement to the Navy.
Ref. Pg. 203

116. Distinguished Achievement in Science Medal

Awarded For: A breakthrough in science for the Navy.
Ref. Pg. 203

117. Air Force Civilian Medal for Valor

Awarded For: Ref. Pg. 204	Civilians serving in any capacity in the Air Force, who demonstrate unusual competence or courage while on duty.

118. Air Force Command Civilian Medal for Valor

Awarded For: Ref. Pg. 204	Civilians who demonstrate unusual courage.

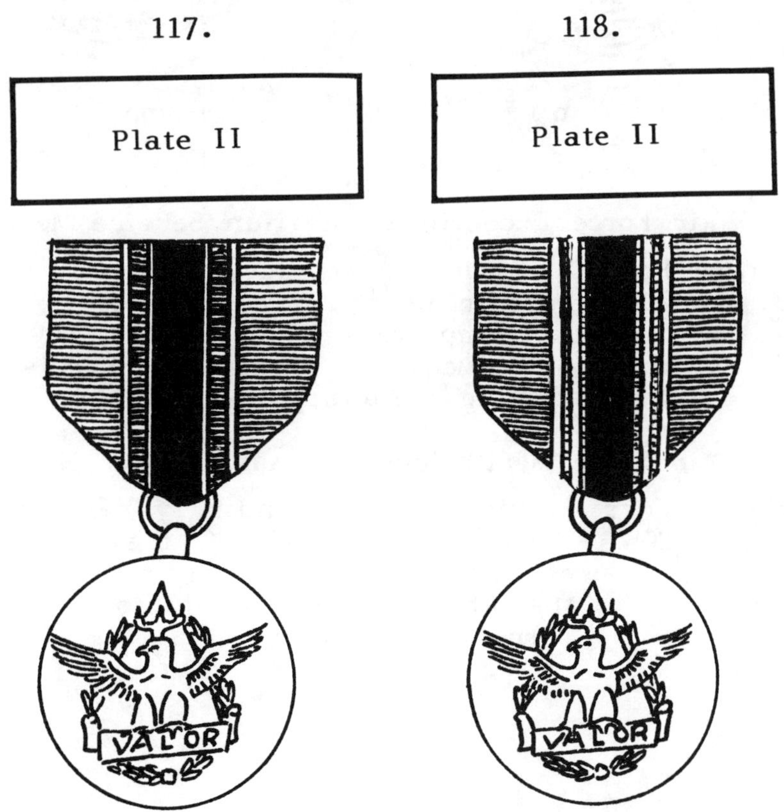

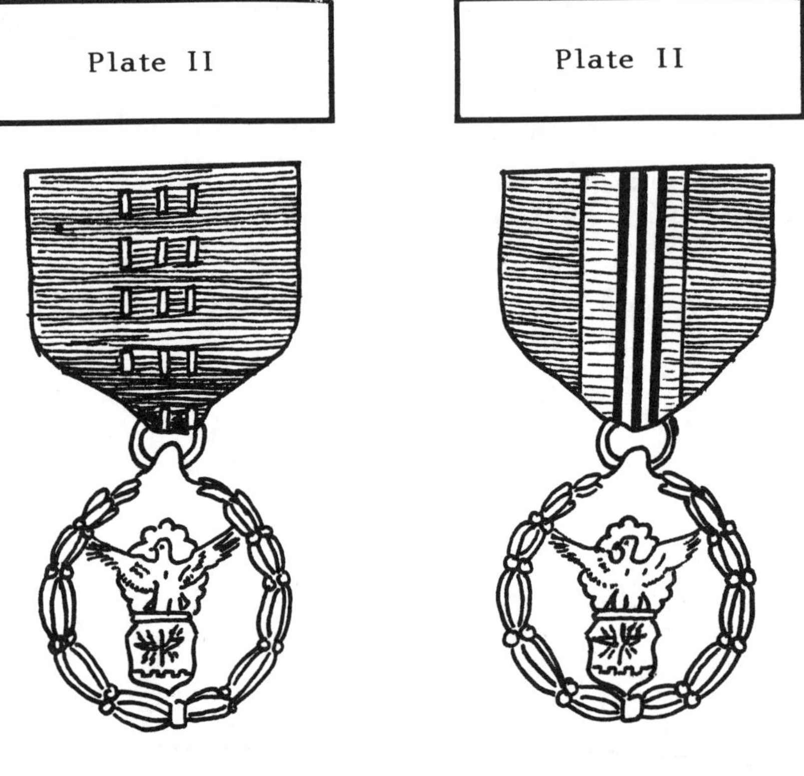

119. 120.

119. Air Force Exceptional Civilian Service Medal

Awarded For: Exceptional service rendered to the Department of the Air Force by civilian employees. This award may also be given for an act of heroism involving voluntary risk of life.
Ref. Pg. 205

120. Air Force Meritorious Civilian Service Medal

Awarded For: Services so outstandingly performed by civilian employees of the Department of the Air Force that recognition of the Chief of Staff, United States Air Force, is merited.
Ref. Pg. 205

121. United States Coast Guard Distinguished Public Service Medal

Awarded For: I have no information on what this medal is awarded for.
Ref. Pg. 206

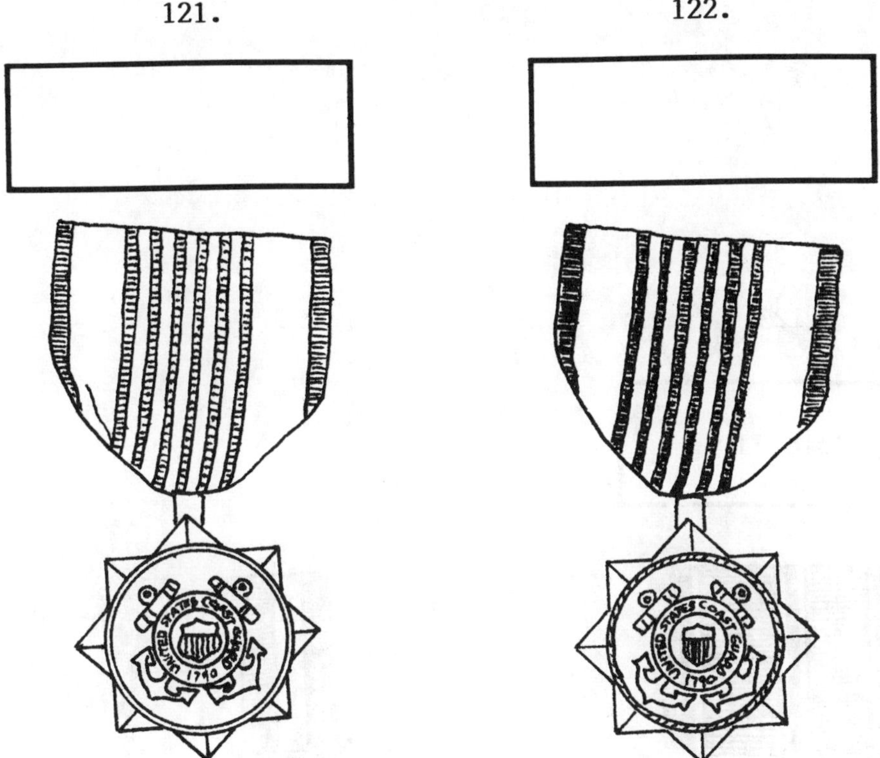

121. 122.

122. United States Coast Guard Meritorious Public Service Medal

Awarded For: I have no information on what this medal is awarded for.
Ref. Pg. 206

123. Vietnam Civilian Service Medal

Awarded For: Ref. Pg. 206	All United States government employees after completion of one full calendar year in Vietnam.

U. Good Conduct Medal, Navy 1869-1884

Awarded For: Ref. Pg. 208	To any seaman holding a continuous service certificate who is distinguished for obedience, sobriety, and cleanliness, and is proficient in seamanship and gunnery.

123.

Plate II

"U".

Plate II

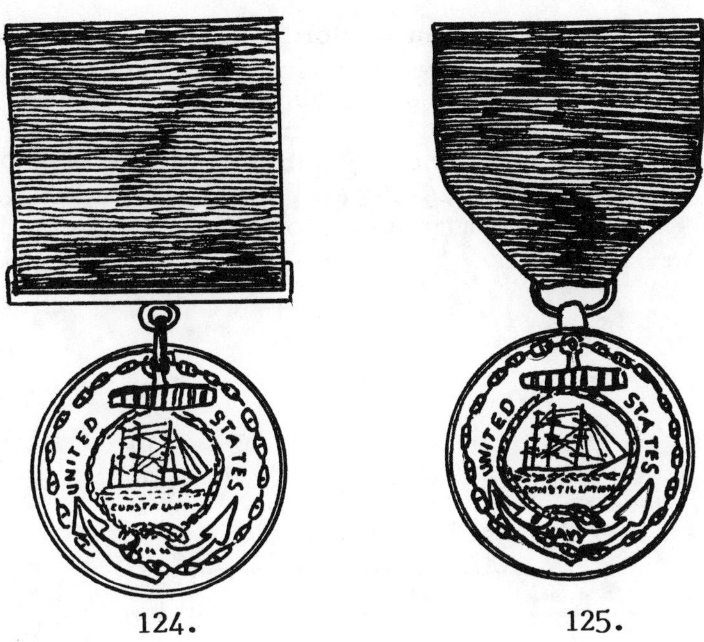

124. 125.

124. Navy Good Conduct Medal–new design old ribbon drape

Awarded For: Fidelity, zeal, and obedience. Men who hold honorable discharges and continuous service certificates, will be entitled to receive the medal.
Ref. Pg. 207

125. Navy Good Conduct Medal – Current

Awarded For: Fidelity, zeal, and obedience. Men who hold honorable discharges and continuous service certificates, will be entitled to receive the medal.
Ref. Pg. 207

126. Marine Corps Good Conduct Medal–First Type

Awarded For: Any man holding an excellent discharge, shall, upon reenlistment, receive a Good Conduct Medal. Only those men who are distinguished for obedience, sobriety, industry, courage, neatness, and proficiency shall be recommended for Good Conduct Medals.

Ref. Pg. 208

127. Marine Corps Good Conduct Medal–Current

Awarded For: Any man holding an excellent discharge, shall, upon reenlistment, receive a Good Conduct Medal. Only those men who are distinguished for obedience, sobriety, industry, courage, neatness, and proficiency shall be recommended for Good Conduct Medals.

Ref. Pg. 208

126. and 127.

Plate II

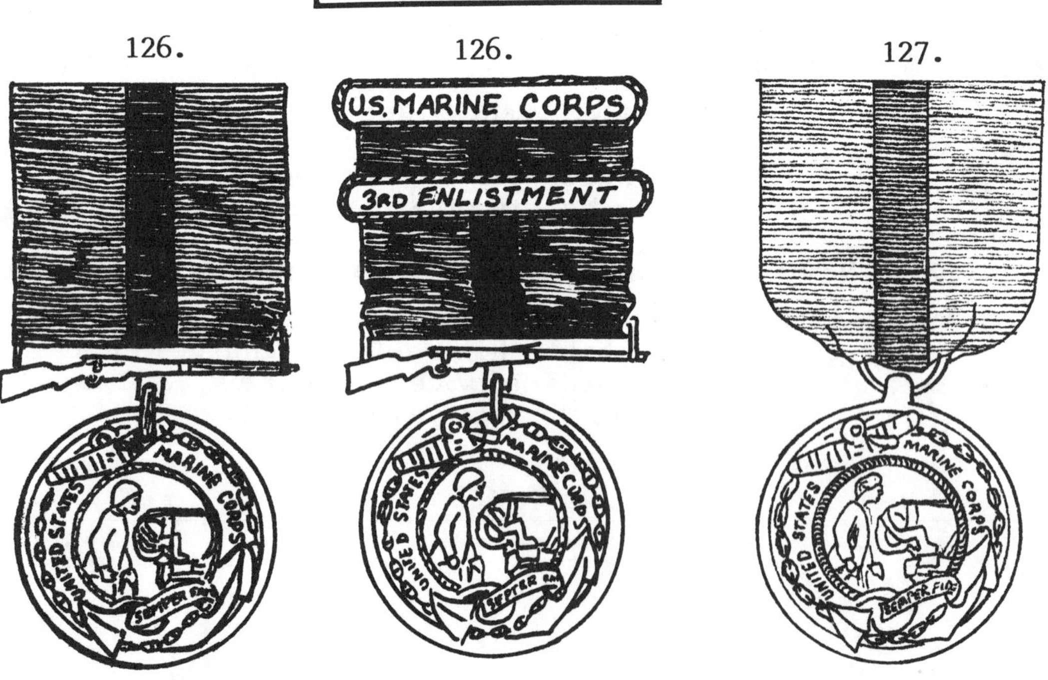

Plate II

128.

129.

128. Army Good Conduct Medal

Awarded For: Ref. Pg. 209	Enlisted personnel, who on or after August 27, 1940, or shall have honorably completed three years of active federal military service, or who after December 7, 1941, have or shall have honorably served one year of federal military service while the United States is at war.

129. Air Force Good Conduct Medal

Awarded For: Ref. Pg. 209	Enlisted personnel, who on or after April 10, 1953, or shall have honorably completed three years of active federal military service.

130. Coast Guard Good Conduct Medal–First Type

Awarded For: Three years of demonstrated proficiency and good conduct.
Ref. Pg. 210

131. Coast Guard Good Conduct Medal–Current

Awarded For: Three years of demonstrated proficiency and good conduct.
Ref. Pg. 210

Plate II

130.

131.

Plate II

Plate III

Plate III

133.

134. and 135.

137.

Plate II

Plate III

132.

136.

132. and 133. **Civil War Campaign Medal, Army**

Awarded For: Those persons who served in the Union
Ref. Pg. 211 forces during the Civil War.

134. and 135. **Civil War Campaign Medal, Navy And Marine Corps**

Awarded For: Those persons who served in the Union
Ref. Pg. 211 forces during the Civil War.

136. and 137. **Indian Wars Campaign Medal, Army**

Awarded For: Service against hostile Indians from
Ref. Pg. 212 1865 to 1891.

138. Sampson Medal, Navy and Marine Corps

Awarded For: To officers and men of the Navy and Marine Corps who participated in the engagements in the West Indies.
Ref. Pg. 213

139. Spanish War Service Medal, Army

Awarded For: Service between April 20, 1898, and April 11, 1899, in the war with Spain, and awarded to those men not eligible to receive the Spanish Campaign Medal.
Ref. Pg. 213

140. and 141. West Indies Campaign Medal Navy and Marine Corps

Awarded For: To Navy and Marine Corps personnel for service aboard ships in the West Indies.
Ref. Pg. 214

138.	139.	140. 141.
Plate III	Plate III	Plate III

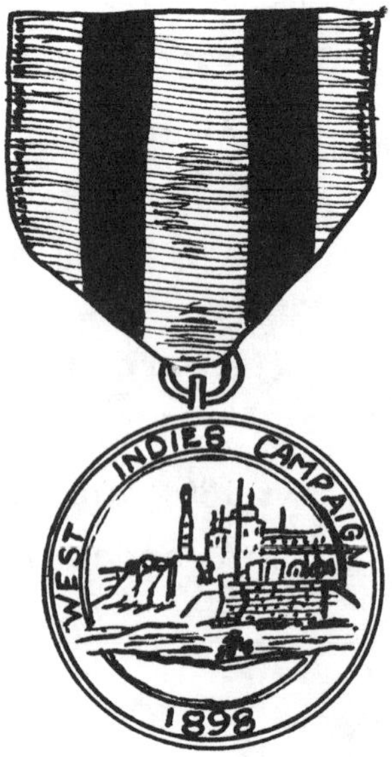

Plate III	Plate III	Plate III

142.

144.

145.146.

143.

142. Dewey Medal, Navy and Marine Corps

Awarded For: Commemorating the battle of Manila Bay. The medal was awarded to officers and men who were with Commodore Dewey at Manila.
Ref. Pg. 215

143. and 144. War with Spain Campaign Medal, Army

Awarded For: Service ashore in Cuba, Puerto Rico, and the Philippine Islands or enroute to on the high seas, during 1898.
Ref. Pg. 216

145. and 146. Spanish Campaign Medal, Navy and Marine Corps

Awarded For: Service afloat or on shore in Cuba, Puerto Rico, the Philippines, or Guam, between May 1 and August 16, 1898.
Ref. Pg. 217

147. Philippine Congressional Medal

Awarded For: Those who served beyond the date on which they were entitled to discharge, during the war with Spain, to help suppress Philippine Insurrection.
Ref. Pg. 217

148. Philippine Campaign, Army

Awarded For: To Army personnel who served in the Philippine Islands against hostile natives between February 4, 1899, and December 31, 1913.
Ref. Pg. 218

149. and 150. Philippine Campaign Medal, Navy and Marine Corps

Awarded For: Issued to Navy and Marine Corps personnel who served in and around the Philippine Islands against hostile natives between February 4, 1899, and December 31, 1904.
Ref. Pg. 218

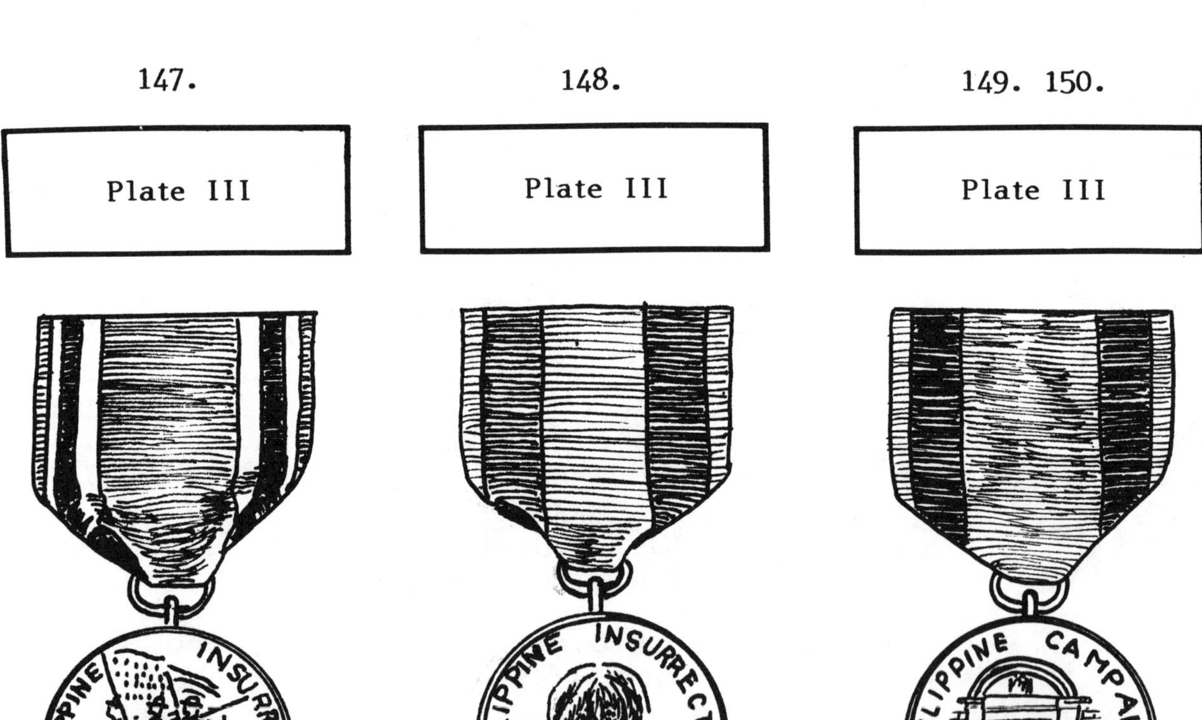

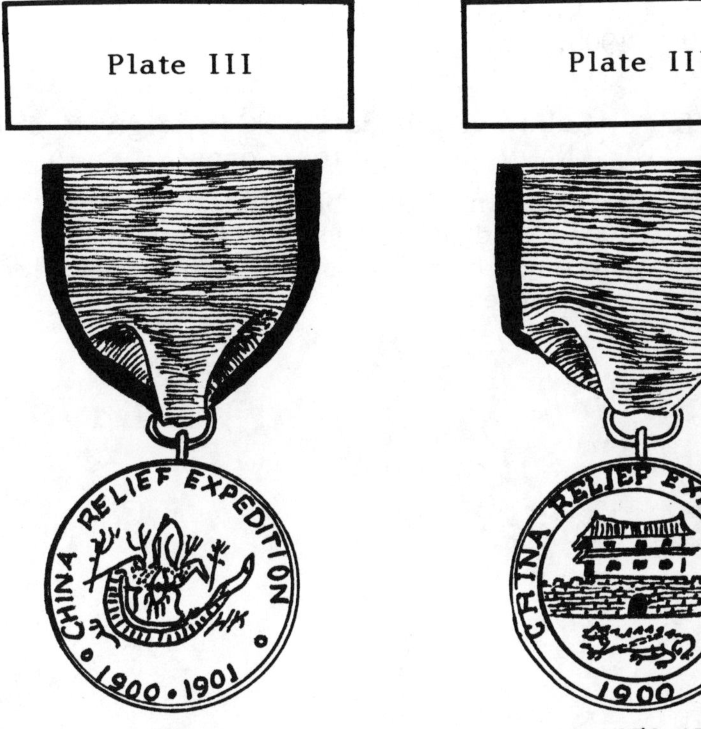

151.

153.154.

Plate III

152.

151. China Relief Expedition Campaign Medal, Army

Awarded For: Service ashore with the Peking Relief Expedition during the Boxer Rebellion, between June 20, 1900, and May 27, 1901.
Ref. Pg. 219

152., 153., and 154. China Relief Expedition Campaign Medal, Navy and Marine Corps

Awarded For: Service ashore with the Peking Relief Expedition or service on naval vessel in that area during the Boxer Rebellion between May 24, 1900, and May 27, 1901.
Ref. Pg. 219

155. Cuban Pacification Campaign Medal, Army

Awarded For: Service in Cuba between October 6, 1906, and April 1, 1909.
Ref. Pg. 220

156. and 157. Cuban Pacification Campaign Medal, Navy and Marine Corps

Awarded For: Service in Cuba between September 12, 1906, and April 1, 1909, by Navy and Marine Corps personnel in expeditionary forces.
Ref. Pg. 220

155.

Plate III

156. 157.

Plate III

Plate III

158.

Plate III

159.160.

158. War with Mexico Campaign Medal, Army

Awarded For: Ref. Pg. 221	To Army personnel who served against hostile Mexicans between April 12, 1911, and June 16, 1919.

159. and 160. War with Mexico Campaign Medal, Navy and Marine Corps

Awarded For: Ref. Pg. 221	To Navy and Marine Corps personnel who served against hostile Mexicans between April 12, 1911, and February 7, 1917.

161. and 162. Nicaraguan Campaign Medal, Navy and Marine Corps

Awarded For: To personnel of the Navy and Marine Corps who served in Nicaragua, or on board certain ships in that area between July 29, 1912, and November 14, 1912.
Ref. Pg. 222

163. and 164. Haitian Campaign Medal, Navy and Marine Corps

Awarded For: To Navy and Navy and Marine Corps personnel who participated in joint expedition to Haiti between July 9, 1915, and December 6, 1915.
Ref. Pg. 222

165. Mexican Border Service Medal, Army

Awarded For: Service in the Mexican Border Patrol by the National Guard from May 9, 1916, to March 24, 1917, and by the Regular Army from January 1, 1916, to April 6, 1917.
Ref. Pg. 222

161. 162.	163. 164.	165.
Plate III	Plate III	Plate III

Plate III	Plate III	Plate III

166. 167. 168. 169. 170. 171.

166. and 167. Dominican Campaign Medal, Navy and Marine Corps

Awarded For: To Navy and Marine Corps personnel who served in operations in Santo Domingo from May 5, 1916, to December 4, 1916.
Ref. Pg. 223

168. and 169. Haitian Campaign Medal, Navy and Navy and Marine Corps

Awarded For: To Navy and Marine Corps personnel who participated in joint expedition to Haiti between April 1, 1919, and June 15, 1920.
Ref. Pg. 224

170. and 171. Second Nicaraguan Campaign Medal, Navy and Marine Corps

Awarded For: To personnel of the Navy and Marine Corps who participated in operations in Nicaragua from August 27, 1926, to January 2, 1933.
Ref. Pg. 225

172. and 173, Yangtze Service Campaign Medal, Navy and Marine Corps

Awarded For: Personnel of the Navy and Marine Corps who participated in operations in the Yangtze River Valley, China, or at Shanghai, between September 3, 1926, and October 21, 1927, or from March 1, 1930, to December 31, 1932.

Ref. Pg. 226

174. and 175. China Service Campaign Medal, Navy and Marine Corps

Awarded For: For participation during operations in China, Taiwan, and the Matsu Straits by Navy and Marine Corps personnel, between the dates July 7, 1937, and September 7, 1939, and a second operation from September 2, 1945, through April 1, 1957.

Ref. Pg. 227

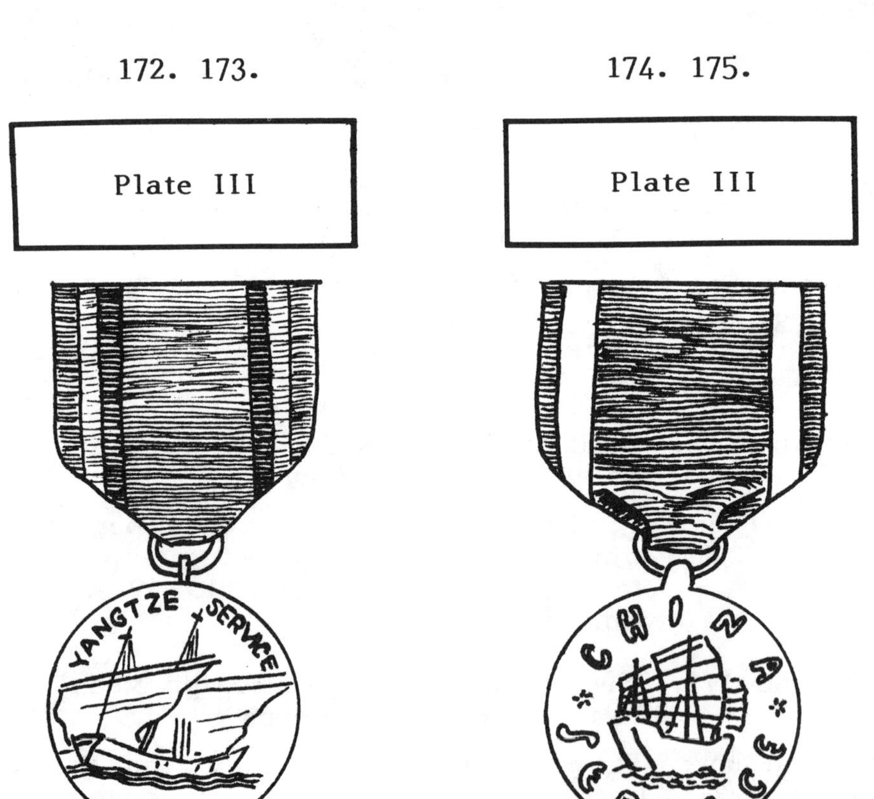

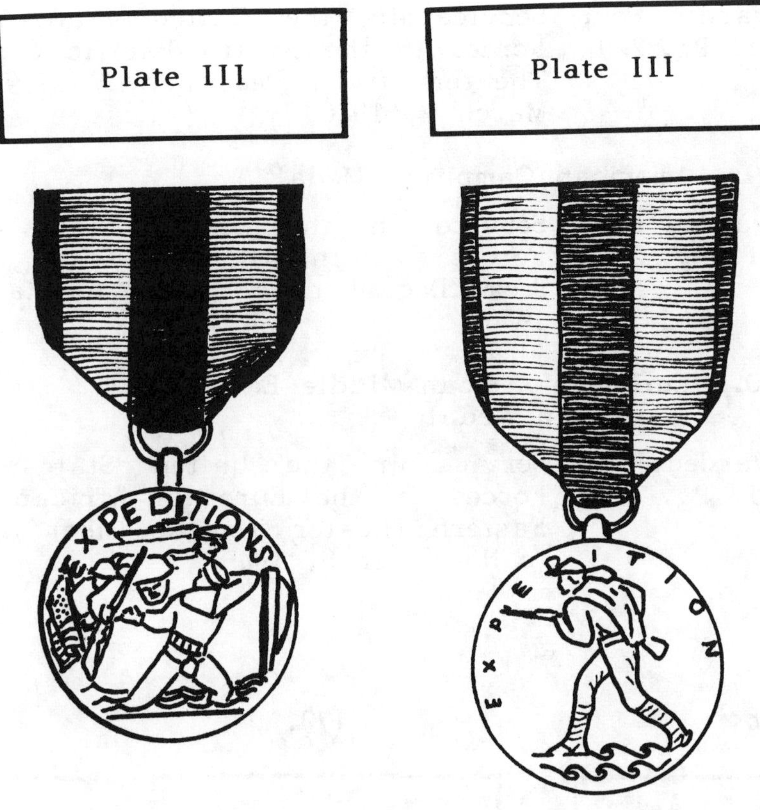

176. 177.

176. Navy Expeditionary Campaign Medal

Awarded For: Ref. Pg. 228	To Navy personnel who have landed on foreign territory and engaged armed enemy opposition under circumstances for which no special medal has been awarded.

177. Marine Corps Expeditionary Campaign Medal

Awarded For: Ref. Pg. 228	To Marine Corps personnel who have landed on foreign territory and engaged armed enemy opposition under circumstances for which no special medal has been awarded.

178. Asiatic-Pacific Campaign Medal

Awarded For: Service in the United States Armed Forces in the Asiatic-Pacific Campaign Theater from December 7, 1941, to March 2, 1946.
Ref. Pg. 229

179. American Campaign Medal

Awarded For: Service in the United States Armed Forces within the American Theater from December 7, 1941, to March 2, 1946.
Ref. Pg. 230

180. European-African-Middle Eastern Campaign Medal

Awarded For: Service in the United States Armed Forces in the European-African-Middle Eastern Theater from December 7, 1941, to November 8, 1945.
Ref. Pg. 231

178.	179.	180.
Plate III	Plate III	Plate III

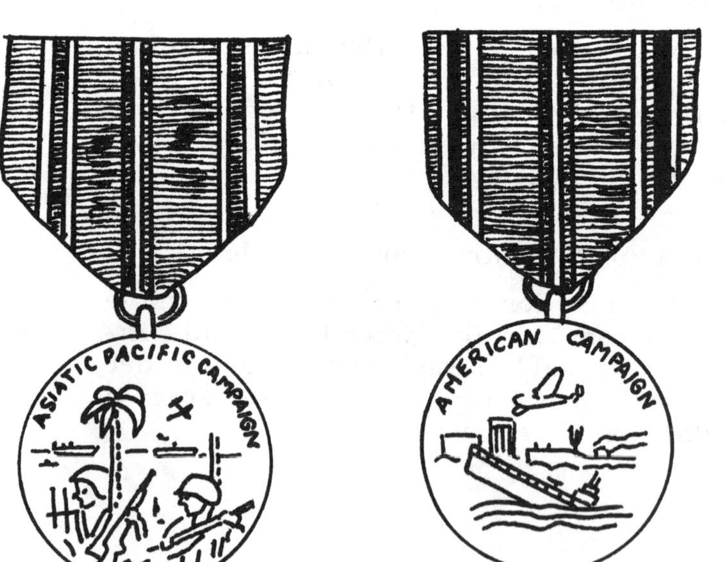

Plate III	Plate III	Plate III

181.	182.	183.

181. Korean Service Campaign Medal

Awarded For: To personnel of the United States Armed Forces for service in the Korean Theater from June 27, 1950, to July 27, 1954.
Ref. Pg. 232

182. Armed Forces Expeditionary Campaign Medal

Awarded For: To any member of the United States Armed Forces who has participated in military operations for which no other service or campaign medal has been authorized.
Ref. Pg. 233

183. Vietnam Service Campaign Medal

Awarded For: Service in the Republic of Vietnam, the waters off Vietnam, and in Thailand.
Ref. Pg. 234

184. Air Force Combat Readiness Service Medal

Awarded For: To members of the Air Force who are combat-ready aircraft-crew members for a four-year period. The term "combat ready" is defined as being professionally or technically qualified in an aircraft-crew position in an aircraft which can be used in combat.
Ref. Pg. 235

185. NC-4 Service Medal

Awarded For: To the officers and men for conceiving, organizing, and commanding the first successful Transatlantic flight in May 1919.
Ref. Pg. 236

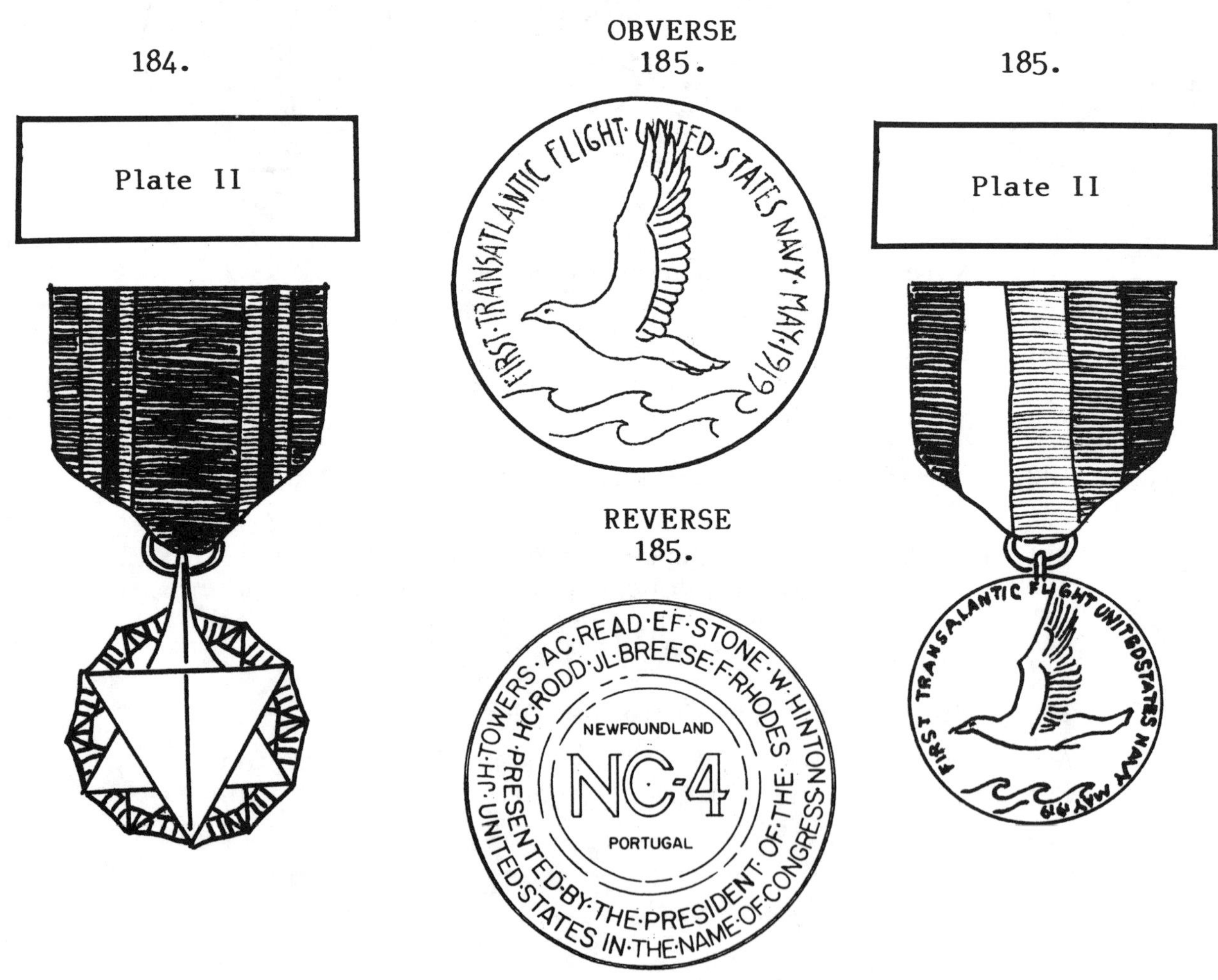

Plate III

186.

Plate III

187.

Plate III

188.

186. American Defense Service Medal

Awarded For:
Ref. Pg. 237

To personnel of the United States Armed Forces, who had one year of service during the Limited Emergency proclaimed by the President on September 8, 1939, or during the Unlimited Emergency proclaimed by the President on May 27, 1941. The one year of service must have been between September 8, 1939, and December 7, 1941.

187. Women's Army Corps Service Medal

Awarded For:
Ref. Pg. 238

To women who served in the Women's Auxiliary Corps from July 20, 1942, to August 31, 1943, and to those who served in the Women's Army Corps from September 1, 1943, to September 2, 1945.

188. Medal for Humane Action - Berlin Air Lift

Awarded For:
Ref. Pg. 239

To personnel assigned to the Berlin Air Lift, or assigned to units that directly supported the Air Lift, for 120 days or more from June 26, 1948, to September 30, 1949.

189. National Defense Service Medal

Awarded For: To any personnel of the United States Armed Forces who served between June 27, 1950, and July 27, 1954, or from January 1, 1961, to January 1, 1974.
Ref. Pg. 239

190. Medal for Humanitarian Service

Awarded For: To honor personnel of the United States Armed Forces who have rendered service to mankind.
Ref. Pg. 240

191. Multinational Force Medal

Awarded For: To personnel of the United States Marine Corps stationed in Lebanon as part of the multi-national peace-keeping force.
Ref. Pg. 240

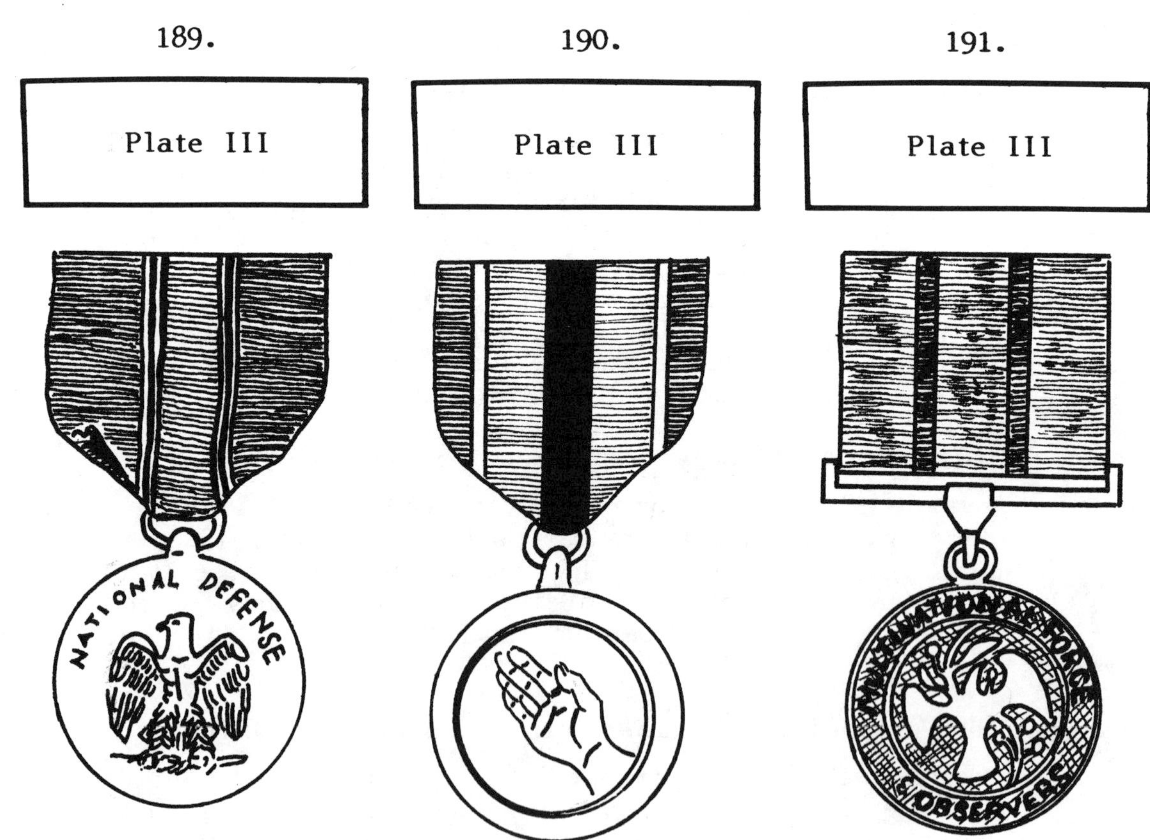

Plate III	Plate III	Plate III

192. 193. 194.

192. Perry Polar Expedition Medal 1908–1909

Awarded For: Ref. Pg. 241	To commemorate members of the Perry Polar Expedition during the years 1908–1909 for the cause of Polar exploration and their service in the field of science by aiding in the discovery of the North Pole.

193. First Byrd Antarctic Expedition Medal 1928–1930

Awarded For: Ref. Pg. 242	To express the high admiration that Congress and the American people held for the members of the first Byrd Antarctic Expedition 1928–1930.

194. Second Byrd Antarctic Expedition Medal 1933–1935

Awarded For: Ref. Pg. 243	To personnel of the Second Byrd Antarctic Expedition who commanded either one of the expedition ships throughout the expedition or who spent the winter night at Little America.

195. United States Antarctic Expedition Medal 1939–1941

Awarded For: To personnel of the United States Antarctic Expedition of 1939–1941 to recognize their valuable services to the nation in Polar exploration and science.
Ref. Pg. 244

196. United States Antarctic Service Medal

Awarded For: To recognize service performed after January 1, 1946, on the Antarctic continent or in support of the United States operations there.
Ref. Pg. 245

197. Arctic Service Medal, United States Coast Guard

Awarded For: I have no information on what this medal is awarded for.
Ref. Pg. 246

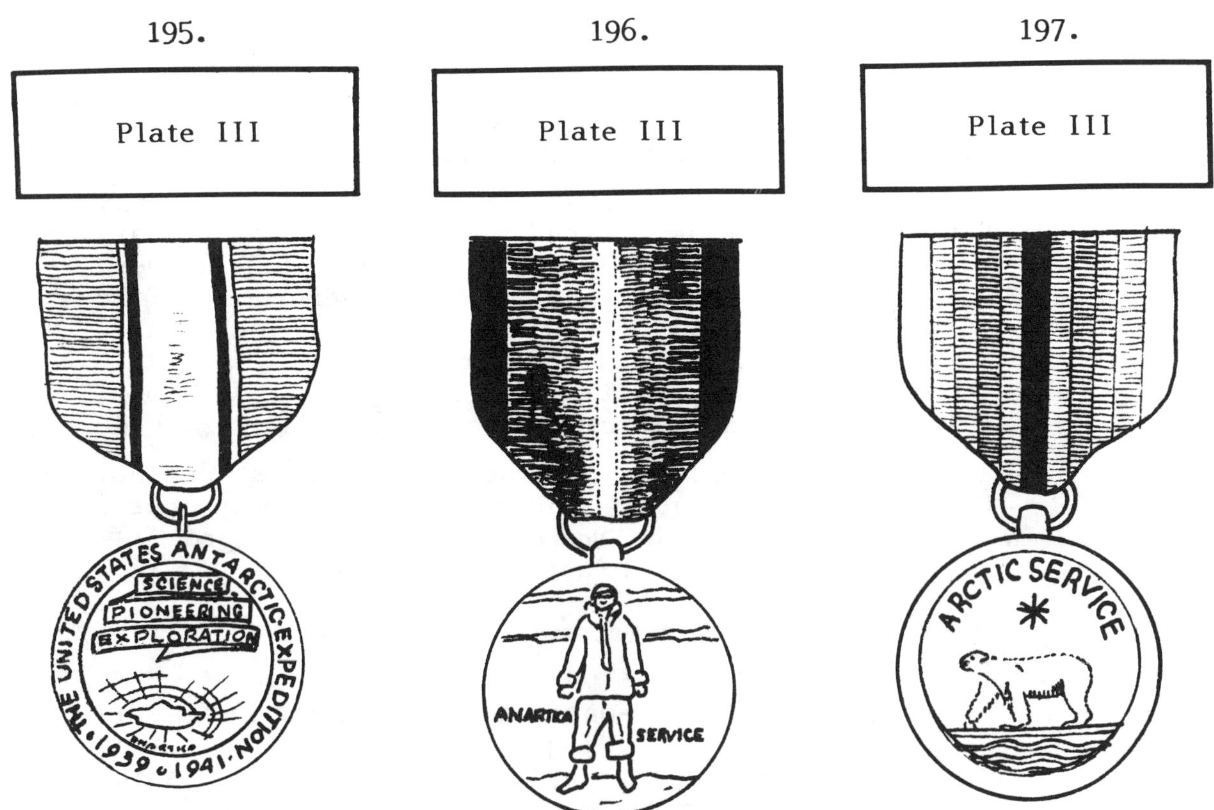

Plate III

198.

Plate III

199.

Plate III

201.

Plate III

200.

198. Army of Occupation of Puerto Rico 1898

Awarded For: To personnel who served in Puerto Rico from August 14, 1898, to December 10, 1898.
Ref. Pg. 246

199. Army of Occupation of Cuba 1898–1902

Awarded For: To personnel who served with the occupation forces in Cuba from July 18, 1898, to May 20, 1902.
Ref. Pg. 247

200. and 201. Army of Occupation of Germany WWI

Awarded For: To personnel of the United States Army, or Navy and Marine Corps with shore duties, for service with the occupation forces in Germany and Austria from November 12, 1918, to July 11, 1923.
Ref. Pg. 248

202. Army of Occupation of Germany and Japan WWII, Army

Awarded For: To Army and Air Force personnel for 30 days or more consecutive service in the occupation forces subsequent to World War II.

Ref. Pg. 249

203. and 204. Army of Occupation of Germany and Japan WWII, Navy and Marine Corps

Awarded For: To Navy and Marine Corps personnel for 30 days or more consecutive service in the occupation forces subsequent to World War II.

Ref. Pg. 250

Plate III

202.

203, 204.

Reverse of the Navy and Marine Corps Medals

174–175 China Service Medal
170–171 Second Nicaraguan Campaign Service Medal
172–173 Yangtze Service Medal
166–167 Dominican Campaign Service Medal
176–177 Expeditionary Medal
203–204 Occupation Service Medal World War II

Reverse of the Navy and Marine Corps Medals

133–134 Civil War Service Medal
156–157 Cuban Pacification Service Medal
161–162 Nicaraguan Campaign Service Medal
163–164 Haitian Campaign Service Medal 1915
168–169 Haitian Campaign Service Medal 1919–1920
149–150 Philippine Campaign Service Medal
159–160 Mexican Service Medal
152 - 153–154 China Relief Expedition Service Medal
140–141 West Indies Campaign Service Medal

Reverse of these Army Medals

155 Cuban Pacification Service Medal
148 Philippine Campaign Service Medal
158 Mexican Service Medal
143 - 144 Spanish Campaign Service Medal
136 - 137 Indian Campaign Service Medal
151 China Campaign Service Medal
198 Army of Puerto Rico Occupation Service Medal
199 Army of Cuba Occupation Service Medal

Plate III	Plate III	Plate III

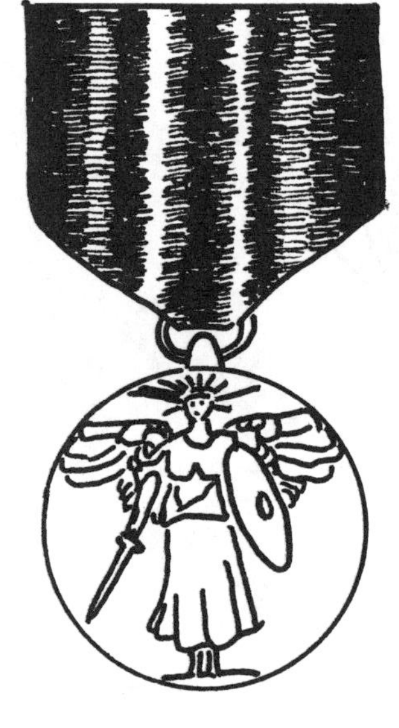

205.	206.	207.

205. Victory Medal World War I

Awarded For: To personnel of the United States Army, Navy, and Marine Corps for service between April 6, 1917, and November 11, 1918, or for later service from November 12, 1918, to August 5, 1919, with the American Expeditionary Forces in European Russia, also awarded for service in Siberia from November 12, 1918, to April 1, 1920.
Ref. Pg. 251

206. Victory Medal World War II

Awarded For: To personnel of the United States Armed Forces who served between December 31, 1946.
Ref. Pg. 252

207. Victory Medal World War II Merchant Marines

Awarded For: To personnel of the Merchant Marines who served between December 7, 1941, and September 3, 1945.
Ref. Pg. 252

Plate III

OBVERSE OF ALL

208.
REVERSE

209.
REVERSE

210.
REVERSE

211.
REVERSE

212.
REVERSE

213.
REVERSE

208. Armed Forces Reserve Medal, Air Force

Awarded For: To personnel of the Reserve components of the United States Air Force, and Air Force Reserve who have completed ten years of honorable and satisfactory service within a twelve year period.
Ref. Pg. 253

209. Armed Forces Reserve Medal, National Guard

Awarded For: To personnel of the Reserve components of the Air National Guard, National Guard in service to the United States, and National Guard of the United States who have completed ten years service and satisfactory service within a twelve year period.
Ref. Pg. 253

210. Armed Forces Reserve Medal, Navy

Awarded For: To personnel of the Reserve components of the United States Naval Reserve, Naval Militia, and National Naval Volunteers who have completed ten years service within a twelve year period.
Ref. Pg. 254

211. Armed Forces Reserve Medal, Coast Guard

Awarded For: To personnel of the Reserve components of the United States Coast Guard who have completed ten years of honorable and satisfactory service within a twelve year period.
Ref. Pg. 254

212. Armed Forces Reserve Medal, Army

Awarded For: To personnel of the Reserve components of the United States Organized Reserve Corps, Army of the United States, and Officers Reserve Corps who have completed ten years of honorable and satisfactory service within a twelve year period.
Ref. Pg. 255

213. Armed Forces Reserved Medal, Marine Corps

Awarded For: To personnel of the Reserve components of the United States Marine Corps who have completed ten years of service within a twelve year period.
Ref. Pg. 255

214. Marine Corps Organized Reserve Medal

Awarded For:	To personnel of the organized Marine
Ref. Pg. 256	Corps Reserve for four years of service after the date July 1, 1925.

214.

Plate III

FLEET MARINE CORPS RESERVE
FOR SERVICE

MARINE CORPS RESERVE
FOR SERVICE

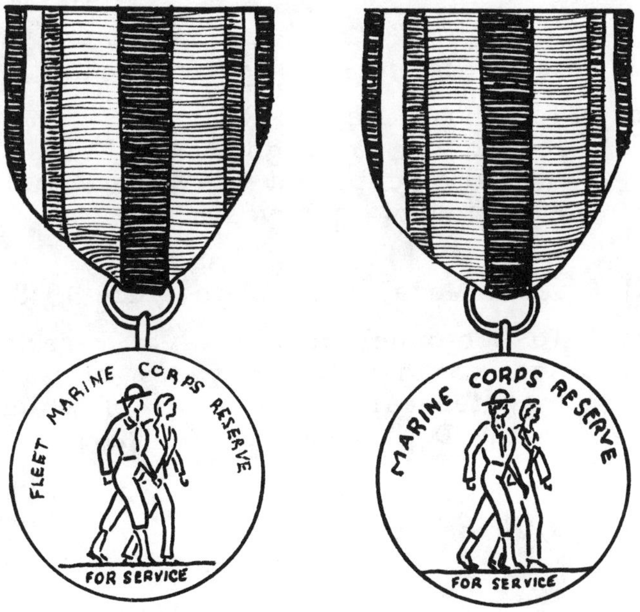

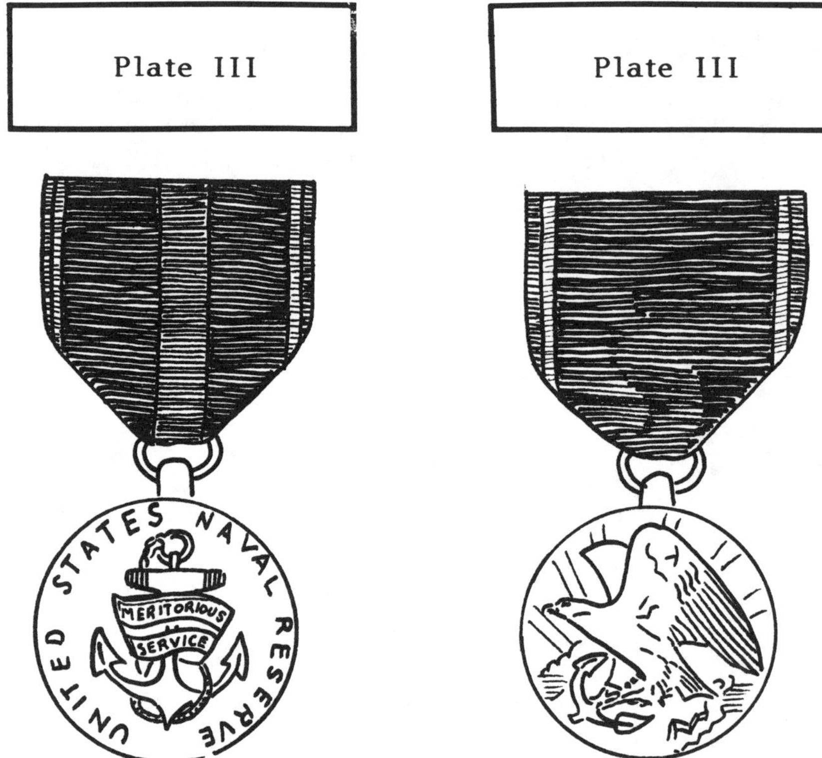

215. 216.

215. Naval Reserve Meritorious Service Medal

Awarded For: To those Naval Reservists who performed at a higher level than that normally expected of a Reservist over a period of four years.
Ref. Pg. 256

216. Naval Reserve Medal – Obsolete since 1958

Awarded For: To personnel of the Naval Reserve who had completed ten years of satisfactory federal service, all of which was to the Department of the Navy.
Ref. Pg. 257

217a. Army National Guard Achievement Medal

Awarded For: Ref. Pg. 258 — Satisfactory service above that expected of a Guardsman in the Army National Guard Troop Program Unit for four years.

217b. United States Army Reserve Achievement Medal

Awarded For: Ref. Pg. 258 — Satisfactory service above that expected of a Reservist in the Army Reserve Troop Program Unit for a period of four years.

218. Department of the Army Commander's Award for Civilian Service

Awarded For: Ref. Pg. 259 — I have no information on this medal.

219. Air Reserve Meritorious Service Medal

Awarded For: Ref. Pg. 259 — Four years of exemplary behavior, efficiency, and fidelity, in the Air Force Reserve.

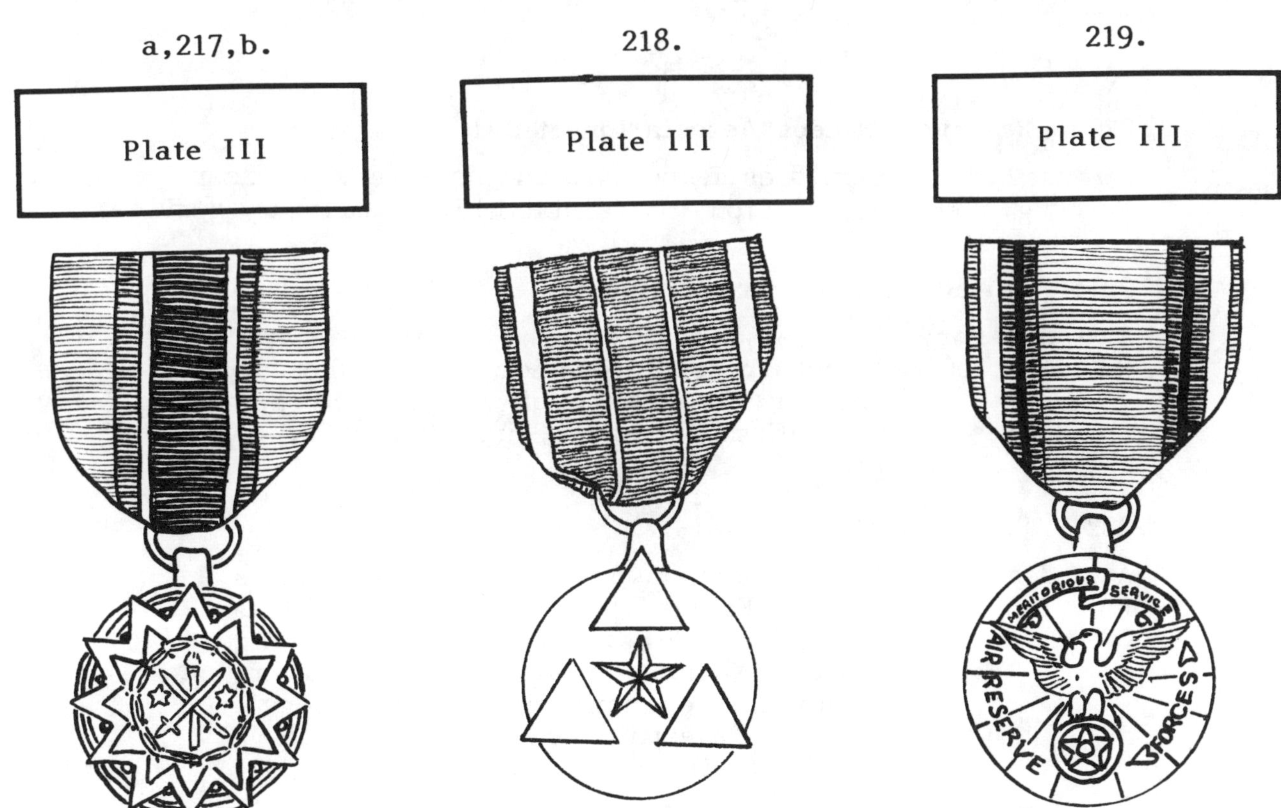

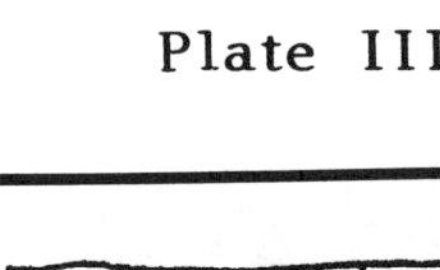

Plate III

Plate III

220. 221. 222.

220. Reserve Officers Association Medal

Awarded For: Signifies membership in the Reserve Officer
Ref. Pg. 260 Association, no relationship to military service.

221. United Nations Service Medal

Awarded For: To personnel of the United States
Ref. Pg. 260 Armed Forces for service in the Korean Theater on behalf of the United Nations Command from June 27, 1950, to July 27, 1954.

222. United Nations Medal

Awarded For: To personnel of the United States
Ref. Pg. 261 Armed Forces for service, not less than six months, with one of following United Nations units: UN Observers Group in Lebanon; UN Truce Supervision in Palestine; UN Military Observers Group in India and Pakistan.

223. United Nations Emergency Force Medal

Awarded For: Authorized for service in Egypt from Nov. 7, 1956 to May 17, 1967.
Ref. Pg. 261

224. Philippine Liberation Medal

Awarded For: To personnel of the United States Armed Forces for service in liberation of the Philippines from October 17, 1944, to September 3, 1945.
Ref. Pg. 262

225. Philippine Defense Medal

Awarded For: To personnel of the United States Armed Forces for service in defense of the Philippines from December 8, 1941, to June 15, 1942.
Ref. Pg. 262

226. Philippine Independence Medal

Awarded For: To personnel of the United States Armed Forces who have been awarded either, or both, Philippine Liberation and Defense medals.
Ref. Pg. 263

223.	224.	225.	226.
Plate III	Plate III	Plate III	Plate III

Plate IV	Plate IV	Plate IV

227.

228.

229.

227. Republic of Vietnam Campaign Medal

Awarded For: Ref. Pg. 264	To United States servicemen who had earned the United States Vietnam Campaign Service Medal and served six months in direct support of military operations in Vietnam.

228. United States Navy Expert Pistol Shot Medal

Awarded For: Ref. Pg. 265	Qualification under rigidly prescribed marksmanship requirements established by the Navy for automatic pistol.

229. United States Navy Expert Rifleman's Medal

Awarded For: Ref. Pg. 265	Qualification under rigidly prescribed marksmanship requirements established by the Navy for either rifle or carbine.

250. **United States Coast Guard Expert Pistol Shot Medal**

Awarded For: Ref. Pg. 266	Qualification under rigidly prescribed marksmanship requirements established by the Commandant, United States Coast Guard.

231. **United States Coast Guard Expert Rifleman's Medal**

Awarded For: Ref. Pg. 266	Qualification under rigidly prescribed marksmanship requirements established by the Commandant, United States Coast Guard.

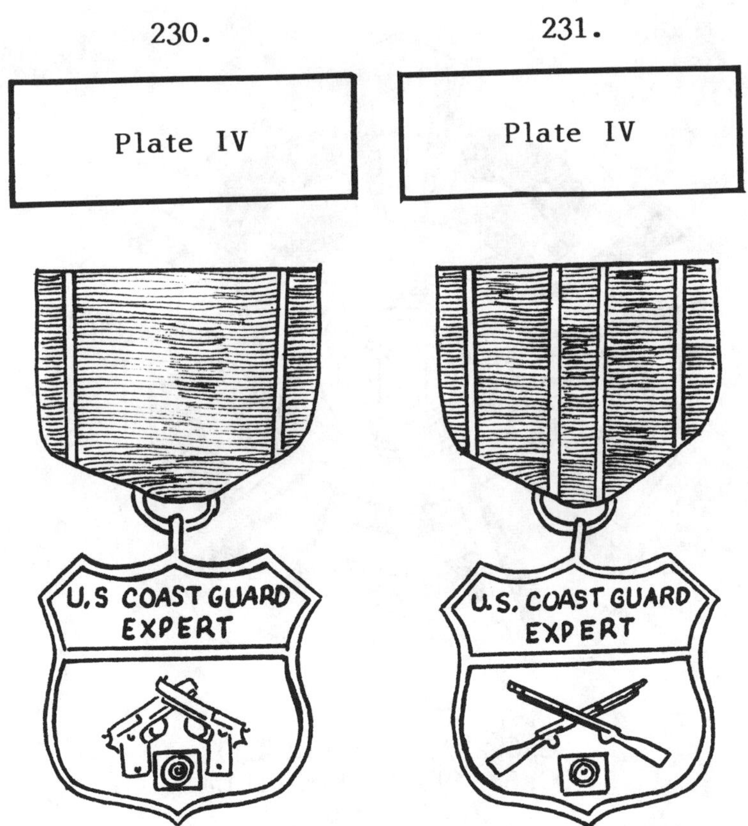

Plate IV

232

Plate IV

233

Plate IV

234

Plate IV

Ribbon 235 only

Plate IV

236

Plate IV

237

Plate IV

238

Plate IV

239

COAST GUARD AUXILIARY
232, 233, and 234

COAST GUARD AUXILIARY
236,237,238, and 239
COAST GUARD FLOTILLA
241 thru 247

Plate IV

Ribbon 240 only

Plate IV

241

Plate IV

242

Plate IV

243

Plate IV

244

Plate IV

245

Plate IV

246

Plate IV

247

232. **Coast Guard Auxiliary Plaque of Merit Medal "A" Award,** Ref. Pg. 267

233. **Coast Guard Auxiliary Certificate of Operational Merit "B" Award,** Ref. Pg. 267

234. **Coast Guard Auxiliary Certificate of Administrative Merit "C" Award,** Ref. Pg. 267

235. **Coast Guard Auxiliary Specialty Training Ribbon Bar,** Ref. Pg. 268

236. **Coast Guard Auxiliary Courtesy Examiner Medal,** Ref. Pg. 268

237. **Coast Guard Auxiliary Instructor Medal,** Ref. Pg. 268

238. **Coast Guard Auxiliary Operational Service Medal,** Ref. Pg. 269

239. **Coast Guard Auxiliary Five Year Membership Medal,** Ref. Pg. 269

240. **Coast Guard Auxiliary District Awards Ribbon Bar,** Ref. Pg. 270

241. **Coast Guard Flotilla Meritorious Achievement Medal,** Ref. Pg. 270

242. **Coast Guard Flotilla CME Achievement Medal,** Ref. Pg. 271

243. **Coast Guard Flotilla PEC Achievement Medal,** Ref. Pg. 271

244. **Coast Guard Flotilla Operations Achievement Medal,** Ref. Pg. 272

245. **Coast Guard Flotilla Training Achievement Medal,** Ref. Pg. 272

246. **Coast Guard Flotilla Growth and Retention Achievement Medal,** Ref. Pg. 273

247. **Coast Guard Flotilla Public Relations Achievement Medal,** Ref. Pg. 273

Awarded For: I have no information on what any of the above medals and ribbon bars are awarded for.

Plate IV	Plate IV	Plate IV
248.	249.	250.
Plate IV	Plate IV	Plate IV
251.	252.	253.
Plate IV	Plate IV	Plate IV
254.	255.	256.
Plate IV	Plate IV	Plate IV
257.	258.	259.
Plate IV	Plate IV	Plate IV
260.	261.	262.

248. **Navy "E" Award,** Ref. Pg. 274
249. **Navy Sea Service,** Ref. Pg. 274
250. **Presidential Unit Citation Army and Air Force,** Ref. Pg. 274
251. **Presidential Unit Citation Navy and Marine Corps,** Ref. Pg. 275
252. **Valorous Unit Citation Army,** Ref. Pg. 275
253. **Meritorious Unit Commendation Army,** Ref. Pg. 276
254. **Meritorious Unit Commendation Navy and Marine Corps,** Ref. Pg. 276
255. **Philippine Republic Presidential Unit Citation,** Ref. Pg. 277
256. **Republic of Korea Presidential Unit Citation,** Ref. Pg. 277
257. **Vietnam Presidential Unit Citation or Friendship Ribbon,** Ref. Pg. 278
258. **Republic of Vietnam Civil Actions Unit Citation,** Ref. Pg. 278
259. **Republic of Vietnam Cross of Gallantry Unit Citation,** Ref. Pg. 279
260. **Merchant Marine Pacific War Zone Bar,** Ref. Pg. 279
261. **Merchant Marine Atlantic War Zone Bar,** Ref. Pg. 280
262. **Merchant Marine Mediterranean-Middle East War Zone Bar,** Ref. Pg. 280

Plate IV	Plate IV	Plate IV
263.	264.	265.
Plate IV	Plate IV	Plate IV
266.	267.	268.
Plate IV	Plate IV	Plate IV
269.	270.	271.
Plate IV	Plate IV	Plate IV
272.	273.	274.
Plate IV	Plate IV	Plate IV
275.	276.	277.

263. Merchant Marine Gallant Ship Citation, Ref. Pg. 281
264. Merchant Marine Defense Bar, Ref. Pg. 281
265. Merchant Marine Combat Bar, Ref. Pg. 281
266. Merchant Marine Korean Service Bar, Ref. Pg. 282
267. Merchant Marine Vietnam Service Bar, Ref. Pg. 282
268. Combat Action Bar–Navy, Marine Corps, and Coast Guard, Ref. 282
269. N.A.T.O., Ref. Pg. 283
270. Air Force Longevity, Ref. Pg. 283
271. Air Force Training Bar, Ref. Pg. 283
272. Air Force Overseas Service Short Term, Ref. Pg. 283
273. Air Force Overseas Service Long Term, Ref. Pg. 284
274. Air Force Outstanding Airman of the Year, Ref. Pg. 284
275. Air Force Outstanding Unit Award, Ref. Pg. 284
276. Air Force Organizational Excellence Award, Ref. Pg. 285
277. Air Force Noncommissioned Officer Academy Graduate, Ref. Pg. 285

Plate IV	Plate IV	Plate IV
278.	279.	280.
Plate IV	Plate IV	Plate IV
281.	282.	283.
Plate IV	Plate IV	Plate IV
284.	288.	289.
Plate IV	Plate IV	Plate IV
287.	288.	289.
Plate IV	Plate IV	Plate IV
290.	291.	293.

278. Air Force Recognition Ribbon Bar, Ref. Pg. 285
279. Air Force Small Arms Expert, Ref. Pg. 285
280. Army N.C.O. Ribbon Bar, Ref. Pg. 286
281. Army Service, Ref. Pg. 286
282. Army Overseas Service, Ref. Pg. 286
283. Navy Unit Commendation, Ref. Pg. 286
284. Coast Guard Unit Commendation, Ref. Pg. 287
285. Reserve Special Commendation-Navy, Ref. Pg. 287
286. Coast Guard Reserve Meritorious, Ref. Pg. 287
287. Marine Corps Reserve Ribbon Bar, Ref. Pg. 288
288. Navy Distinguished Marksman Distinguished Pistol Shot, Ref. Pg. 288
289. Navy Distinguished Marksman, Ref. Pg. 288
290. Navy Distinguished Pistol Shot, Ref. Pg. 288
291. National Matches Marksmanship Medals, Ref. Pg. 289
293. United States Coast Guard Reserve Unit Commendation, Ref. Pg. 289

Plate IV

292.

292. Organization of American States

Awarded For: In 1965 United States troops were sent into the Dominican Republic. All troops involved were to receive this medal but it was never issued.

Ref. Pg. 289

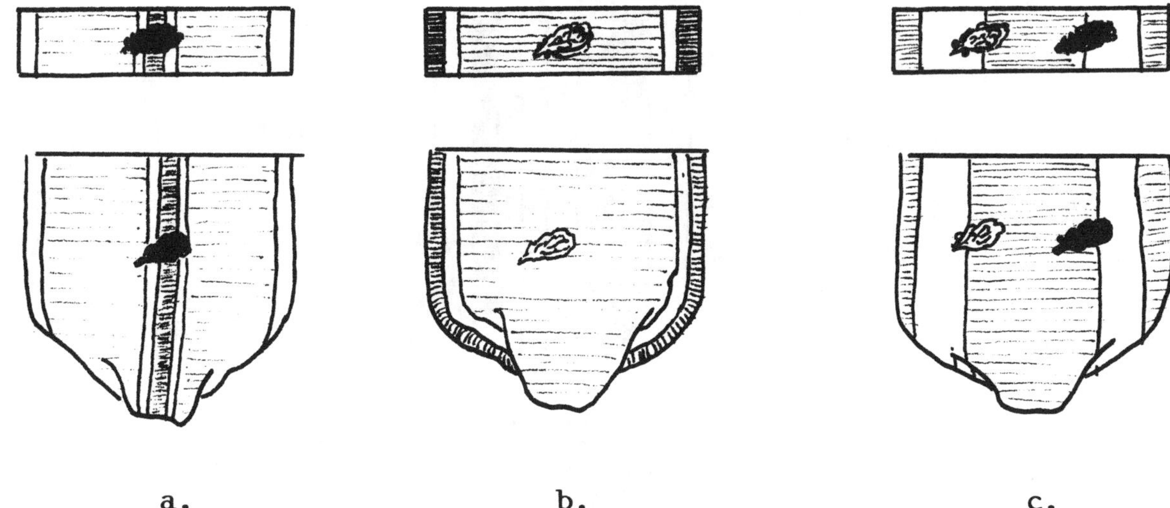

a. b. c.

Oak Leaf Clusters, Army and Air Force

a. A Bronze Oak Leaf Cluster denotes each subsequent award of the same decoration.

b. A Silver Oak Leaf Cluster denotes five Bronze Oak Leaf Clusters earned.

c. When an Oak Leaf Cluster is worn on a decoration, it will be centered on the ribbon. When two or more are worn, they are arranged an equal distance apart from the ends of the ribbon centered as much as possible. When both a Silver and a Bronze Oak Leaf Cluster are worn, the Silver one will be to the wearer's right.

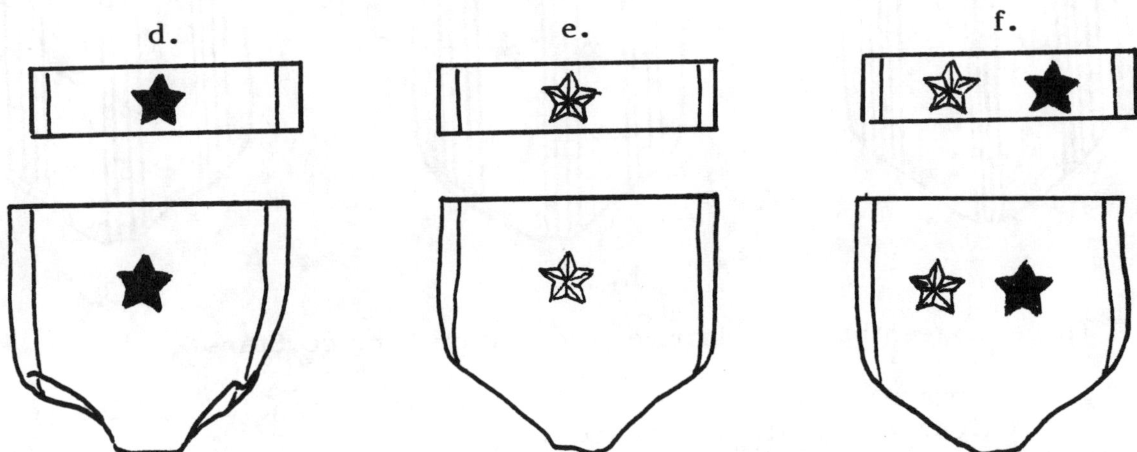

Five-sixteenths inch Gold and Silver Stars, Navy, Marine Corps, and Coast Guard

d. A Gold Star denotes each subsequent award of the same decoration.

e. A Silver Star denotes five Gold Stars earned.

f. When a five-sixteenths inch Star is worn, it will be centered on the ribbon. When two or more are worn they are arranged an equal distance apart from the ends of the ribbon and centered as much as possible. When both a Gold and Silver Star are worn, the Silver one will be to the wearer's right.

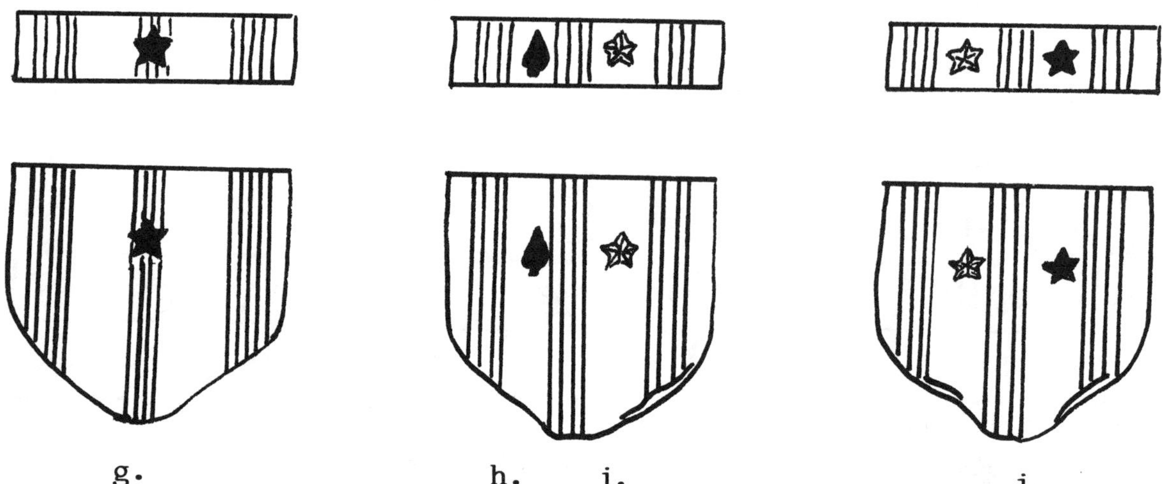

g. h. i. j.

Three-sixteenths Inch Bronze and Silver Service Stars

g. A Bronze Service Star is awarded for designated battles, campaigns or additional awards.

h. A Silver Service Star is awarded to denote five Bronze Stars earned.

j. When a three-sixteenths inch Service Star is worn on a ribbon, it will be centered on the ribbon. When two or more are worn they are arranged an equal distance apart from the ends of the ribbon and centered as much as possible. When both a Silver and a Bronze Star are worn, the Silver Star will be worn to the wearer's right.

Bronze Arrowhead

h. A Bronze Service Arrowhead, one quarter inch high, was authorized December 23, 1944, for wear on the appropriate campaign service and suspension ribbon. Worn with the point up, this Arrowhead indicates that a man has participated in a combat parachute jump, combat glider landing, or initial assault landing on a hostile shore. This device will be awarded to all personnel who have taken part in any such operation subsequent to December 7, 1941. Only one Arrowhead may be worn on any service or suspension ribbon, and they are placed to the right of all other devices on the ribbon.

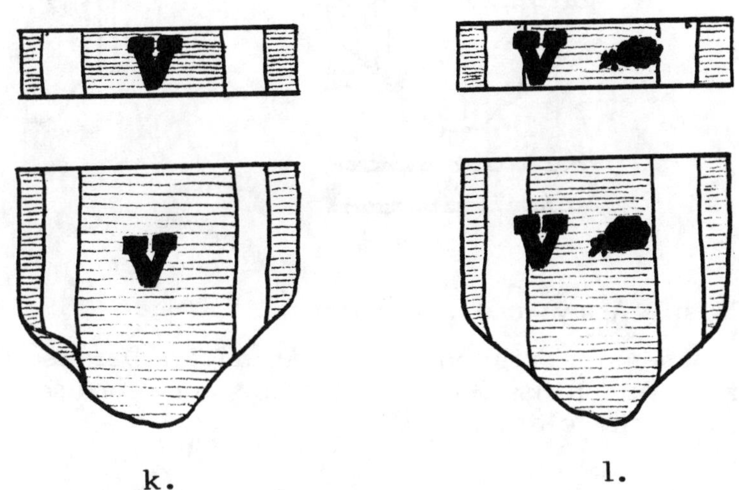

k. l.

Bronze V

k. A Bronze V denotes an award for valor or combat.

l. When a Bronze V is worn, it will be centered on the ribbon. When another device such as an Oak Leaf Cluster or Star is worn, the two devices are arranged an equal distance apart from the ends of the ribbon and centered as much as possible with the V device always worn to the right of the ribbon.

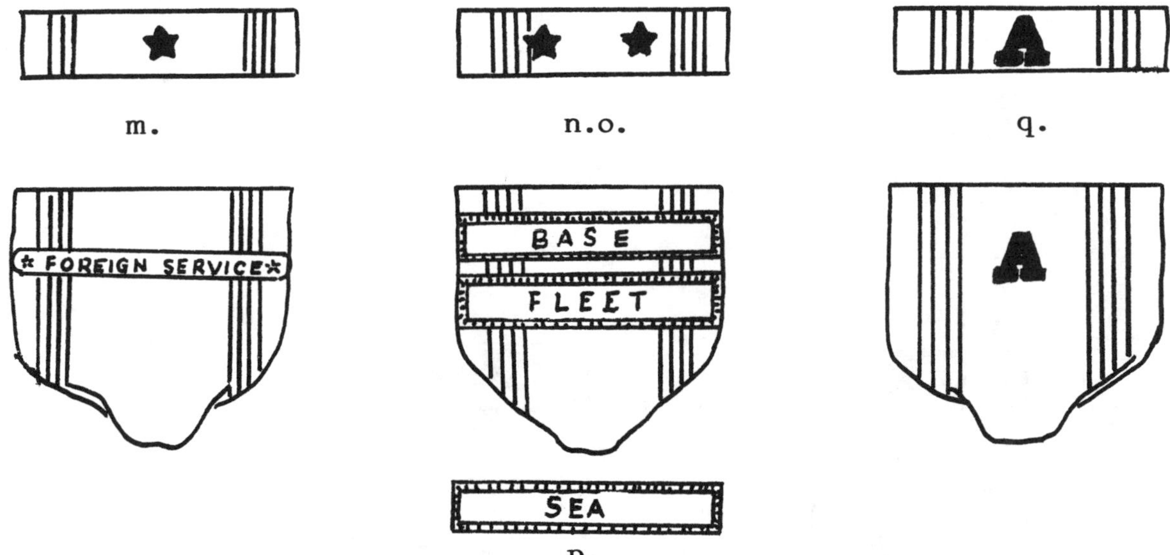

p.

Foreign Service Clasp, Army and Air Force

m. Worn on the suspension ribbon of the American Defense Service Medal. A three-sixteenths Service Star is worn on the service ribbon in lieu of the clasp.

Fleet and Base Clasp, Navy, Marines, and Coast Guard

n.o. Worn on the suspension ribbon of the American Defense Service Medal. A three-sixteenths service star is worn on the service ribbon in lieu of the clasp.

Sea Service Clasp, Coast Guard

p. Worn on the suspension ribbon of the American Defense Service Medal. A three-sixteenths Service Star is worn on the service ribbon in lieu of the clasp.

Bronze A

q. Worn on the service and suspension ribbons of the American Defense Service Medal by personnel of designated vessels with the Atlantic Fleet for service between June 22, 1941, and December 7, 1941. When wearing the A device, no Service Star can be worn on the ribbon.

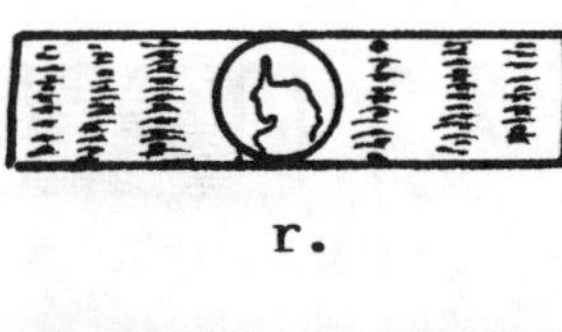

r.

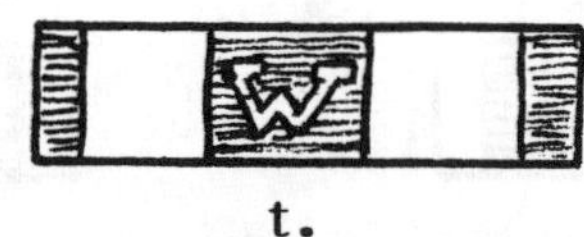

t.

s.

u.

Wintered Over Disk

r. Worn on the service ribbon of the Antarctica Service Medal to show that a person remained on the Antarctica continent through a winter. Bronze for one winter, Gold for two winters, and Silver for three winters.

Wintered Over Clasp

s. Worn on the suspension ribbon of the Antarctica Service Medal to show that a person remained on the Antarctica continent through a winter. Bronze for one winter, Gold for two winters, and Silver for three winters.

Silver W

t. A Silver W worn on the service ribbon indicates possession of the Wake Island clasp worn on the suspension ribbon.

Wake Island Clasp

u. Awarded to Navy personnel who served in defense of Wake Island December 7, 1941. The Wake Island Clasp is worn on the Navy Expeditionary Medal suspension ribbon only.

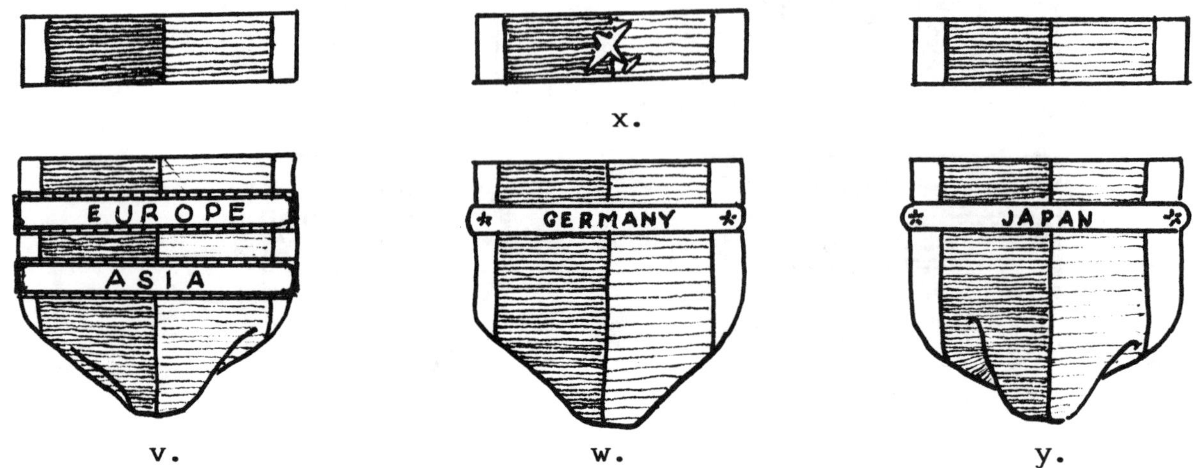

Europe and Asia Clasps, Navy, Marines, and Coast Guard

v. Worn on the suspension ribbon of the Navy Occupation Service Medal. May not be worn on the ribbon bar.

Germany Clasp, Army and Air Force

w. Worn on the suspension ribbon of the Army Occupation Service Medal. May not be worn on ribbon bar.

Japan Clasp, Army and Air Force

y. Worn on the suspension ribbon of the Army Occupation Service Medal. May not be worn on the ribbon bar.

Berlin Airlift Device

x. Awarded for 90 consecutive days service in direct support of the Berlin Airlift from June 26, 1948, to September 30, 1949. Worn on the service and suspension ribbons of the Army of Occupation Medal or Navy Occupation Medal. When wearing the device, the nose of the aircraft is pointed at a 30-degree angle toward the wearer's right.

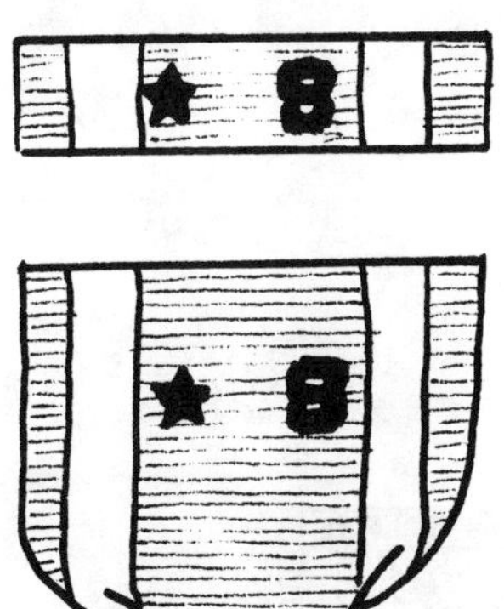

z. aa.

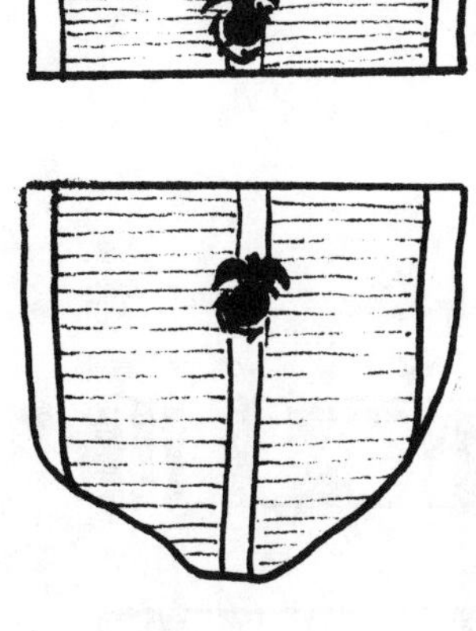

bb.

Navy and Marine Corps Air Medal, Three-sixteenths inch Service Star

z. Worn to denote the initial heroic award of the medal subsequent to April 9, 1962.

Bronze Arabic Numeral, Army
Strike/Flight Device, Navy and Marine Corps

aa. Worn to denote subsequent awards of the Air Medal, Army. When worn by Navy and Marine Corps personnel it denotes the total number of strike/flight awards of the Air Medal earned subsequent to April 9, 1962.

Fleet Marine Force Combat Operations Insignia

bb. For Navy personnel attached to Fleet Marine Force units participating in combat operations. Worn on the service and suspension ribbons of the appropriate campaign or service medal. When this device is worn on a ribbon it is centered and Battle Stars are placed alternately, the first to the right of the device, the second to the left of the device, etc.

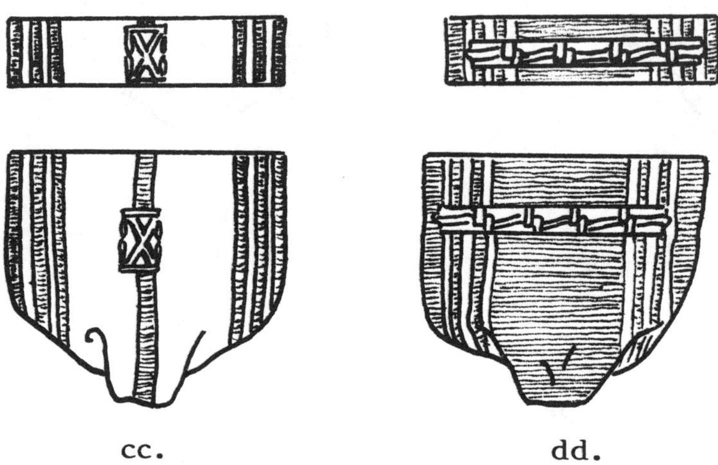

cc. dd.

Hour Glass Device

cc. Worn to denote each succeeding award of the Armed Forces Reserve Medal. When two or more are worn, they are arranged an equal distance apart from the ends of the ribbon and centered as much as possible.

Good Conduct Medal Clasp, Army

dd. The number of loops and color denote the number of awards of the Army Good Conduct Medal, Bronze 2nd through 5th awards, Silver 6th through 10th awards, and Gold 11th through 15th awards. Only one color may be worn at a time, centered on the ribbon.

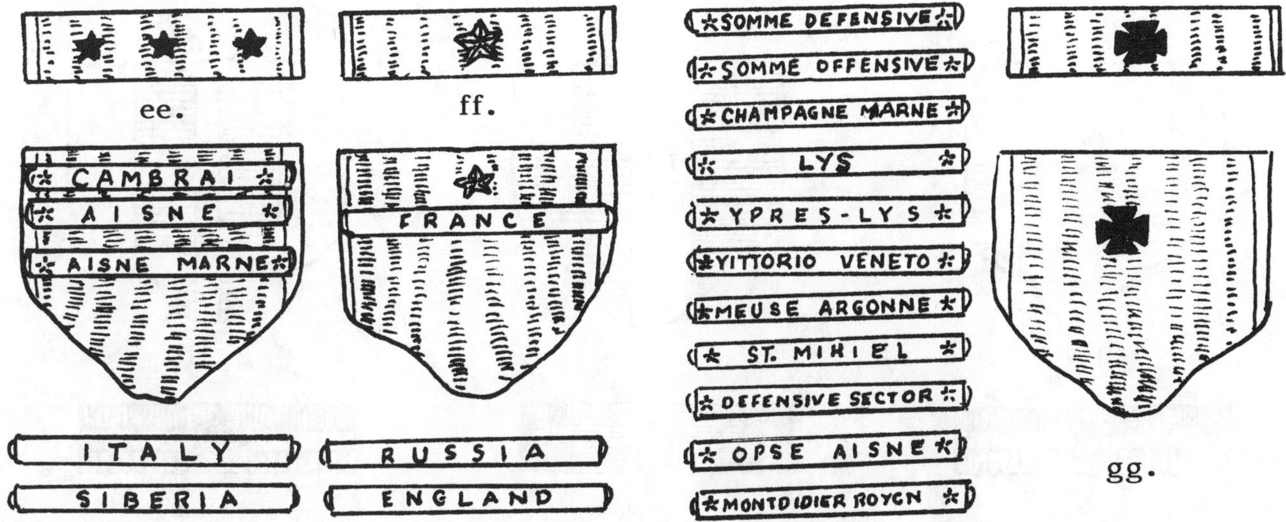

Bronze Service, Defense Sector, and Battle Clasps

ee. Worn on the suspension ribbon of the World War I Victory Medal. A three-sixteenths inch Service Star is worn on the service ribbon in lieu of the clasps.

Silver Citation Star, Obsolete

ff. By Act of Congress July 9, 1918, for each citation of an Army officer or enlisted man for gallantry in action, a Silver Star three-sixteenths inch in diameter was authorized for wear on the suspension and service ribbon of the appropriate service medal, shown here on the World War II Victory Medal. In 1932 the Citation Star was replaced by the Silver Star Medal.

Bronze Maltese Cross

gg. The Bronze Maltese Cross is worn centered on the World War I Victory Medal. This device was awarded to Marine Corps, Medical Corps, and Navy personnel who served with the A.E.F. in France between April 6, 1917, and November 11, 1918, and did not participate in any engagement for which battle clasps were authorized by the Army.

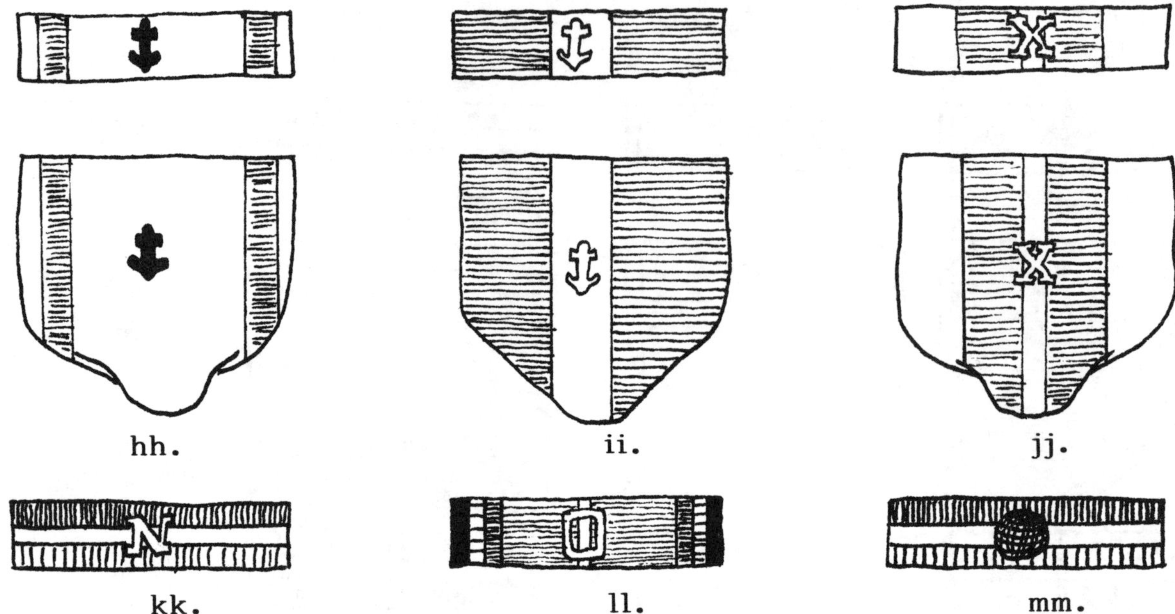

Bronze Anchor, United States Coast Guard

hh. Awarded to denote additional awards on the Coast Guard Auxiliary and Flotilla Service medals.

Silver Anchor, United States Coast Guard

ii. Awarded to denote four additional awards of the Coast Guard Auxiliary and Flotilla Service medals.

Silver X

jj. Awarded to those who qualified with ten years cumulative service, worn on the Coast Guard Auxiliary Courtesy examiner, instructor, and operational service medals.

Gold N

kk. Worn on the Navy Presidential Unit Citation Ribbon by personnel of the U.S.S. Nautilus who were on board the ship when it was cited.

Silver O

ll. Worn on the United States Coast Guard Unit Commendation Ribbon to denote distinguished operational performance.

Bronze Globe

mm. Worn on the Navy Presidential Unit Citation Ribbon by personnel of the U.S.S. Triton who were on board the ship when it was cited.

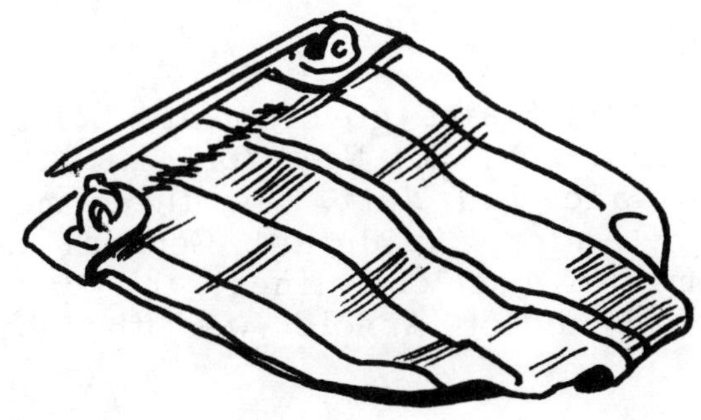

1898 to 1920

1920 to 1940

1940's

CURRENT
FLAT PIN

CURRENT CLUTCH BACK

A.

Andre Medal

The only decoration given by the United States government, before the Civil War, was given to three privates of the New York Militia, John Paulding, David Williams, and Isaac Van Wart. The three men intercepted and captured Major John Andre, Adjuntant General of the British Army, on his return from the American lines; the dangerous and traitorous conspiracy of Benedict Arnold was thereby brought to light.

Obverse. A silver, oval shaped, medallion. In the center an elaborately ornamented shield. Above, a banner ininscribed with the word, **"Fidelity"**, the whole encircled by a branch of laurel and a stem of a lily, bearing leaves and blossom.

Reverse. A wreath of two stems with leaves and blossoms, similar to the one on the obverse, surrounding a plain field; Legend, **"Vincit Amor Patrie"**.

The medal is then topped with a loop for suspension.

Note: Some people refer to this medal as the Fidelity Medal and others the Andre, but to my knowledge it was never given a formal name.

B.

The Kearny Medal for Officers

On November 29, 1862, a meeting of officers adopted a resolution to the effect that a **"Medal of Honor"** to be known as the **"Kearny Medal"**, presented to all officers who had **"Honorably served in battle under General Kearny in his Division."** Major General Philip Kearny, commander of the First Division, Third Army Corps, was killed at the Battle of Chantilly, September 1, 1862.

Obverse. A gold cross patte, in center of which is a circular medallion, with a banner draped horizontally across center, bearing the word **"Kearny"**, in black enamel. Encircling this one-eighth of an inch distance is a plain black enamel band, with the inscription **"Dulce Et Decorum Est Pro Patria Mori"**, in gold letters.

Reverse. The number of the medal, name, and rank of the recipient. The medal is then suspended from a gold bar attached to a ribbon.

Ribbon. Red.

Designer. Ball, Black, and Company, Jewelers and Silversmiths of New York.

Note: This medal is also to apply to soldiers promoted to commissioned officers prior to January 1, 1863.

C.

The Kearny Cross
For Non-Commissioned Officers and Privates

On March 13, 1863, Brigadier General Birney issued an order to the effect that a **"Cross of Valor,"** to be known as the **Kearny Cross"** would be bestowed upon Non-Commissioned officers and privates who had distinguished themselves in battle.

Obverse. A bronze cross patte, at center on a ribbon bearing the words **"Kearny Cross"**.

Reverse. On the horizontal arm of the cross in a straight line the words **"Birney's Division"**. At the top of the cross in very small letters the inscription **"Jacobus Phila"**.

D.

Gillmore or Fort Sumter Medal

On October 28, 1863, Major General Quincy A. Gillmore issued an order that **"Medals of Honor for Gallant and Meritorious Conduct during the Operations Before Charleston"** be awarded by the Commanding General to a number of enlisted men of the command who had been in action or on duty in the batteries and trenches.

Obverse. A bronze medallion that bears the representations of Fort Sumter surrounded by water. Above the fort inscribed in an arc the words **"Fort Sumter"**. Below the fort and water the inscription **"Aug. 23d 1863"**. Around the outside edge of the medal are thirteen stars.

Reverse. Around the outside edge the inscription **"For Gallant and Meritorious Conduct"** ending with three tiny stars. At top, the word **"Presented"** and under that the word **"By"**. Centered a facsimile of General Gillmore's signature signed **"Q.A. Gillmore"** below that **"Maj. Gen."**

The medal is suspended by a swivel from a plain clasp pin.

Ribbon. None.

Designer. Ball, Black, and Company, New York.

E.

Butler or Colored Troops Medal

On October 11, 1864, Major-General Benjamin F. Butler, the Commander of the Army of the James, announced that a special medal would be struck in honor of certain black soldiers of his command for gallantry in action in the storming of New Market Heights, September 29, 1864.

Obverse. A bronze medallion that portrays a Bastion Fort charged upon by black soldiers, and bears the inscription **"Ferro iis Libertas Perveniet"**, on a ribbon at top. Below this in very small letters the words **"Butler. Del. Paquet. F."** Under the representation of the attack, at the base of the medal the inscription of the attack, at the base of the medal the inscription **"U.S. Colored Troops."**

Reverse. Centered the inscription **"Campaign Before Richmond 1864"**, encircled by an oak wreath, around the outside of the medal the words **"Distinguished for Courage"** with a small star starting and ending.

The medal is suspended from a ribbon by an eagle's claw grasping a sphere to which was attached the ring that passes through the medal. The medal is attached to the clothing by a strong pin, having in front an oak leaf, with the inscription on a ribbon placed horizontally **"Army of the James."**

Ribbon. Starting at left red, white, and blue in equal stripes.

Designer. Medal dies by Anthony C. Paquet. The ribbon and attachments supplied by Charles W. Kennard & Co.

Note: In this one action there were nearly two hundred medals presented.

Congressional Medal of Honor

This is the highest honor the United States can bestow on members of its Armed Forces. It is usually presented by the President and is awarded in the name of the Congress of the United States.

Awarded **"For Conspicuous Gallantry and Intrepidity at the Risk of Life, Above and Beyond the Call of Duty, in Action Involving Actual Conflict with an Enemy"** and without detriment to his mission - Congress, February 4, 1919.

Each branch of the United States Armed Forces has its own distinctive type of decoration.

F.

Navy and Marine Corps Medal of Honor 1861 - 1913

Until 1861 the United States Navy had no medals or decorations. At the outbreak of the Civil War, Senator James Grimes of Iowa, Chairman of the Senate Naval Committee, introduced a bill to create a Navy award **"To seaman and petty officers of the United States Navy who distinguished themselves by their gallantry in action and seaman-like qualities."** This bill was passed by both Houses of Congress and approved by President Abraham Lincoln on December 21, 1861, thereby establishing the first decoration formally authorized by the United States government. Naval and Marine officers were not eligible for this decoration until March 3, 1863.

Obverse. Five-pointed star, tipped with trefoils containing crown of laurel and oak in the middle of each point. In the center of the star is a ring of 34 stars, the number of states in 1862. Inside the ring of stars is Minerva, personifying the United States, she stands with right hand holding a shield blazoned with the U.S. Arms. She repulses discord, represented by snakes. All suspended by small anchor wrapped loosely with rope (or fouled anchor), suspended from a Bronze frame centered by a star just over the anchor. Clasp is bronze frame just like lower one but without star.

Ribbon. Top half blue field bottom half red and white striped; 7 red, 6 white.

Designer. Anthony C. Paquett.

G.

Navy and Marine Corps Medal of Honor 1913 - 1919

Same as 1861-1913 version with two changes.

Change One. Fouled anchor is replaced by anchor.

Change Two. Ribbon is changed to blue moire in color with thirteen white stars in this pattern starting at top of ribbon: 1-2-3-2-3-2.

H.

Navy and Marine Corps Medal of Honor 1919–1942

Congress, on February 4, 1919, authorized the President to present in the name of Congress a Medal of Honor to any person in the Naval Service who shall **"In action involving actual conflict with the enemy, distinguish himself conspicuously by gallantry and intrepidity at the risk of his life above and beyond the call of duty"** and without detriment to his mission.

Awarded for service during World War I.

Obverse. Gold cross patée: on each arm a free anchor. A wreath between each arm encircling an octagonal medallion containing U.S. Coat of Arms within the legend, United States Navy 1917–1918. Clasp bar inscribed **"Valour."**

Ribbon. Blue moire with thirteen white stars in this pattern starting at top of ribbon: 1-2-3-2-3-2.

Designer. Tiffany and Company.

I.

Medal of Honor – Navy and Marine Corps 1942 to Present

Obverse. Five-pointed star, tipped with trefoils containing crown of laurel and oak in the middle of each point. In the center of the star is a ring of 34 stars, the number of states in 1862. Inside the ring of stars is Minerva, personifying the United States. She stands with right hand holding a shield blazoned with the United States Coat of Arms. All suspended by a small anchor.

This pendant is just the same as the 1913–1919 except it is now worn from a neck ribbon.

Ribbon. 1 3/16 inches wide and 21 3/4 inches long of blue moire. A pad of blue moire bares thirteen white stars in this pattern starting at top: 1-2-3-2-3-2.

Designer. Anthony C. Paquet.

I.

Army Medal of Honor 1862 - 1896

Until the outbreak of the Civil War those individuals who distinguished themselves during war received battlefield or brevet promotions. On February 17, 1862, Senator Henry Wilson of Massachusetts introduced a Senate resolution providing for presentation of Medals of Honor to be presented **"In the name of Congress, to such non-commissioned officers and privates as shall most distinguish themselves by their gallantry in action, and other soldier-like qualities"**, during the Civil War. President Abraham Lincoln's approval on July 12, 1863, made the resolution a Law and on March 3, 1863, Congress provided that Commissioned Officers might also receive the Medal. The time limit was removed, leaving **"Gallantry in Action"** the only qualification.

Obverse. Five-pointed star, tipped with trefoils containing crown of laurel and oak in the middle of each point. In the center of the star is a ring of 34 stars, the number of states in 1862. Inside the ring of stars is Minerva, personifying the United States, stand with right hand holding a shield blazoned with U.S. Arms. She repulses discord, represented by snakes. All suspended by a trophy of crossed cannons, balls, sword, and American eagle. Clasp is two cornucopias and arms of the United States.

Ribbon. Top half blue field, bottom half red and white striped; 7 red, 6 white.

Designer. Anthony C. Paquet.

J.

Army Medal of Honor 1896 - 1904

Same as 1862-1896 version with one difference. On May 2, 1896, Congress authorized a change in the ribbon.

Ribbon. Changed to a vertical white center strip. Flanked by blue and red at each edge.

K.

Medal of Honor 1904 - 1945

On April 23, 1904, Congress provided for a new design and five months later, September 20, 1905, an Executive order of President Theodore Roosevelt, provided that presentation of a Medal of Honor always be made with **"Formal and Impressive Ceremonial".** The President ordered **"The recipient of a Medal of Honor will, whenever practicable, be ordered to Washington and the presentation will be made by the President".**

The New Design.

Obverse. A Gold five-pointed star, 1 9/16 inches in diameter, each point tipped by trefoils with a green enamel oak leaf in the center of each point. In the center of the star, Minerva's head surrounded by the words, **"United States of America".** This star is superimposed on a green enamel and gold laurel wreath. The star and wreath is suspended from a gold bar inscribed **"Valor",** surmounted by an eagle.

Reverse. Bar engraved **"The Congress to".**

Ribbon. Light blue moire with thirteen white stars in this pattern starting at top: 1-2-3-2-3.

Designer. Major General George L. Gillespie.

2.

Army Medal of Honor 1945 to Present

Same as the 1904 to 1945 version with one difference. At the end of World War II the ribbon was changed so that the decoration would be worn on the neck ribbon.

Ribbon. Light blue moire worn from a neck cravat. A pad of blue moire bares thirteen white stars in this pattern starting at top: 1-2-3-2-3-2. The ribbon is 1 3/16 inches wide and 21 3/4 inches long.

3.

Air Force Medal of Honor 1963 to Present

From 1907 to September 18, 1947, the Air Force was part of the Army and Air Force personnel received the Army type decoration. In 1963, Air Force Secretary Eugene M. Zuckert approved a new design.

Obverse. A five-point bronze star, 2 inches in diameter, each point tipped by trefoils. In each ray of the star appears a crown of laurel and oak surrounded by green enamel. The center of the medallion portrays the head of the Statue of Liberty surrounded by a ring of thirty-four stars. The entire medallion is superimposed on a green enamel and gold laurel wreath. The star is suspended from bronze portion of the Air Force Coat of Arms, thunderbolts, aviator's wings, and talons, topped by a bronze plaque inscribed **"Valor"**.

Ribbon. Light blue moire worn from a neck cravat. A pad of blue moire bares thirteen white stars in this pattern starting at top: 1-2-3-2-3-2. The Ribbon is 1 3/16 inches wide and 21 3/4 inches long.

Designer. By the Institute of Heraldry, U.S. Army.

4.

Congressional Space Medal of Honor

Established by Act of Congress on September 29, 1969. The President may award this decoration, in the name of Congress, to any astronaut, civil or military, who, in performance of his duties, distinguishes himself, or herself, by exceptionally meritorious contributions to the welfare of a mission, and/or of the nation, and/or of mankind.

Obverse. On a bronze circular medallion a green-enameled laurel wreath on which is superimposed a five-pointed, gold star. Between the arms of the star is portrayed a light blue enamel cloud bank with five lobes edged in gold. In the center of this is a five-pointed, dark enamel star edged in gold, with a one-quarter carat diamond in its center. The wreath is topped by a gold eagle with outstretched wings.

Reverse. In a semi-circle at the top it has the inscription **"Congressional"**, at the bottom **"Space Medal Presented to"**, in the center is an area for the recipient's name. Both inscription and name are surrounded by a circle of fifty stars.

Ribbon. Center stripe of red flanked by a narrow white stripe, a wide blue stripe, a medium-dark-blue stripe, and edged in gold.

Rank. With the word **"Congressional"** in its title some rank it just above the branch distinguished service crosses. Others feel it is a non-military decoration and rank it just under the Purple Heart, when worn on a military uniform.

Rank. Note: This is the only precious jewelled U.S. decoration. Also from what information I could gather, this decoration has yet to be awarded.

5.

U.S.M.C. Brevet Medal

Established by the Secretary of the Navy on June 7, 1921, as an award to Marines who had received Brevet Commissions issued by the President and confirmed by the Senate for distinguished conduct in the presence of the enemy. This decoration was not awarded posthumously.

Definition of the word Brevet - A commission nominally promoting an officer to a higher honorary rank without higher pay or greater authority.

Obverse. Bronze cross pattée with building ends. On medallion, the word **"Brevet"** encircled by the words **"United States Marine Corps."** A small star separates the words United and Corps. The Marine Corps insignia joins the cross to the ribbon.

Reverse. Inscription, **"For Distinguished Conduct in Presence of Enemy."**

Ribbon. Red moire with thirteen white stars in this pattern starting at top of ribbon: 2-3-2-3-2-1.

Designer. Q.M. Sgt. Joseph A. Burnett, U.S.M.C.

6.

Certificate of Merit - Army

Created during the War with Mexico by Act of Congress, March 3, 1847, for Army privates only. In 1854 Non-Commissioned officers were also made eligible.

Awarded for - having distinguished himself in the services of the United States in battle or peacetime for heroism involving saving life or property at the risk of one's own or for other services that the President of the United States thought were deserving of this certificate.

On January 11, 1905, Congress authorized all former recipients of the Certificate of Merit to receive a medal. The medal was discontinued by Congress on July 9, 1918, and holders of the medal could at that time upon request exchange it for the Distinguished Service Medal. In 1934 this was again changed and the Distinguished Service Medal awarded under these circumstances could be exchanged for the higher ranking Distinguished Service Cross.

Obverse. Roman war eagle, surrounded by the inscription, **"Virtutis Et Audaciae Monumentum Et Praemium"** translation (Virtue and Courage are their Own Monument and Reward.).

Reverse. **"For Merit"** in oak wreath joined at bottom by a knot, all in a circle of words **"United States Army"** in upper half, and 13 stars in lower half.

Ribbon. White center stripe with red, white, and blue on either side.

Designer. Francis D. Millet.

L.

Revenue Cutter Service Cardenas Medal of Honor

By joint resolution of Congress approved May 3, 1900, in recognition of the gallantry of the officers and men of the Hudson, who in the face of the enemy under heavy fire towed the Winslow out of range of enemy fire. First Lieutenant Frank H. Newcomb received a Gold Medal, his officers a Silver, and to his men a Bronze.

Obverse. The medallion is 3 1/8 inches in diameter not intended for wear. It portrays a draped winged female figure wearing a winged helmet holding sword and palm branch. At bottom right is the scene of the Hudson towing the Winslow. Below the inscription **"Cardenas May 11, 1898."**

Reverse. At left an oak wreath superimposed over a palm branch extending beyond the oak wreath. To the right of this is a nude figure inscribing with chisel and mallet the inscription **"Joint Resolution of Congress Approved May 3, 1900, in Recognition of the Gallantry of the Officers and Men of the Hudson Who in Face of the Enemy's Gun."** Below this is an area for the recipient's name framed by sprays of laurel.

Ribbon. None.

Note: Revenue Cutter Service is the former name of the U.S. Coast Guard.

M.

Bailey Medal

On December 1, 1885, the Navy Department announced that a Medal of Gold would be awarded annually to one Naval apprentice with an outstanding record. The Medal was named in Honor of Theodorus Bailey.

Obverse. Bust of Admiral Bailey, surrounded by the inscription **"Endowed in Memoriam Theodorus Bailey, Obit. 1877."**

Reverse. Has the words **"Conferred on"** a space for the recipient's name; and **"For Merit in"** (duties specified)**"by Trustees."**

The medal is edged with a rope design that goes up through a single eye rigging block by which it is attached to a ribbon. At the top of the ribbon is a plain gold bar with pin back.

Ribbon. Blue.

Distinguished Service Crosses

Awarded to any individual, male or female, regardless of rank, serving with the Armed Forces who distinguishes himself by extraordinary heroism in connection with military operations against an armed enemy. The act or acts of heroism must have been so notable and involved risk of life so extraordinary as to set the individual apart from his comrades. Also can be awarded to members of Allied Forces during wartime.

Each service has its own distinctive decoration.

7.

Distinguished Service Cross - Army

By Presidential order January 2, 1918, confirmed by Congress July 9, 1918, the President was authorized to present, but not in the name of Congress, this medal to any person serving in the Army after April 6, 1917, who distinguishes himself or herself by **"Exceptionally Meritorious Service to the Government in a Duty of Great Responsibility."**

Obverse. Bronze cross 2 inches high and 1 13/16 inches wide with a bronze American eagle with wings outstretched, superimposed. Beneath the eagle is a scroll inscribed **"For Valour"**, on the reverse is a space for the name of the recipient surrounded by a laurel wreath.

Ribbon. Dark blue, narrow white stripe and red on the edges.

Ribbon. Army's second highest decoration; just under the Army Medal of Honor.

Designer. Capt. Aymar Embury. Sculptor Corp. Gaetano Cecere.

Note: There is an early variation of this Medal, known as the French type, in which the arms of the cross are heavily ornamented with oak leaves and the eagle is mounted on a diamond shaped plaque. The scroll below the eagle, instead of being inscribed **"For Valour"** had the motto **"E Pluribus Unum."** These are quite rare as only about 100 of this type were presented.

8.

Distinguished Service Cross - Navy

Authorized by Act of Congress February 4, 1919, for the United States Navy and Marine Corps. The Navy Cross could be granted also for peacetime heroism until the Act of Congress of August 7, 1942, which revised the conditions to read: **"While Serving in any Capacity with the Naval Service of the United States, Distinguishes Himself or Herself by Extraordinary Heroism in Connection with Military Operations Against an Armed Enemy."**

Obverse. Bronze cross with rounded ends, with four leaves and betties in each re-entrant angle; in center a medallion charged with a sailing vessel on waves.

Reverse. Same as obverse, except medallion is charged with cross cabled anchors between letters **"U.S.N."** The early examples of the Navy Cross were almost black and as a large number were issued posthumously, they are commonly called the **"Black Widow"**. Post WWI issues are of lighter colored bronze.

Ribbon. Navy blue with white center stripe.

Rank. The Navy's second highest decoration; just under the Navy Medal of Honor.

Designer. James E. Fraser.

9.

Distinguished Service Cross - Air Force

Created July 6, 1960, to take the place of the Army Distinguished Service Cross. For combat action only; can also be awarded to Air Force personnel while serving with a friendly foreign force engaged in armed conflict against an opposing armed force in which the U.S. is not a belligerent party.

Obverse. A 1 13/16 inch bronze cross, in oxidized satin finish. In the center is a gold American bald eagle with wings outstretched resting on a gold plaque symbolic of a cloud (part of the Air Force Coat of Arms). Eagle is surrounded by a green enamel and gold laurel wreath.

Reverse. A raised plaque for the recipient's name.

Ribbon. Light blue edge with white and red stripes.

Rank. The Air Force's second highest decoration just under the Air Force Medal of Honor.

Designer. Eleanor Cox, Awards Division, Headquarters United States Air Force.

Distinguished Service Medals

Created as an award to any individual, male or female, while serving in any capacity in the United States Armed Forces, who distinguishes himself or herself by exceptionally meritorious service to the government in a duty, combat or non-combat, of great responsibility. The performance must be such as to merit recognition which is clearly exceptional. Outstanding performance of normal duty does not alone justify an award. This decoration may be presented to persons other than members of the Armed Forces of the United States for wartime services only, and then only under exceptional circumstances with the express approval of the President of the United States.

Each service has its own distinctive decoration.

10.

Distinguished Service Medal - Army

By Presidential Order January 2, 1918, confirmed by Congress July 9, 1918, the President was authorized to present, but not in the name of Congress, this medal to any person serving in the Army who distinguished himself or herself by **"Exceptionally Meritorious Service to the government in a Duty of Great Responsibility"**. This decoration was made retroactive to April 6, 1917, and was also awarded to the Air Force until 1960.

Obverse. U.S. Coat of Arms in bronze, surrounded by a circle of dark blue enamel band 1 1/2 inches in diameter, inscribed in gold **"For Distinguished Service"** and the date **"MCMXVIII.**

Reverse. A space for the recipient's name bordered on each side with a trophy of flags and weapons.

Ribbon. Center of white flanked each side by blue, edged in in red.

Rank. Third highest Army decoration; just under the Army Distinguished Service Cross.

Designer. Capt. Aymar Embury. Sculptor Corp. Gaetano Cecere.

11.

Distinguished Service Medal – Navy

On February 4, 1919, Congress authorized this decoration for any person in the Naval Service who after April 6, 1917, distinguishes himself or herself by **"Exceptionally Meritorious Service to the Government in a Duty of Great Responsibility."**

There are two variations of the decoration.

Type 1 – Circular bronze medallion portraying a fouled anchor with waves and a rising sun in the background. On the right flank of the anchor is a spray of laurel. At the top of the medallion are the words **"Distinguished Service."** The medallion is suspended from an eagle with wings outspread; the eagle's talons support a scroll with the dates 1917 – 1918.

This type was never actually authorized to be awarded.

Type II – as follows:

Obverse. A medallion 1 3/8 inches in diameter; in the center is an eagle standing on olive branch and arrows, all gold, within blue enamel annulet with words in gold, **"United States of America – Navy."** Gold wave scroll border. pendant is suspended by a white star with gold ball tips, charged with gold anchor. Gold rays emit from re-entrant angles of star.

Reverse. Neptune's trident within laurel wreath, all gold, encircled by blue enamel annulet with words, **"For Distinguished Service"**; gold wave scroll border.

Ribbon. Same for both types. Gold center; flanks Navy blue.

Rank. Third highest Navy decoration; just under the Navy Cross.

Designer. Paul Manship.

12.

Distinguished Service Medal - Air Force

Established by Congress on July 6, 1960, to replace the Army Distinguished Service Medal for Air Force personnel.

Obverse. Bronze, thirteen-pointed star, 2 1/4 inches in diameter. Between each ray appears a small gold rimmed, white enamel star. Center medallion is a circular dark blue stone.

Ribbon. Center of white flanked by gold stripe and a wide blue stripe, and edged in gold.

Rank. Third highest Air Force decoration; just under the Air Force Distinguished Service Cross.

Designer. Institute of Heraldry, U.S. Army.

13.

Distinguished Service Medal - Coast Guard

Established in 1962 to replace the Navy Distinguished Service Medal which up to that point had been awarded to Coast Guard personnel.

Obverse. A 1 3/8 inch gold circular medal. In the center of the medallion is portrayed the **"Massachusetts"** in full sail the first vessel of the U.S. Revenue Cutter Service (organized in 1790 it later became the Coast Guard). This ship is surrounded by a gold rim inscribed **"U.S. Coast Guard Distinguished Service."**

Reverse. Coast Guard seal upon crossed anchors and an area for the recipient's name.

Ribbon. Light blue center flanked by thin white stripes with purple on either edge.

Rank. As in all other branches, it is the highest peacetime decoration and third highest war time decoration; just under the Distinguished Service Cross of the Navy.

14.

Merchant Marine Distinguished Service Medal

Joint Resolution of Congress, April 11, 1943. Awarded to any person in the American Merchant Marine, who on or after September 3, 1939, **"Has Distinguished Himself in the Line of Duty."** Awarded by the U.S. Maritime Commission.

Obverse. Silver compass rose imposed on compass card, suspended by an eagle in front of crossed anchors. An arch of leaves over the eagle's head.

Reverse. Disk within compass rose, charged with shield of U.S. Coat of Arms, with words, **"Distinguished Service"** and **"United States Merchant Marine."**

Ribbon. Red center flanked by stripes of white and dark blue edges.

Rank. Highest decoration for the U.S. Merchant Marines.

Designer. Paul Manship.

15.

Defense Distinguished Service Medal

Established July 9, 1970, by the Secretary of Defense and Executive Order as an award to military officers who perform exceptionally meritorious service in a degree of great responsibility with the Office of the Secretary of Defense, the Organization of the Joint Chiefs of Staff, special or outstanding command in a Defense Agency or for other Joint Activities as may be designated by the Secretary of Defense. Very rarely awarded.

Obverse. Gold circular medal. In the center is a gold-rimmed, light blue enameled pentagon. Surrounding this at the top are thirteen stars and at the base a wreath, superimposed on the wreath is an eagle with wings outstretched holding three arrows in its talons.

Reverse. Inscribed at the top: **"For Distinguished Service,"** and on the Pentagon: **From The Secretary of Defense To."**

Ribbon. Center of red flanked by gold light blue edges.

Rank. Third highest decoration; just under the Distinguished Service Crosses.

16.

Silver Star

By Act of Congress, July 9, 1918, for each citation of an officer or enlisted man for gallantry in action not sufficient to warrant the Medal of Honor or the Distinguished Service Cross, a Silver Star 3/16 inch in diameter was authorized for wear on the suspension and service ribbons of appropriate service medals. This award was called the Citation Star and on August 8, 1932, this decoration was revised by Act of Congress and redesigned to present form. Its purpose remained the same.

Obverse. A bronze five-pointed star 1 1/4 inches across. In the center of which the 3/16 inch five-pointed Silver Citation Star mentioned above with rays which extend to the inner edges of a surrounding wreath.

Reverse. Inscribed **"For Gallantry in Action"** and place for the recipient's name.

Ribbon. Red center flanked on each side by white, blue, white, and blue.

Rank. Third highest U.S. combat decoration.
Note: The Silver Star was made a Navy Decoration August 7, 1942, by Act of Congress.

Designer of Pendant. Bailey, Banks, and Biddle.

Legion of Merit

The Legion of Merit was created by Congress July 10, 1942, in four degrees: Chief Commander, Commander, Officer, and Legionnaire; for award to personnel of armed forces of friendly foreign nations, and personnel of the Armed Forces of the United States and Philippines.

The recipients must **"Have Distinguished Themselves by Exceptionally Meritorious Conduct in the Performance of Outstanding Services"** since the Presidential Proclamation of Emergency, September 8, 1939.

This is as close as the United States has come to creating an Order of the European type. It is the first specific decoration awarded to foreigners; and the first decoration of the United States to be awarded in different degrees.

17.

Legion of Merit, Chief Commander

Usually awarded to Heads of Foreign States who have distinguished themselves by exceptionally meritorious conduct in the performance of outstanding service to the United States.

Obverse. A 3 inch plaque of a five-pointed American star of heraldic form, which has centered 13 white stars on a blue enamel field emerging from a circle of clouds; the stars are in the following pattern starting at top: 1-4-3-4-1. Taken from the U.S. Coat of Arms to represent the "**New Constellation,**" as the founding fathers described the young republic. The large heraldic star is white enamel outlined with purple red enamel. Each tip of the star has a gold ball. The star is superimposed over a green enamel laurel wreath. Between each point of the star are crossed war arrows pointing out to represent armed protection to the nations.

Reverse. Basically as just described except there are no stars in the center, where the wreath would have been is a banner with the words: **"United States of America."** This decoration has a pin back and not suspended from a ribbon. Worn on the left side of the tunic.

Ribbon Bar. Purple-red moire edge with a thin white stripe. Has a small narrow horizontal gold bar with replica of pendant in center.

Designer. Col. Townsend Heard, U.S. Army.

18.

Legion of Merit, Commander

Usually awarded to Supreme Commanders of foreign military who have distinguished themselves by exceptionally meritorious conduct in the performance of outstanding service to the United States.

Obverse. A gold 2 1/4 inch medallion of a five-pointed American star of heraldic form, which has centered thirteen white stars on a blue enamel field emerging from a circle of clouds. The stars are in the following pattern starting at top: 1-4-3-4-1. Taken from the U.S. Coat of Arms to represent the **"New Constellation,"** as the founding fathers described the young republic. The large heraldic star is white enamel outlined with purple-red enamel. Each tip of the star has a gold ball. The star is then superimposed over a green enamel laurel wreath. Between each point of the star are crossed war arrows pointing out to represent armed protection to the nation.

Reverse. Basically as just described except replacing the thirteen stars at center is the motto taken from the reverse of the great seal of the United States **"Annuit Coeptis,"** (He-God-has favored our undertakings). Together with the date MDCCLXXXIII or 1782, the year of the founding of our first military award, the Purple Heart. Replacing the wreath is a banner with the words **"United States of America"**. The heraldic star is white enamel outlined in purple-red.

The medallion has a gold wreath between the two top tips of the upper point of the star by means of which it is attached to a neck ribbon two inches in width.

Ribbon. Purple-red moire with thin white stripe at each edge with a small, narrow horizontal silver bar with a replica of pendant in the center.

Designer. Col. Townsend Heard, U.S. Army

19.

Legion of Merit, Officer

Usually awarded to officers of foreign military who have distinguished themselves by exceptionally meritorious conduct in the performance of outstanding service to the United States.

Obverse. A gold 1 7/8 inch medallion of a five-pointed American star of heraldic form, which has centered thirteen white stars on a blue enamel field emerging from a circle of clouds. The stars are in the following pattern starting at top: 1-4-3-4-1. Taken from the U.S. Coat of Arms to represent the **"New Constellation"** as the founding fathers described the new republic. The large heraldic star is white enamel outlined with purple-red enamel. Each tip of the star has a gold ball. The star is then superimposed over a green enamel laurel wreath. Between each point of the star are crossed war arrows pointing out to represent armed protection to the nation.

Reverse. Basically as just described except replacing the thirteen stars at center is the motto taken from the reverse of the great seal of the United States **"Annuit Coeptis"** (he-God-has favored our undertakings). Together with the date MDCCLXXXII or 1782, the year of the founding of our first military award, the Purple Heart. Replacing the wreath is a banner with the words **"United States of America"**. The heraldic star is not enameled, although earliest types were.

The medallion has simply a gold loop for the breast ribbon between the two top tips of the upper point of the star.

Ribbon. Purple-red moire edged with thin white stripes.

Ribbon Fixture. A fixed to the middle of the ribbon drape is a 11/16 inch bronze replica of the medal pendant.

Ribbon Bar. Purple-red moire edged with thin white stripes, centered is a 7/16 inch bronze replica of the medal pendent.

Designer. Col. Townsend Heard, U.S. Army.

20.

Legion of Merit, Legionnaire

Usually awarded to officers of the United States military who have distinguished themselves by exceptionally meritorious conduct in the performance of outstanding service to the United States.

Obverse. A gold 1 7/8 inch medallion of a five-pointed American star of heraldic form, which has centered thirteen white stars on a blue enamel field emerging from a circle of clouds. The stars are in the following pattern starting at top: 1-4-3-4-1. Taken from the U.S. Coat of Arms to represent the **"New Constellation"** as the founding fathers described the young republic. The large heraldic star is white enamel outlined with purple-red enamel. Each tip of the star has a gold ball. The star is then superimposed over a green enamel laurel wreath. Between each point of the star are crossed war arrows pointing out to represent armed protection to the nation.

Reverse. Basically as just described except replacing the thirteen stars at center is the motto taken from the reverse of the great seal of the United States **"Annuit Coeptis"** (he-God-has favored our undertakings). Together with the date MDCCLXXXII or 1782, the year of the founding of our first military award, the Purple Heart. Replacing the wreath is a banner with the words **"United States of America."** The heraldic star is not enameled, although earliest types were.

The medallion has simply a gold loop for the breast ribbon between the two top tips of the upper point of the star.

Ribbon. Purple-red moire edged with thin white stripes.

Ribbon Bar. Purple-red moire edged with thin white stripes with no replica of pendant, but worn with a bronze V if awarded to a U.S. officer in combat service.

Rank. Just below the Silver Star.

Designer. Col. Townsend Heard, U.S. Army.

21

Defense Superior Service Medal

Established by the Secretary of Defense and Executive Order as an award to military officers who perform exceptionally meritorious service in a degree of great responsibility with the Office of the Secretary of Defense, the Organization of the Joint Chiefs of Staff, special or outstanding command in a defense agency or for other Joint activities as may be designated by the Secretary of Defense, but not to the degree to merit a Defense Distinguished Service Medal.

Obverse. Silver circular medal. In the center is a silver-rimmed, light blue enameled pentagon. Surrounding this at the top are thirteen stars and at the base a wreath. Superimposed on the wreath is an eagle with wings outstretched holding three arrows in its talons.

Reverse. Inscribed at top **"For Superior Service"** and on the pentagon: **"From The Secretary Of Defense To"**.

Ribbon. Centered flanked by white, light blue, yellow.

Rank. Just under the Distinguished Service Medal.

22.

Distinguished Flying Cross

Authorized by Act of Congress on July 2, 1926, established for award to any person who, serving any branch of the service including National Guard and the Organized Reserves after April 6, 1917, **"Distinguishes himself or herself by heroism or extraordinary achievement while participating in an aerial flight."**

Obverse. On a bronze cross pattee 1 1/2 inches across, a four-bladed propeller; in the re-entrant angles, rays forming a one inch square.

Reverse. Area for recipient's name and date awarded.

Ribbon. Blue with narrow stripe of red bordered by white in center and near each edge a stripe of white.

Rank. Just under the Legion of Merit and Department of Defense Superior Service Medals.

Designer. Elizabeth Will and Arthur E. DuBors.

Branch Service Medals

These are awards to individuals serving in the various services including Reserves and National Guard who distinguish themselves by heroism not involving actual armed conflict with an enemy. Each service branch has its own individual decoration.

23.

Soldiers Medal - Army

Established by Act of Congress, July 2, 1926.

Obverse. On a 1 3/8 inch Bronze octagon. In the center is an eagle with wings upraised perched on a fasces (The Ancient Roman Symbol of United Authority) between two groups of stars, looking at the pendant, six left - seven right; above the group of six is a spray of leaves.

Reverse. Shield of the United States with letters **"U.S."** on chief between sprays of laurel and oak. Around upper edge, words **"Soldiers Medal"**, across face **"For Valor."**

Ribbon. Two outside stripes of blue and a center of seven white and six red stripes of equal width.

Rank. Just under the Distinguished Flying Cross.

Designer. Gaetano Cecere.

24.

Navy and Marine Corps Medal

Authorized by Act of Congress, August 7, 1942, and made retroactive to December 6, 1941.

Obverse. Octagonal bronze medallion which portrays an eagle with wings outstretched perched on an anchor below which is a globe of the world and below the globe the inscription **"Heroism."**

Reverse. Area for recipient's name.

Ribbon. Equal stripes of navy blue, gold, and red.

Rank. Just under the Distinguished Flying Cross.

Designer. Lt. Comdr. McClelland Barclay, U.S.N.R.

25.

Coast Guard Medal

Created in 1951, but was not awarded until 1958.

Obverse. Bronze octagonal medallion with crossed anchors in the center upon which has been superimposed the Coast Guard Seal.

Reverse. Has inscription **"For Heroism."**

Ribbon. Center and edges light blue, three red stripes and four white stripes on each side of center blue.

26.

Airman's Medal - Air Force

Established by Act of Congress July 6, 1960, to take the place of the Soldier's Medal for Air Force personnel.

Obverse. Circular bronze medallion portraying Hermes (in Greek mythology the messenger of the gods) resting on one knee after releasing a falcon shown rising into flight. Surrounding Hermes is the inscription **"Airman's Medal."**

Reverse. Has inscription **"For Valor"** with area for recipient's name surrounded by a laurel wreath.

Ribbon. Edges of light blue and alternating in the center 13 stripes: 7 yellow and 6 dark blue.

Rank. Just under the Distinguished Flying Cross.

Designer. Institute of Heraldry, U.S. Army.

27.

Bronze Star

Established February 4, 1944, as an award to any individual, male or female, in the Armed Forces of the United States, who on or after December 7, 1941, shall have distinguished himself for heroic or military achievement or service not involving aerial flight.

Obverse. A 1 1/2 inch bronze five-pointed star. In the center is a small raised 3/16 inch bronze star.

Reverse. Inscribed **"Heroic or Meritorious Achievement"**.

Ribbon. Red with blue center, flanked on each side by thin white stripes, edges thin white stripes.

Rank. Just under branch medals such as Soldiers Medal and Airman's Medal.

Designer of Pendant. Bailey, Banks, and Biddle.

28.

Department of Defense Meritorious Service Medal

Established by the Secretary of Defense and Executive Order as an award to military officers who perform exceptionally Meritorious Service in a degree of great responsibility with the Office of the Secretary of Defense, the Organization of the Joint Chiefs of Staff, special or outstanding command in a defense agency or for other joint activities as may be designated by the Secretary of Defense, but not to the degree to merit a Defense Superior Service Medal.

Obverse. A bronze circular medal. In the center is a pentagon, surrounding this is a wreath. Superimposed on the wreath is an eagle with wings outstretched standing on the bottom edge of the pentagon.

Reverse. Inscription **"Defense Meritorious Service"** and along the bottom the words **"United States of America."**

Ribbon. Three light blue and two white stripes down the center flanked by a 1/4 inch white stripe, a 1/4 inch purple-red stripe edged by a 1/16 inch white stripe.

Rank. Just under the Bronze Star.

Note: You may have noticed that this is the third of three Department of Defense Medals.

1st Department of Defense Distinguished Service Medal.

2nd Department of Defense Superior Service Medal.

3rd Department of Defense Meritorious Service Medal.

29

Meritorious Service Medal

Founded January 16, 1969, as an award primarily for outstanding meritorious achievement or service to the United States by any member of the Armed Forces. Some portion of the completed service or achievement must have been made on or after January 16, 1969. In actuality this decoration could be described as a fifth class or grade of the Legion of Merit. This is exemplified by the reversal of the color (red-purple instead of purple-red) of the ribbon of the Legion of Merit.

Obverse. A 1 1/2 inch bronze medallion portraying an eagle with wings outstretched holding in his talons branches of laurel. Eagle is topped by the upper part of a five-pointed star on an incised plaque with six points starting at the top of each wing of the eagle.

Reverse. Has inscribed: **"United States of America - Meritorious Service."**

Ribbon. Red-purple with 1/4 inch white stripe towards each edge.

Rank. Just under the Defense Meritorious and Bronze Star.

30.

Merchant Marine Meritorious Service Medal

Authorized August 29, 1944, as an award to any individual serving on U.S. vessels or any foreign vessel operated by the War Shipping Administration of the United States Maritime Commission who was commended for meritorious conduct not of a sufficient nature to warrant the Merchant Marine Distinguished Service Medal.

Obverse. A bronze medallion portraying an eagle perched on the flukes of an anchor.

Reverse. Has the inscription **"For Meritorious Service in the United States Merchant Marine"** and an area for the recipient's name.

Ribbon. Light blue with center stripe of dark blue edged with narrow stripes of white, red, and yellow.

Rank. Just under the Bronze Star.

Designer. Paul Manship.

31.

Specially Meritorious Medal

Authorized March 3, 1901, by Act of Congress. This award was created to recognize officers and men for acts of specially meritorious service, other than in battle, during the War with Spain; was seldom awarded.

Obverse. A 1 1/4 inch bronze cross patfee, in center a medallion charged with anchor encircled by wreath of oak and laurel within inscription, **U.S. Naval Campaign West Indies."** Arms of Cross inscribed, **"Specially Meritorious Service - 1898."**

Reverse. Bare.

Ribbon. Bright scarlet silk moire without pattern or design.

Rank. Some rank it as high as the Meritorious Service Medal, or just under the Bronze Star.

Note: Personnel who qualified for the award a second time were presented with an inscribed bronze bar to be attached to the suspension ribbon.

32.

Medal for Merit

Authorized by the President of the United States, July 20, 1942, as an award to civilians of foreign nations who distinguish themselves in the performance of outstanding service to the United States. This decoration has not been awarded since World War II.

Obverse. Gold American eagle with outstanding wings standing on a sheaf of arrows. Surrounding the sheaf of arrows is a band inscribed **"Novus Ordo Seclorum"** (New Order of the Ages). Eagle and arrow are superimposed on a gold-rimmed blue enamel band with thirteen stars, three above the eagle's head and five on each side of its body.

Reverse. Has the inscription **"United States of America for Merit."**

The pendant is suspended from a small green enamel laurel wreath.

Ribbon. Magenta moire with two narrow white stripes in the center.

Designer. Col. Townsend Heard.

Rank. Just under the Meritorious Service Medal.

Note: Some people also consider this decoration to be a lesser degree of the Legion of Merit and rank it somewhere between the Legion of Merit and the Bronze Star.

33. Air Medal

Executive Order, May 11, 1942. Recipients, members of the Armed Forces, must have distinguished themselves, after September 8, 1939, by meritorious achievement in flight. The Air Medal is awarded where the service does not warrant a Distinguished Flying Cross.

Obverse. Bronze compass rose with 16 points 11/16 inches in diameter, suspended by a pointer and charged with a diving American eagle with thunderbolts in his talons.

Reverse. Area for recipient's name.

Ribbon. Blue with orange stripe near each edge.

Designer. Walker K. Hancock.

Rank. Just under the Meritorious Service Medal.

Commendation Medals

These decorations were created as an award to officers and men of the United States Armed Forces who perform outstandingly either in combat or non-combat and receive letters of commendation from a superior grade officer. Each service has its own individual decoration.

Note: A bronze **"V"** is worn on the suspension ribbon of the medal and on the ribbon bar to show that it was earned while participating in operations against an armed enemy.

34.

Joint Service Commendation

Founded June 25, 1963, as an award to any member of the United States Armed Forces who distinguishes himself or herself by meritorious achievement or service. It is awarded by the Secretary of Defense and normally the individual must be serving with either the Joint Chiefs of Staff, National Security Agency, Defense Supply or in a Joint Task Force Control Group of Command. The degree of merit does not need to be unique but must be distinctive.

Obverse. Is 1 5/8 inches in diameter; has an unusual shaped green enameled cross; in the center is a gold eagle with wings outstretched holding three arrows in its talons. Above the eagle are thirteen gold stars in a pattern 1-4-3-2-3 and at the base a heraldic emblem representing land, sea, and air. The cross is superimposed on a gold laurel wreath.

Reverse. Has the inscription **"For Military Merit"** and has a plaque for the recipient's name between the words military and merit.

Ribbon. Green center, on either side are stripes of white, green and again white, with edges of light blue.

Rank. Just under the Air Medal.

Designer. Institute of Heraldry, U.S. Army.

35.

Army Commendation

Originally created as a ribbon in 1945, the medal was added in 1949. Awarded to individuals who were commended on or after December 7, 1941.

Obverse. A 1 3/8 inch hexagonal bronze medallion portraying an American eagle with wings outstretched holding three arrows in his talons. In the center of the eagle's breast is the U.S. Shield.

Reverse. Has inscription **"For Military"** with a plaque for the recipient's name; below this is the word **"Merit"**.

Ribbon. Green with five thin stripes in center and white on each edge.

Rank. Just under the Air Medal.

Designer. Institute of Heraldry, U.S. Army.

36.

Navy Commendation

Established January 11, 1944, as a ribbon, the medal was added March 22, 1950.

Obverse. A 1 3/8 inch hexagonal bronze medallion portraying an American eagle with wings outstretched holding three arrows in his talons. In the center of the eagle's breast is the U.S. Shield.

Reverse. Has inscription **"For Military"** with a plaque for the recipient's name; below this is the word **"Merit"**.

Ribbon. Green with white stripe toward each edge.

Rank. Just under the Air Medal.

Designers. Institute of Heraldry, Quartermaster Corps, U.S. Army.

37.

Coast Guard Commendation

Authorized by the Secretary of the Treasury on August 26, 1947, as a ribbon. The medallion was added July 5, 1951.

Obverse. A 1 3/8 inch bronze hexagonal medallion with American eagle with wings arched. On the eagle's breast are crossed anchors topped by the seal of the Treasury Department surrounded by a ring with the inscription **"United States Coast Guard - 1790."**

Reverse. Has the inscription **"For Outstanding"** a plaque for the recipient's name, and below this the word **"Service."**

Ribbon. Green with white stripe toward each edge and a narrow white stripe in center.

Rank. Just under the Air Medal.

Designers. Institute of Heraldry, U.S. Army.

38.

Air Force Commendation

Authorized by the Secretary of the Air Force on March 28, 1959, for those individuals commended after March 24, 1958. Prior to this date, Air Force recipients received the decoration from the Army or the Navy.

Obverse. A 1 3/8 inch bronze hexagonal medallion which portrays the seal of the Air Force topped by an American eagle with wings outstretched perched on a torse (twisted ribbon).

Reverse. Has inscription **"For Military"** with a plaque for the recipient's name; below this is the word **"Merit."**

Ribbon. Yellow with a wide and two thin stripes of blue in the center and blue edges.

Rank. Just under the Air Medal.

Designers. Institute of Heraldry, U.S. Army.

39.

Navy Achievement Medal

Was formerly titled the "**Navy Commendation For Achievement**" and was previously only a ribbon. This medal was authorized by the Secretary of the Navy on January 24, 1962. It is awarded to junior officers of the Navy or Marine Corps, including reserves, who are serving in the grade of lieutenant commander or major and below or enlisted personnel serving in any capacity with the Navy or Marine Corps. It is earned by officers for outstanding professional achievement or leadership and by enlisted men only for leadership. This award is strictly for non-combat service.

Obverse. A bronze 1 1/4 inch square medal with a 1/4 inch star at each of its four blunted corners. At the center is the stylized fouled naval anchor.

Ribbon. Green with an orange stripe toward each edge.

Rank. Just under the Navy Commendation Medal.

40.

Coast Guard Achievement Medal

This award has borne two different names in the past.

1. Secretary of the Treasury Commendation for Achievement Award founded January 29, 1963.
2. Secretary of Transportation Commendation Award. Founded March 13, 1967.

On June 11, 1968, this award was renamed the Coast Guard Achievement medal by the Commandant of the Coast Guard. The design of the ribbon and pendant have remained the same throughout, with no changes made.

It is presented for outstanding achievement and superior performance of duty to commissioned and enlisted men of the U.S. Coast Guard and Coast Guard Reserve in the grade of lieutenant Commander and under, on or after April 1, 1967. This is strictly for non-combat service.

Obverse. A bronze, 1 1/4 inch, circular medallion bearing the inscription, **"U.S. Coast Guard,"** superimposed on the U.S. Coast Guard Seal, consisting of crossed anchors, which is surrounded by a laurel wreath.

Ribbon. Green, with narrow white central stripe, and wide orange stripe toward each edge.

Rank. Just under Coast Guard Commendation Medal.

41.

Air Force Achievement Medal

One of the Air Force's newest awards. It is presented for outstanding achievement and superior performance of duty to commissioned and enlisted men of the U.S. Air Force and Air Force Reserve in the grade of major and under.
grade of major and under.

Obverse. A silver medallion portraying an adaption of the thunderbolts and wings from the U.S. Air Force Coat of Arms, inside a circle. Around the outside edge are eleven square points with rounded edges.

Reverse. In a circle the inscription, **Air Force-Meritorious Achievement".**

Ribbon. A thin silver stripe flanked by a thin blue stripe, a thin silver stripe, a narrow blue stripe, a wide silver stripe, a narrow blue, a thin silver, · a thin blue, thin silver, edged in a narrow blue.

42.

Army Achievement Medal

One of the newest awards from the Army. It is presented for outstanding achievement and superior performance of duty to commissioned and enlisted men of the U.S. Army and Army Reserve in the grade of major and under.

Obverse. A 1 1/2 inch, bronze, octagonal medallion portraying breast armor, flanked by United States flag, cannon, and cannon balls, to the left looking at it, to the right by U.S. Army flag, mortar, and powder jars. At bottom the date **"1775"**. At top a snake holding a banner in its mouth with the inscription **"This We'll Defend"** and just under this is a spear, a sword with helmet over point, and musket. Affixed with bayonet.

Reverse. Has inscription **"For Military Achievement"** and area for recipient's name, at bottom a crossed spray of laurel leaf.

Ribbon. A 1/16 inch center white stripe, flanked by a 5/16 inch blue stripe, a 1/16 inch white stripe, a 1/8 inch green stripe, a 1/16 inch white stripe, edged by a 1/8 inch green stripe.

43.

The Purple Heart

Originally established by General George Washington on August 7, 1782, at Newburg on the Hudson, New York, as an award for outstanding military merit, or the badge of military merit. The decoration was in the form of a cloth badge and only three non-commissioned officers received the order at that time. Though never officially abolished it was not again awarded for almost one hundred and fifty years.

Upon its revival in 1932, as the Purple Heart, the decoration was to be awarded in two categories:

A. For being wounded in action in any war or campaign under conditions which entitle the wearing of a wound chevron.

B. For those persons who perform any singularly meritorious act of extraordinary fidelity or essential service.

In 1942, President Franklin D. Roosevelt issued Executive Orders which provided that the Purple Heart would be made available to members of all the Armed Services who were wounded in action. Since then the Purple Heart has become one of the most highly respected decorations of the United States Armed Forces. The decoration holds a very unique position in that it can be earned only one way, by being wounded. An attendant requirement is that the wound must have been received as a direct result of enemy actions.

Stemming directly from General George Washington's Badge of Military Merit, the Purple Heart is our oldest military decoration.

Currently, the Purple Heart may be awarded to members of the United States Armed Forces and to civilian citizens of the U.S., male or female, who, while serving with the Armed Forces, are wounded due to the result of a direct enemy action.

Obverse. A 1 11/16 inch gold-rimmed, heart-shaped, purple enamel medallion. In the center is a gold bust of George Washington. Above this are the red, white, and green enamelled coat of arms of the Washington family.

Reverse. Below shield and leaves, a raised bronze heart with words, **"For Military Merit"**, and an area for the recipient's name.

Ribbon. Purple moire edged in white.

Rank. Just under the branch Achievement Medals.

Designer. Elizabeth Will. Modeled by John R. Sinnock.

44.

Mariners Medal - Merchant Marines

Established by Act of Congress, May 10, 1943. Awarded to **"Any person who, while serving on any vessel in the American Merchant Marine during the war period is wounded, suffers physical injury, or suffers through dangerous exposure as a result of an enemy of the United States."**

Obverse. Eight-pointed gold plaque upon which has been superimposed a silver medallion portraying an eagle resting on an anchor.

Reverse. Inscribed **"United States Merchant Marines"** surrounding a wreath which in turn has a hand carrying a flaming torch above the ocean.

Ribbon. Equal stripes of blue and red, separated by a narrow stripe of white in center.

Rank. This decoration serves the same purpose as and is equal to the Purple Heart of the Armed Forces.

Designer. Paul Manship.

Lifesaving Medals

The Lifesaving Medals are available to members of the United States Armed Forces, but they are rarely awarded to Military personnel because of the existence of medals in all services whose criteria for award are very similar.

Since their creation, there have been several changes. The width of the ribbons and the pendants has been reduced in size, and the ribbon has been changed in design and color.

Note: The measurements given on the medallion are the new size. The old medals were 1 3/4 inches in diameter. Also the U.S. Armed Forces classify these to be a non-military decoration and when worn on a military uniform it ranks just under the Purple Heart.

45. and 46.

Gold Lifesaving Medal First Class

The Gold Lifesaving Medal is awarded by the Transportation Department to civilians and members of the U.S. Armed Forces who endanger their lives in saving or attempting to save lives of others from dangers of the sea. Established by Act of Congress on June 20, 1874.

Obverse. A gold medallion 1 1/2 inches in diameter in the center; three men in a boat in a heavy sea. One is rescuing a person who has hold of a spar. Another is casting a rope. A third is rowing. In the distance, the wreck of a large vessel. Around the outer edge the inscription **"United States of America Act of Congress June 20, 1874."** The medallion is suspended by an eagle's head.

Reverse. Around the outer edge the inscription **"In testimony of heroic deeds in saving life from the perils of the sea."** In the center a female figure, standing, holding in left hand a wreath of oak. With her right hand she is preparing to inscribe the name of the recipient on a monument surmounted by an eagle. To her right are a mast, a yard with its sail bent, an anchor, a sextant, and a laurel branch.

Ribbon. Original #45 - scarlet red moire
New #46 - Wide gold center flanked on each side by thin stripe of white and a red stripe at either edge.

Rank. When worn on a military uniform it comes after the Purple Heart.

Designer. Anthony C. Paquet, a designer of the Medal of Honor.

47. and 48.

Silver Lifesaving Medal Second Class

The Silver Lifesaving Medal is awarded under the same general conditions as the Gold Lifesaving Medal; however, it is secondary in importance and permits a lesser degree of heroism for award. Established by Act of Congress June 20, 1874.

Obverse. A silver medallion 1 1/2 inch in diameter in the center. Centered is a female figure hovering in the air, and saving a man from the deep. Around the edge of the medallion the inscription **"United States of America, Act of Congress, June 20, 1874"**. The pendant is suspended by an eagle's head.

Reverse. Around the outer edge the inscription **"In testimony of heroic deeds in saving life from perils of the sea."** With a wreath further in.

Ribbon. Original #47 - light blue moire.
New #48 wide silver center flanked on each side by a thin stripe of white and a blue stripe at either edge.

Rank. When worn on a military uniform it is worn just after the Purple Heart.

Designer. Anthony C. Paquet, a designer of the Medal of Honor.

49.

National Security Medal - Obsolete

Established by Act of Congress January 19, 1953, for any individual U.S. or foreign, military or civilian, for distinguished achievement or acts of valor on or after July 2, 1947, in the field of intelligence relating to National Security.

Obverse. A gold medallion surrounded by a wreath. Just inside the wreath a gold-rimmed, red enamel band inscribed in gold: **"United States of America National Security".** The center of the medallion is white enamel and has an eight-pointed star with a four-pointed star superimposed over it; superimposed over these two stars is another larger four-pointed star, all stars are of blue enamel and make up one large star with sixteen points. The wreath is topped with an eagle with outstretched wings.

Reverse. Has the inscription **"presented to"** and an area for the recipient's name.

Ribbon. Dark blue with a gold pattern in the center forming what looks like a diagonal ladder in center.

Rank. With the words **"Distinguished, Achievement, and Valor"** in its description, some rank it with the branch Distinguished Service Medals just under the Distinguished Service Crosses. Others feel that it is a non-military decoration and rank it just under the Purple Heart, when worn on a military uniform. The U.S. Armed Forces classify this award as non-military and when worn on a militry uniform it ranks just under the Purple Heart.

50.

National Security Agency Exceptional Service Medal

Awarded for Exceptional Services.

Obverse. A gold medallion, 1 1/4 inches in diameter, portrays an eagle perched on a large key. Surrounding the edge are inscribed the words: **"National Security Agency - U.S.A."**

Reverse. I have no information on this.

Ribbon. Has a center stripe of wine red flanked by thin yellow stripes, wide green stripes then edged in white.

Note: This decoration is not readily acknowledged and little is known about it. I could not confirm the date in which it was established.

51. 52. 53. and 54.

Medal of Freedom

Founded by President Truman, established July 6, 1945, amended by Executive Order on April 5, 1952, to be awarded to any person other than a member of the Armed Forces of the United States who, after December 6, 1941, performed a meritorious act or service which aided the United States or its allies in the prosecution of a war against an armed enemy or during any period of national emergency declared by the President or the Congress furthered the interests or security of the United States or its allies during such period when the award of any other United States Military decoration was not deemed appropriate. Under special circumstances, without regard to the existence of a state of war or National Emergency, the Medal of Freedom was awarded by or at the direction of the President for performance of a meritorious act or service in the interest of the United States.

Obverse. A medallion which has the profile of the top of the statue of freedom facing left, with the word "**freedom**" inscribed below.

Reverse. The Liberty Bell in center, surrounded by the inscription: "**United States of America.**"

Ribbon. Red with four narrow white stripes toward the center; when awarded to foreigners, it is divided into four degrees.

Grade 1 #51 **Gold Palm,** equivalent to the Legion of Merit chief Commander.

Grade 2 #52 **Silver Palm,** equivalent to the Legion of Merit, Commander.

Grade 3 #53 **Bronze Palm,** equivalent to the Legion of Merit Officer.

Grade 4 #54 **Without Palm,** equivalent to the Legion of Merit Legionnaire, or some feel that the Legionnaire degree is included in Grade 3 or this decoration along with officer and Grade 4 is equivalent to the Bronze Star.

When this decoration is awarded to United States citizens, it is awarded without palm. The Medal of Freedom could be considered as a lower grade of the Legion of Merit.

Note: The Medal of Freedom was reestablished as the Presidential Medal of Freedom by President Kennedy on February 22, 1963, and no awards of the Medal of Freedom after that date were authorized.

N.

Presidential Medal of Freedom

The Medal of Freedom was reestablished as the Presidential Medal of Freedom by President Kennedy on February 22, 1963. The new medal was revised to include those who should be honored for meritorious contributions to security or national interests of the United States, world peace, cultural or other significant public or private endeavors. Awarded by the President of the United States at his discretion to either civilian or military Americans or foreigners.

This is primarily a diplomatic order available for presentation to distinguished individuals for services to the United States that are not precisely designated.

It comes in three classes:

1st Class **(With distinction")** comes with sash, breast badge, and breast medal, 2 3/4 inches in diameter.

2nd Class Is worn on a neck cravat, 2 inches in diameter.

3rd Class Is a breast medal, 1 3/4 inches in diameter.

When worn on a military uniform this decoration takes precedence directly after the Purple Heart.

Obverse. A star of five white enamel points with a gold eagle with wings spread between each pair of points. Each eagle stands on a red enamel triangle which has its apex toward the center of the star. In the center of the medal is a constellation of thirteen gold stars, in this pattern: 1-4-3-4-1 or the same as the Legion of Merit, all with one point upward, set in a field of blue enamel surrounded by a gold rim.

Reverse. Bears a serial number and is inscribed with the words **"Presidential Medal of Freedom"** in incised letters.

Ribbon. Blue moire, edged in white. Sash of 1st Class is closed by a large rosette bearing a replica of center medallion (blue field with thirteen white stars). On the suspension ribbon of the 3rd Class is a gold replica of one of the five eagles between the points of the pendent.

O.

Chaplain's Medal for Heroism

During World War II, four Chaplains showed extreme heroism and made a great sacrifice when the Army Transport S.S. Dorchester was torpedoed and sunk, with the loss of 681 lives, 100 miles off the coast of Greenland on February 3, 1943. The four men, Rev. George L. Fox, Rabbi Alexander D. Goode, Rev. Clark W. Bowing, and Father John R. Washington aided troops into lifeboats, and when life preservers were exhausted, they gave their own to others. As the ship went down, the four were seen, arms linked, singing a Hymn.

Obverse. An oval, bronze, medallion. Superimposed is an eagle with wings outstretched beyond the rim.

Reverse. At top is a Cross and a Tablet of Moses topped by the Star of David. Below this is an open book across the pages of which are inscribed the names of the four chaplains. Under their names is the date of founding **"July 14, 1960."**

Ribbon. Medium blue, edged in black.

This must be one of the rarest, if not the rarest, of all U.S. Medals, as only twelve were made. It was established by Act of Congress July 14, 1960, and awarded only to the next of kin.

Note: Among their honors, the four Chaplains have been posthumously awarded the Army Distinguished Service Cross.

55.

NASA Distinguished Service Medal Type I

This is the Agency's highest honor. It is awarded to individuals with distinguished service who contributed to substantial progress in U.S. Aeronautical and Space Explorations. Created on July 29, 1959, there are two designs and ribbons of the particular medal. The first design was superseded by the second.

First Design

Obverse. A gold medallion portraying the official seal of NASA, a planet with a natural satellite and another planet in the distance. In the background are numerous stars. Along the outside edge of the medal surrounding the seal is the inscription: **"National Aeronautical and and Space Administration, U.S.A."**

Reverse. Has the inscription **"Distinguished Service"** surrounded by oak leaves. At the base of the medal is a blank area for the recipient's name.

Ribbon. A thin white stripe in center, flanked by light blue, then medium blue, edged with navy blue.

56.

NASA Distinguished Service Medal Type II

Obverse. A gold cross with four large arms and four alternate smaller ones. The arms have fluted edges and are jointed together with a cloud design. The center is light blue enamel and portrays a stylized satellite streaking through the skies surrounded by a laurel wreath. Surrounding the wreath is the inscription: **"Distinguished Service N.A.S.A."**

Reverse. I have no information on this.

Ribbon. Wide dark blue stripe flanked by narrow light blue stripes, edged in wide medium blue stripes.

Rank. Just after the Purple Heart between the Gold and Silver Life Saving Medals.

57.

NASA Medal for Exceptional Bravery

Created on July 29th, 1959, to recognize particularly exemplary and courageous handling of an emergency in activities by individuals, regardless of personal danger, which saves lives and/or government property.

Obverse. A circular gold wreath tied at the bottom. Extending upward from the bottom of the wreath is a hand reaching up to hold a five-pointed star. Behind this star is a scroll on which are the letters **"N.A.S.A."**

Reverse. I have no information on this.

Ribbon. A narrow center stripe of scarlet flanked by a thin stripe of white, wide stripe of navy blue, a thin stripe of light blue and edged in medium blue.

Rank. Just under the Purple Heart between the Gold and Silver Life Saving Medals.

58.

NASA Exceptional Service Medal

Established July 29, 1959, as an award for unusual services or creative ability in engineering, administrative, or space-related activities which contribute to a NASA mission.

Obverse. A gold laurel wreath, across which is superimposed a scroll centered by a globe of the earth with latitudes and longitudes. Upward from the base of the wreath extend two hands, each holding a spray of laurel, which together surround the globe. At left of the globe on the scroll appears the letters **"N.A."** and at right **"S.A."**

Reverse. I have no information on this.

Ribbon. Medium blue, edged in thin stripes of gold, black, and gold.

Rank. Just under the Purple Heart between the Gold and Silver Life Saving Medals.

59.

NASA Medal for Exceptional Scientific Achievement

Established July 29, 1959, as an award for a high order of creative scientific accomplishments.

Obverse. Circular gold laurel wreath with a bow at bottom. From the bow extending upward is a hand balancing a globe behind which is a horizontal scroll inscribed at left **"N.A."** and at right **"S.A."**

Reverse. I have no information on this.

Ribbon. A white center stripe flanked by a thin light blue stripe, a wide stripe of dark blue, a thin stripe of light blue and edged with a medium blue stripe.

Rank. Just under the Purple Heart between the Gold and Silver Life Saving Medals.

60.

NASA Outstanding Leadership

Founded July 29, 1959, to award outstanding leadership which results in technological or administrative improvements for the Agency.

Obverse. At center is a hand holding a lighted torch which is superimposed over a horizontal scroll which bears at left the letters **"N.A."** and to the right **"S.A."** This again is superimposed over a gold laurel wreath.

Reverse. I have no information on this.

Ribbon. A narrow center stripe of medium blue flanked by a thin stripe of light blue, wide stripe of navy blue, a thin stripe of light blue, edged by medium blue.

Rank. Just under the Purple Heart between the Gold and Silver Life Saving Medals.

Note: May be awarded for a single accomplishment or for sustained performance.

61.

NASA Medal for Distinguished Public Service

Established July 29, 1959, and awarded for meritorious contributions that have aided work or scientific progress of NASA's mission by any U.S. citizen not employed by the U.S. government.

Obverse. A gold seven-pointed star, in the center of each point appears a flame. Between each point of the star are three laurel leaves. At the center of the star is a globe on which the longitudes and latitudes of earth are delineated.

Reverse. I have no information on this.

Ribbon. A wide navy blue center stripe flanked by a narrow light blue stripe, a thin gold stripe and edged in light blue.

Central Intelligence Agency Table Medals

These are also referred to as plaques and sometimes, though, incorrectly, as paper weights. We have included these because of the tremendous interest in the Central Intelligence Agency. Despite the fact that they are not worn, they carry with them the same degree of respect for achievement or valor as the more usual medals.

P.

Distinguished Intelligence Cross

Awarded for extraordinary heroism in the line of duty.

Obverse. The medallion portrays a multi-rayed star on a shield, which is topped by the head of an eagle, surrounded by the inscription: **"Central Intelligence Agency-For Valor"**. This is then superimposed over a cross with four large arms, between each arm of the cross are three laurel leaves.

Reverse. In the center of the medallion there is a plaque with the inscription **"Awarded to"** with an area just below for the recipient's name. This is superimposed on a laurel wreath, surrounded by the inscription **"United States of America."**

Q.

Intelligence Star

Awarded for courageous action in the line of duty.

Obverse. A large five-pointed star in the center of which is a multi-rayed star on a shield, topped by the head of an eagle, between each point of the star are rays. The star is then superimposed over a laurel wreath. Along the outside edge of the medallion between each point of the star appears the inscription: **"Central Intelligence Agency - For Valor."**

Reverse. In the center of the medallion there is a plaque with the inscription **"Awarded to"** with an area just below for the recipient's name. This is superimposed on a laurel wreath, surrounded by the inscription **"United States of America."**

R.

Distinguished Intelligence Medal

Awarded for outstanding service.

Obverse. An American eagle with wings and legs outstretched, in its left talon, arrows, in the right, a branch of laurel. Above the eagle's head are thirteen stars in a cloud pattern. In the eagle's mouth a banner with the inscription **"E Pluribus Unum."** In the center of the eagle's breast appears a multi-rayed star on a shield. Along the outside edge of the medallion is the inscription **"Central Intelligence Agency for Distinguished Service."**

Reverse. In the center of the medallion there is a plaque with the inscription **"Awarded to"** with an area just below for the recipient's name. This is superimposed on a laurel wreath, surrounded by the inscription **"United States of America."**

S.

Intelligence Medal for Merit

Awarded for meritorious service.

Obverse. In the upper right corner is a shield with a multi-rayed star, topped by an eagle's head, and to the left is the inscription: **"for Merit."** Surrounding the shield at bottom right is a branch of oak, at bottom left is a branch of laurel. At the base of the medallion appears the inscription: **"Central Intelligence Agency."**

Reverse. In the center of the medallion there is a plaque with the inscription **"Awarded to"** with an area just below for the recipient's name. This is superimposed on a laurel wreath, surrounded by the inscription **"United States of America."**

T.

Career Intelligence Medal

Awarded for outstanding achievement in the field of intelligence.

Obverse. In the center is a multi-rayed star superimposed over a shield. Along the upper outside edge of the medallion is the inscription **"Central Intelligence Agency"** and just under the shield across the bottom the inscription **"for career achievement."**

Reverse. In the center of the medallion there is a plaque with the inscription **"awarded to"** with an area just below for the recipient's name. This is superimposed on a laurel wreath, surrounded by the inscription **"United States of America."**

62.

U.S. State Department Distinguished Honor Award

The Distinguished Honor Award is for exceptionally outstanding service to the department or the government for achievements of marked national or international significance; for exceptionally outstanding service or leadership in administering programs which result in successful accomplishments of mission, or in major attainment of objectives, or specific accomplishment to meet unique or emergency situations; or for outstanding accomplishments over a prolonged period that involve the exercise of authority or judgment in the public interest.

Obverse. A gold circular medallion, on which is the seal of the United States, surrounded by the inscription: **"Department of State, United States of America"** and at the base, a plaque with the inscription **"Distinguished Honor Award."** At each side upward from the base is a laurel branch.

Reverse. An area for the recipient's name and date received.

Ribbon. White overall with three thin navy blue stripes evenly spaced down the center.

Note: Founded in 1968.

63.

U.S. Department of State Superior Honor Award

The Superior Honor Award is given for outstanding service to the department or government, -service of significance where the interests of the United States are involved, or which has aided the department in furthering its objectives; for outstanding results in increasing productivity, efficiency and economy of operations resulting in a substantial contribution in accomplishing the department's mission; for outstanding leadership and/or professional competence in successful attainment of the department's goals; for superior creative service or contribution, such as the development of a new and highly effective product, program or method for accomplishing an objective of the department.

Obverse. A silver circular medallion, on which is the seal of the United States, surrounded by the inscription: **"Department of State, United States of America"** and at the base, a plaque with the inscription **"Superior Honor Award."** At each side upward from the base is a laurel branch.

Reverse. An area for the recipient's name and date awarded.

Ribbon. A wide stripe of white which in turn contains three thin black stripes. The white stripe is flanked by maroon to the edge.

Note: Founded in 1968.

64.

U.S. Department of State Meritorious Honor Award

The Meritorious Honor Award is conferred for: outstanding service in the conduct or improvement of the program or operations of the department; for accomplishing assigned responsibilities in an exemplary manner and establishing a record of achievement; for demonstration of unusual initiative in contributing to efficiency; improved management, or outstanding executive or technical ability; or for unusual devotion to duty under adverse conditions.

Obverse. A bronze, circular medallion, on which is the seal of the United States, surrounded by the inscription: "**Department of State, United States of America**" and at the base, a plaque with the inscription **Meritorious Honor Award.**" At each side upward from the base is a laurel branch.

Reverse. An area for the recipient's name and date awarded.

Ribbon. Navy blue with three thin white stripes in the center.

Note: Founded in 1968.

65.

Environmental Protection Agency Exceptional Service Medal

The gold medal for exceptional service was established October 7, 1971, to be awarded for one of the following:

1. Outstanding service to the mission of environmental protection.
2. Outstanding leadership, skill, or ability in devising and implementing or administering programs.
3. Major contributions to scientific and technological knowledge.
4. Distinguished authorship.
5. Notable creative service.
6. Heroic action.

Obverse. A gold medallion. In center is a stylized sun, land, and water; underneath are spreading leaves. Around the outside edge of the medal the inscription, **"United States Environmental Protection Agency."**

Reverse. Has the inscription, **"For Exceptional Service"**.

Ribbon. Center stripe is hunter green flanked by stripes of mint green, lemon-yellow, edged with oriental blue.

66.

Environmental Protection Agency Superior Service Medal

The silver medal for superior service was established October 7, 1971, and may be awarded for one of the following.

1. Highly meritorious service to environmental protection.
2. The demonstration of exceptional initiative or creative ability in the development of new or improved work methods, procedures, or devices for which monetary award would provide inadequate recognition.
3. Unusual courage or competence in an emergency relating to employment.
4. Meritorious authorship.
5. The performance of assigned task in such an outstanding manner that monetary recognition is inadequate.

Obverse. A silver medallion. In the center is a stylized sun, land, and water; underneath are spreading leaves. Around the outside edge of the medal the inscription, **"United States Environmental Protection Agency".**

Reverse. Has the inscription, **"For Superior Service".**

Ribbon. Center stripe is oriental blue flanked by stripes of mint green, white, and edged in hunter green.

67.

Environmental Protection Agency Commendable Service Medal

The bronze medal for commendable service was established October 7, 1971, and is awarded for highly competent performance of duties in the agency over a long period of time. Examples of such services are as follows:

1. Performance of assigned tasks in superior manner, setting a record of achievement and inspiring other employees to improve the quality or quantity of their work.
2. Demonstration of unusual initiative or creative ability in the development and improvement of methods, procedures, or devices.

Obverse. A bronze medallion. In the center is a stylized sun, land, and water; underneath are spreading leaves. Around the outside edge of the medal the inscription, **"United States Environmental Protection Agency".**

Reverse. Has the inscription **"For Commendable Service".**

Ribbon. The center stripe is moss green, flanked by stripes of white, blue, white and edged in mint green.

Note: The gold, silver, and bronze medallions are identical, except for the medal used and the inscription on the reverse.

68.

Agency for International Development Distinguished Honor Medal

Established March 12, 1964; awarded for exceptionally outstanding service to the agency or the government or for achievements of national or international significance.

Obverse. A gold medallion on which has been superimposed a shield showing clasped hands topped by four stars. Beneath are thirteen vertical stripes.

Reverse. Has the inscription: **"Distinguished Honor Award"** and an area for the recipient's name.

Ribbon. Has a wide center stripe of pale blue, flanked by stripes of royal blue, followed by thin stripes of white, royal blue, then white, and edged in red.

69.

Agency for International Development Superior Honor Medal

Established March 12, 1964; awarded for outstanding service or increased productivity for the agency or the government.

Obverse. A silver medallion on which has been superimposed a shield showing clasped hands topped by four stars. Beneath are thirteen vertical stripes.

Reverse. Has the inscription: **"Superior Honor Award"** and an area for the recipient's name.

Ribbon. Has a wide center stripe of pale blue, flanked by stripes of royal blue, followed by thin stripes of white, royal blue, then white, and edged in red.

70.

Agency for International Development Meritorious Honor Medal

Established March 12, 1964; awarded for outstanding service in conducting or improving programs or unusual devotion to duty under adverse conditions.

Obverse. A bronze medallion on which has been superimposed a shield showing clasped hands topped by four stars. Beneath are thirteen vertical stripes.

Reverse. Has the inscription: **"Meritorious Honor Medal"** and an area for the recipient's name.

Ribbon. Has a wide center stripe of pale blue, flanked by stripes of royal blue, followed by thin stripes of white, royal blue, then white, and edged in red.

Note: The gold, silver, and bronze medallions are identical, except for the metal used and the inscription on the reverse.

71.

Veterans Administration Exceptional Service Medal

Established in 1951; awarded for outstanding leadership, skill or ability in administration or for performance of duty, acts of heroism or creation of major programs benefiting the Veterans Administration or the government or science.

Obverse. A gold medallion portraying the seal of the V.A. topped by the inscription: **"Veterans Administration"** and along the bottom **"Exceptional Service."**

Reverse. Bears the recipient's name, the month and year awarded.

Ribbon. Dark blue.

73.

Veterans Administration Meritorious Service Medal

Established in 1956; awarded for performance of duty in such an outstanding manner that other recognition is inadequate, for developing new work methods or for courage in emergencies.

Obverse. A silver medallion portraying the seal of the V.A. topped by the inscription **"Veterans Administration"** and along the bottom **"Meritorious Service"**.

Reverse. Bears the recipient's name, the month and year awarded.

Ribbon. Red.

73.

Veterans Administration Distinguished Career Medal

Established in 1965; awarded to employees who have earned this recognition on their retirement or on resignation, for work characterized by outstanding efficiency, integrity and dedication.

Obverse. A bronze medallion portraying the seal of the V.A. topped by the inscription: **"Veterans Administration"** and along the bottom: **"Distinguished Career."**

Reverse. Bears the recipient's name, the month and year awarded.

Ribbon. Green.

Note: The gold, silver, and bronze medallions are identical, except for the metal used and the inscription at bottom on the obverse.

74.

General Accounting Office Distinguished Service Medal

Established June 14, 1967, and is awarded for exceptional efficiency, usually over a period of ten years or more. Not more than five persons may receive it in any one year.

Obverse. A gold medallion with nine scallops around its edge. In the center is the seal of the Comptroller General of the U.S.A. and has the inscription: **"Distinguished Service Award"** around its edge. At center are the initials: **"GAO."**

Reverse. Plain.

Ribbon. Center stripe navy blue flanked by a thin stripe of green, white, green, red, gold, red, and again a thin white stripe, edged in blue.

75.

General Accounting Office Career Development Medal

Established June 14, 1967; awarded to recognize employees who have contributed significantly to public service. Not more than ten persons may receive it in any one year.

Obverse. A gold medallion with twelve scallops around its edge. In the center is the seal of the Comptroller General of the U.S.A. and has the inscription: **"Career Development"**, around its edge. At the bottom are the initials: **"GAO."**

Reverse. Plain.

Ribbon. At center is a wide stripe of blue, flanked by thin stripe of green, thin white, wide blue, thin black, thin gold, edged with a wide stripe of blue.

76.

General Accounting Office Meritorious Service Medal

Established June 14, 1967; awarded for superior outstanding performance of work far above that ordinarily expected; and may be received by either an individual or a group. Not more than 20 are usually conferred in one year.

Obverse. A silver medallion framed by a wavy edge. In the center is the seal of the Comptroller General of the U.S.A. and has the inscription **"Meritorious Service"** around its edge. At bottom are the initials: **"G.A.O."**

Reverse. Plain.

Ribbon. Center stripe navy blue flanked by a thin stripe of green, white, green, red, gold, red, and again a thin white stripe, edged in blue.

77.

Department of Transportation Outstanding Achievement Medal

Established October 1968 and is awarded by the Secretary for outstanding leadership or other achievements as deemed appropriate.

Obverse. A gold medallion, marked in a grid pattern, surrounded by a laurel wreath. Superimposed at center is a stylized triangle.

Reverse. Bears the name of the award.

Ribbon. Blue center flanked by white, orange, black, white, black, and edged with orange.

78.

Department of Transportation Meritorious Achievement Medal

Established October 1968; awarded by the Secretary for completing assigned duties in an outstanding manner, developing new ideas, eminent authorship, outstanding ideas or other contributions.

Obverse. A silver medallion, marked in a grid pattern, surrounded by a laurel wreath. Superimposed at center is a stylized triangle.

Reverse. Bears the name of the award.

Ribbon. A blue center stripe flanked by white, orange, white, orange, blue, and edged with orange.

79.

Department of Transportation Medal For Valor

Established October 1968; awarded by the Secretary for acts of heroism involving great personal risk under unusual circumstances.

Obverse. A gold medallion, marked in a grid pattern, surrounded by a laurel wreath. Superimposed at center is a stylized triangle. The triangle and laurel wreath are superimposed on a six-pointed star, which in turn is superimposed on a second six-pointed star.

Reverse. Bears the name of the award.

Ribbon. A center stripe of blue flanked by orange, white, orange, white, black, orange, black on either side edged in white.

80.

Department of Transportation Superior Achievement Medal

Established November 1972; awarded by the Secretary or Under Secretary for performance of assigned tasks in exemplary fashion, for unusual skills or for improving work methods or for inventions which result in savings of manpower, time, etc., for notable authorship, exceptional achievements, and for significant achievement in support of the department's equal opportunities program.

Obverse. A bronze medallion, marked in a grid pattern, surrounded by a laurel wreath. Superimposed at center is a stylized triangle.

Reverse. Bears the name of the award.

Ribbon. A center stripe of red flanked by blue, white, red, blue, red on each side then edged by white.

81.

U.S. Information Agency Distinguished Honor Medal

Established in 1955; awarded for exceptional service in matters of marked national or international significance.

Obverse. A gold medallion showing the seal of the United States surrounded by the inscription **"United States Information Agency."**

Reverse. Bears the name of the award.

Ribbon. Blue.

82.

U.S. Information Agency Superior Honor Medal

Established in 1955; awarded for outstanding service to the U.S. government or for furthering the mission of the U.S. Information Agency in a superior manner.

Obverse. A silver medallion showing the seal of the United States surrounded by the inscription **"United States Information Agency."**

Ribbon. Bears the name of the award.

Ribbon. Red.

83.

U.S. Information Agency Meritorious Honor Medal

Established in 1955; awarded for outstanding service to the agency in improving its products, initiating new programs or carrying out projects which surpass usual requirements. Groups as well as individuals may receive the awards.

Obverse. A bronze medallion showing the seal of the United States surrounded by the inscription **"United States Information Agency."**

Reverse. Bears the name of the award.

Ribbon. White.

84.

H.E.W. U.S. Public Health Service Distinguished Service Medal

Established in 1961; awarded to commissioned officers of the U.S. Public Health Service only, for distinguished accomplishment or for heroism in saving life or property.

Obverse. A gold medallion bearing in the center the shield of the U.S. Public Health Service, surrounded by the inscription: **"Public Health Service - United States of America."**

Reverse. Has the inscription: **"Department of Health, Education, and Welfare,"** with a small star at the top.

Ribbon. Has a yellow center stripe flanked by purple, edged in black with inner thin stripe of white.

85.

H.E.W. U.S. Public Health Service Meritorious Service Medal

Established in 1961; awarded to commissioned officers of the U.S. Public Health Service only, for important achievement, technical or professional accomplishment, or leadership.

Obverse. A silver medallion bearing in the center the shield of the U.S. Public Health Service, surrounded by the inscription: **"Public Health Service - United States of America."**

Reverse. Has the inscription: **"Department of Health Education, and Welfare,"** with a small star at the top.

Ribbon. Has a white center stripe flanked by purple, edged in black with inner thin stripe of white.

86.

H.E.W. Public Health Service Commendation Medal

Established in 1961; awarded to commissioned officers of the U.S. Public Health Service only, for recognized levels of proficiency or dedication greater than that expected of the average commissioned officer, sustained high performance, or unique skills.

Obverse. A bronze medallion bearing in the center the shield of the U.S. Public Health Service, surrounded by the inscription: **"Public Health Service – United States of America."**

Reverse. Has the inscription: **"Department of Health, Education, and Welfare,"** with a small star at the top.

Ribbon. Purple flanked by thin white stripes, edged with black.

87.

Selective Service System Medal WWII

Awarded for exceptionally meritorious service or for significant achievements or inspiration to others which contributes to the goals of the Selective Service System.

Obverse. A bronze medallion which portrays the seal of the Selective Service System, which is the American eagle with wings and legs outstretched. In the right talons a branch of laurel, in the left arrows. Above the eagle's head are thirteen stars, in the following pattern starting at top: 1-4-3-4-1. In the eagle's mouth a banner with the words: **"E Pluribus Unum."** In the center of the eagle's chest is a shield with the letters S.S.S. at top. Around the outside edge the words: **"Selective Service System"** separated by tiny stars forming the words: **"World War II."**

Reverse. The words: **"Awarded in the Name of Congress of the United States for Faithful and Loyal Service."**

Ribbon. A wide blue stripe at center, flanked by a stripe half its size of orange-yellow, a thin stripe of blue, and edged by another stripe of orange-yellow the same width as the first.

Note: Civilian and military personnel are both eligible for this award.

88.

Selective Service System Distinguished Service Medal

Established October 1, 1971; awarded for extraordinary performance or contribution to the Selective Service System Administration.

Obverse. A gold medallion, which portrays the seal of the Selective Service System, which is the American eagle with wings and legs outstretched. In the right talons a branch of laurel, in the left arrows. Above the eagle's head are thirteen stars, in this pattern starting at top: 1-4-3-4-1. In the eagle's mouth a banner with the words **"E Pluribus Unum."** In the center of the eagle's chest is a shield with the letters S.S.S. at top. Around the upper outside edge the words: **"Selective Service System"** with a tiny star beginning and ending.

Reverse. Blank.

Ribbon. A wide center stripe of yellow, flanked by dark blue to each edge.

Note: Civilian and military personnel are both eligible for this award. Also the ribbon and pendant are incased together in Lucite, making the award unwearable.

89.

Selective Service System Exceptional Service Medal

Established October 1, 1971; awarded for exceptional service, and/or improvements of methods, or great acts of courage.

Obverse. A silver medallion which portrays the seal of the Selective Service System, which is the American eagle with wings and legs outstretched. In the right talons a branch of laurel, in the left, arrows. Above the eagle's head are thirteen stars in the following pattern starting at top: 1-4-3-4-1. In the eagle's mouth a banner with the words: **"E Pluribus Unum."** In the center of the eagle's chest is a shield with the letters S.S.S. at top. Around the upper outside edge the words: **"Selective Service System"** with a tiny star beginning and ending.

Reverse. Blank.

Ribbon. Left half, dark blue, right half yellow, looking at it.

Note: Civilian and military personnel are both eligible for this award. Also the ribbon and pendant are incased together in Lucite, making the award unwearable.

90.

Selective Service System Meritorious Service Medal

Established October 1, 1971; and awarded for exceptionally meritorious service, for significant achievements or inspiration to others which contributes to the goals of the Selective Service System.

Obverse. A bronze medallion which portrays the seal of the Selective Service System, which is the American eagle with wings and legs outstretched. In the right talons a branch of laurel, in the left arrows. Above the eagle's head are thirteen stars, in the pattern starting at top: 1-4-3-4-1. In the eagle's mouth a banner with the words: **E Pluribus Unum."** In the center of the eagle's chest is a shield with the letters S.S.S. at top. Around the upper outside edge the words: **"Selective Service System"** with a tiny star beginning and ending.

Reverse. Blank.

Ribbon. Yellow-edged in dark blue.

Note: Civilian and military personnel are both eligible for this award. Also the ribbon and pendant were incased together in Lucite, making the award unwearable.

91.

Defense Nuclear Agency Exceptional Service Medal

I have no information on what this decoration is awarded for.

Obverse. A gold medallion, centered is a nucleus surrounded by three orbits, through which are three war arrows, pointing upward. All this is then superimposed over a laurel wreath.

Reverse. Around the outside of the medallion the inscription: **"For Exceptional Service - Defense Nuclear Agency."** Just inside the inscription is a ring; inside the ring at top is the word: **"To"** with an area for the recipient's name.

Ribbon. At center is a narrow gold stripe, flanked by a thin navy blue stripe, a narrow light blue stripe, a narrow white stripe, a narrow navy blue stripe edged with a narrow gold stripe.

92.

Defense Nuclear Agency Meritorious Service Medal

I have no information on what this decoration is awarded for.

Obverse. A silver medallion, centered is a nucleus surrounded by three orbits through which are three war arrows pointing upward. All this is then superimposed over a laurel wreath.

Reverse. Around the outside of the medallion the inscription: **"For Meritorious Service - Defense Nuclear Agency."** Just inside the inscription is a ring; outside the ring at top is the word: **"To"**, with an area for the recipient's name.

Ribbon. A white stripe, flanked by a thin dark blue stripe, a light blue stripe, a white stripe, a dark blue stripe, edged by a white stripe.

93.

Presidential Citizens Medal

Established November 13, 1969, as a personal award of the President of the United States, in recognition of exemplary deeds of service performed by any of the country's citizens. It differs from the Medal of Freedom in that it honors service beyond the call of duty. Comes in one class and can be awarded posthumously.

Obverse. A gold medallion encircled by laurel wreath of green enamel. At center is the American eagle against a background of dark blue enamel on which are thirteen stars. Above the stars are clouds of white enamel.

Reverse. Carries the shield of the presidential coat of arms between two oak sprays and is inscribed: **"To** (the recipient's name) **from the President of the United States."**

Ribbon. Has a center stripe of light blue flanked by dark blue, edged in white.

94.

Presidential Award for Distinguished Federal Civilian Service

Established on July 27, 1957. This is the highest honor awarded to a career employee for extraordinary achievement in federal service. The award is granted annually to selected individuals whose achievements exemplify to an exceptional degree, imagination, courage, and high ability in carrying out the mission of the government.

Obverse. A gold medallion in the center is the American eagle with outstretched wings surrounded by a laurel wreath.

Reverse. Has these words inscribed: **"Award of the President of the United States to"** (recipient's name).

Ribbon. Worn from a neck cravat in the colors of dark blue with thin stripes of white and light blue toward each edge.

95.

Air Mail Flyers Medal of Honor

Established by Act of Congress, February 14, 1931, but was not presented until February 13, 1933. This bronze medal is awarded by the President but not in the name of Congress. It is awarded to civilian pilots for acts of outstanding bravery while carrying the mail.

This medal is very rare and has been conferred only ten times. Although apparently not rescinded, the last time this medal was awarded appears to have been in 1948.

Obverse. A bronze medallion portraying a nude male figure clasping a bag of mail, walking over clouds. In the background is a lightning bolt. Around the outside edge of the medallion are the words, **"Air Mail Flyers Medal of Honor".** A small triangle separates each word.

Reverse. Has the inscription, **"Presented by the President of the the United States to** (recipient's name) **for Distinguished Service as an Air Mail Pilot, Authorized by Congress February XIV, MCMXXI"** or 14, 1931.

Ribbon. Equal stripes of red, white, and blue.

96.

American Typhus Commission Medal

Established December 24, 1942. Awarded by the President, but not in the name of Congress, for meritorious service in connection with the work of the Typhus-Control Commission.

Obverse. A bronze medallion 1 and 1/4 inches in diameter. Centered are the profiles of Charles J.H. Nicolle (1866-1936) and Howard Taylor Ricketts (1871-1910), contributors to modern knowledge of cause and transmission of typhus fever.

Reverse. At right looking at the medal, the staff of Aesculapius, the Roman God of medicine. In straight lines the inscription, **"United States of America-Typhus Commission for"** separated slightly **"Meritorious Service".**

Ribbon. Equal stripes of gold centered, flanked by red-purple.

Designer. Edmond R. Amateis.

97.

Department of Defense Distinguished Civilian Service Medal

Established November 26, 1954, this is the highest award given by the Secretary of Defense to civilian employees of the Department. Awarded for exceptional devotion to duty and for contribution to the operation of the department. Succeeding awards to the same individual are shown by a bronze palm attached to the ribbon.

Obverse. A gold octagonal medallion portraying an arm and fist, vertical from bottom, clutching three arrows. Thirteen stars are scattered as background, seven above the fist, and three to each side of the arm. Around the outer edge is inscribed: **"Department of Defense."**

Reverse. I have no information on this.

Ribbon. Blue with three thin gold stripes of broken lines in center.

98.

Secretary of Defense Meritorious Civilian Service Medal

Established March 4, 1955, this is the second highest award given by the Secretary of Defense to civilian employees of the government. It recognizes exceptionally meritorious service to the Department of Defense. Succeeding awards to the same individual are shown by a bronze palm attached to the ribbon.

Obverse. A bronze medallion, with an arc of laurel leaves around its base. The center bears the seal of the Defense Department, which is the American eagle, wings outstretched, with three arrows in its talons and the U.S. shield on its breast. Around the eagle is the inscription: **"Office of the Secretary of Defense."**

Reverse. I have no information on this.

Ribbon. Gold with three thin stripes of blue stripes of broken lines in center.

Note: In addition to personnel of the office of the Secretary of Defense and the organization of the Joint Chiefs of Staff. The award may be received by employees of other Department of Defense activities and other government agencies.

99.

Department of Defense Distinguished Public Service Medal

Presented to civilians who do not derive their principal livelihood from government employment, but who have rendered especially meritorious service to the Department of Defense and/or one of its components.

Obverse. A gold medallion, in center of which is an eagle with wings outstretched holding three arrows in its talons. Above the eagle are thirteen stars. Below the eagle is a half circle of laurel coming almost to the tip of each wing, and the whole is surrounded by a laurel wreath.

Reverse. Has the inscription: "To (recipient's name) **for Distinguished Public Service to the Department of Defense,"** encircled by a laurel wreath at the medallion's edge.

Ribbon. A maroon center stripe flanked by a thin stripe of white, a wider stripe of blue, and edged in white.

Note: May be presented posthumously.

100.

Department of Defense Civil Preparedness Agency Director's Award for Distinguished Civilian Service

This is the department's highest award for civilian employees. It is granted to bestow major recognition for meritorious performance, acts or services of pre-eminent importance and value to the agency, the Department of Defense, of the U.S. government. It can also be conferred for acts of unusual courage or competence in the agency.

Obverse. A gold medallion, bearing the shield of the United States, the eagle and equilateral triangle of the Defense Civil Preparedness Agency, superimposed over an open wreath of two olive branches, the stems of which pass beneath the point of the shield.

Reverse. Has the inscription **"Distinguished Service"** and in smaller letters, **"Defense Civil Preparedness Agency"**, each word on a separate line.

Ribbon. A central panel of light blue flanked by dark blue, golden yellow, thin stripes of light blue, edged in golden yellow.

101.

Defense Communications Agency Director's Exceptional Civilian Service Medal

Established in 1967; awarded for outstanding performance.

Obverse. A bronze plaque that has a rounded base with scroll which in black enamel is engraved **"Defense Communications Agency."** The top corners of the plaque are scalloped. In the center is the shield of the Department of Defense, which is an eagle with wings outstretched, perched atop a globe. In the top half is a half circle of thirteen stars going over the top of the eagle. Coming from each talon is three thunderbolts.

Reverse. Has inscription: **"For Exceptional Civilian Service."**

Ribbon. Royal blue with six gold stripes.

Note: When established this award was conferred only upon an employee leaving the agency, if merited, or for heroism or exceptionally meritorious service. The criteria were changed in September, 1973, and now six civilian employees are honored with this decoration each year.

102.

Defense Supply Agency Exceptional Civilian Service Medal

I have no information on the criteria the medal is awarded for.

Obverse. A triangular silver shield above which is perched an an eagle, modified from the device of the agency. The whole is superimposed on a gold base, roughly triangular in shape, on which are three arrow heads symbolic of the three departments comprising the Department of Defense, and a laurel wreath, one branch at each side.

Reverse. Inscribed: **"Defense Supply Agency, Awarded to"** (recipient's name), and **"For Exceptional Civilian Service."**

Ribbon. Maroon center stripe, flanked by wide blue stripes centered by a thin yellow stripe.

103.

Defense Supply Agency Meritorious Civilian Service Medal

I have no information on the criteria the medal is awarded for.

Obverse. A triangular, green bronze, shield above which is perched an eagle, modified from the device of the agency. The whole is superimposed on a red bronze base, roughly triangular in shape, on which are three arrow heads symbolic of the three departments comprising the Department of the Defense, and a laurel wreath, one branch at each side.

Reverse. Inscribed **"Defense Supply Agency, Awarded to"** (recipient's name), and **"For Meritorious Civilian Service."**

Ribbon. Center stripe of yellow flanked by a blue stripe, a broad yellow stripe, edged with a wide maroon stripe.

104.

Defense Contract Audit Agency Distinguished Civilian Service Medal

I have no information on the criteria the medal is awarded for, but it was established August 1967.

Obverse. A gold medallion consisting of a triangular shield on which is represented a quill pen and scroll. Above them is a torch. Forming the border is a circle bearing a laurel wreath. The area between the border and the shield is open.

Reverse. Bears the inscription: **"Defense Contract Audit Agency - Distinguished Civilian Service."**

Ribbon. Center stripe of yellow, flanked in white, edged with turquoise with a thin black stripe centered in the turquoise.

105.

Defense Contract Audit Agency Meritorious Civilian Service Medal

I have no information on the criteria the medal is awarded for but it was established August 1967.

Obverse. A silver medallion consisting of a triangular shield on which is represented a quill and pen and scroll. Above them is a torch. Forming the border is a circle bearing a laurel wreath; the area between the border and shield is open.

Reverse. Bears the inscription: **"Defense Contract Audit Agency – Meritorious Civilian Service."**

Ribbon. Center stripe of white, flanked in yellow, edged with turquoise with a thin black stripe centered in the turquoise.

106.

Defense Intelligence Agency The Director's Award for Exceptional Civilian Service

Established October 1970; awarded to civilian employees who have distinguished themselves by notable performance or an act of great scope and significance to the agency. The Department of Defense and/or the federal government.

Obverse. A gold medallion, edged in a blue enamel ring with thirteen gold stars in the top half, and a laurel wreath tied with a bow at the base, in the bottom half of the ring. At the center of the ring is a globe surrounded by the axes. The globe and ring are then superimposed over a gold torch.

Reverse. I have no information on this.

Ribbon. A wide light blue center stripe flanked by navy blue, gold, and edged by navy blue.

107.

Defense Intelligence Agency Meritorious Civilian Service Medal

Established October 1970; awarded to civilian employees of the Defense Intelligence Agency for meritorious performance, for an act of service of pre-eminent importance and value to the agency, the Department of Defense and/or the federal government.

Obverse. An odd-shaped cross outlined in gold formed by placing a hexagon over a Latin cross. Inside the gold rim is white enamel. Between each arm of the cross are gold laurel leaves. In the center of the cross is a globe surrounded by two axes. The globe and axes are then superimposed over a gold torch.

Reverse. I have no information on this.

Ribbon. Centered by light blue, flanked by gold, and edged by a wide stripe of navy blue.

108.

Army Distinguished Civilian Service Medal

Established September 17, 1956, was made retroactive to July 26, 1947. Awarded by the Secretary of the Army to private citizens, federal government officials, and technical personnel who serve the Army in an advisory capacity or as consultants. All of these must have rendered distinguished service or made a substantial contribution to the Army's mission.

Obverse. A gold medallion bearing a triangle within which is the American eagle with wings and legs outstretched, in the center of the eagle's chest is the great shield of the U.S., in its right talons is a branch of laurel, in its left are arrows. At the base of the medallion is a laurel wreath.

Reverse. Has the inscription: **"Awarded to** (recipient's name) **For Distinguished Service to the United States Army."**

Ribbon. White overall with thin blue, red, blue stripes toward each edge.

Note: May also be awarded to foreigners.

109.

Army Outstanding Civilian Service Medal

Awarded by the Secretary of the Army to private citizens, federal government officials, and technical personnel who serve the Army in an advisory capacity or as consultants. All of these must have rendered distinguished service or made a substantial contribution to the Army's mission, but not to a degree high enough to merit the Distinguished Civilian Service Medal.

Obverse. A bronze medallion bearing a triangle within which is the American eagle with wings and legs outstretched, in the center of the eagle's chest is the great shield of the U.S., in its right talons is a branch of laurel, in its left are arrows. At the base of the medallion is a laurel wreath.

Reverse. Has the inscription: **"Awarded to"** (recipient's name) **"For Meritorious Service to the United States Army."**

Ribbon. White with six equal stripes of red; down the center of each white stripe is a very thin stripe of blue. Edged in white with a thin stripe of blue centering each.

Note: May be awarded to foreigners.

110.

Army Meritorious Civilian Service Medal

Awarded to United States Army civilian employees who have rendered exceptional services to the Department of the Army. It can also be awarded for an act of heroism involving voluntary risk of life in direct benefit to the government or its personnel.

Obverse. A bronze medallion bearing a triangle within which is the American eagle with wings and legs outstretched, in the center of the eagle's chest is the great shield of the U.S., in its right talons is a branch of laurel, in its left are arrows. At the base of the medallion is a laurel wreath.

Reverse. Has the inscription: **"Awarded to** (recipient's name) **for Outstanding Service to the United States Army."**

Ribbon. Blue with three solid white threads, center.

111.

Army Exceptional Civilian Service Medal

Established by the Secretary of the Army in 1960, as an award to private citizens, federal officials and technical personnel including consultants, who render outstanding service to the major command concerned, but not to a degree high enough to merit the Army Meritorious Civilian Service Medal.

Obverse. A gold medallion centered by the great Seal of the United States. The medallion is edged by a laurel wreath.

Reverse. Has the inscription **"For Department of the Army Exceptional Civilian Service - - to"** (recipient's name).

Ribbon. Blue with three dotted white stripes down the center.

112.

Navy Distinguished Civilian Service Medal

Awarded for contributions of such an extraordinary nature that recognition is deserved over that of headquarters command level. It can also be awarded for great courage in the face of danger which results in direct benefit to the government or its personnel.

Obverse. A gold medallion upon which is centered the Seal of the Department of the Navy, which is an American eagle with wings outstretched and perched on the flukes of a vertical anchor; all this then is superimposed over a background of the sea in the lower, and clouds in the upper part of the disc. Around the outside edge of the medallion is a blue enamel ring containing the words: **"Department of the Navy - Distinguished Service."**

Reverse. Has the inscription: **"Awarded to"** (recipient's name), resting on a spray of laurel.

Ribbon. Blue with three gold stripes at center.

Note: This is the highest honorary award conferred by the Secretary of the Navy to civilian employees of the Department of the Navy. This award may also be awarded posthumously.

113.

Navy Superior Civilian Service Medal

Awarded for superior civilian service or contributions which have resulted in exceptional benefit to the Navy.

Obverse. A silver medallion on which is centered the seal of the Department of the Navy, which is an American eagle with wings outstretched and perched on the flukes of a vertical anchor; all this is then superimposed over a background of the sea in the lower, and clouds in the upper part of the disc. Around the outside edge of the medallion is a blue enamel ring containing the words: **"Department of the Navy - Superior Civilian Service."**

Reverse. Blank.

Ribbon. Blue with three thin stripes of white down the center.

Note: This is the second highest honorary award conferred by the Secretary of the Navy to civilian employees of the Department of the Navy. This award may also be awarded posthumously.

114.

Navy Distinguished Public Service Medal

Established July 1951; awarded for heroic acts and significant contributions which help to accomplish the Navy's mission.

Obverse. A gold medallion which bears in its center an American eagle, with wings outstretched, perched on the flukes of an anchor that is slightly tilted. The eagle and anchor are then superimposed over a sailing ship rigged in full sail. Around the outside edge of the medallion is a ring of blue enamel which has the words: **"Department of the Navy - United States of America."**

Reverse. Has the inscription: **"Awarded to"** (recipient's name) on a tablet resting on a spray of laurel.

Ribbon. Left half blue, right half gold, looking at it.

Note: This is the highest award the Secretary of the Navy may give a U.S. citizen who is not employed by the Navy during the period when the award was earned.

115.

Captain Robert Dexter Conrad Medal
Awarded for Distinguished Achievement in Science

Established December 1956; awarded by the Secretary of the Navy for outstanding scientific achievement to the Navy. Named in honor of Robert Dexter Conrad, first director of the Planning Division of the Office of Naval Research. Born March 20, 1905, died July 26, 1949.

Obverse. A gold medallion, in center of which is the bust in left profile of Captain Conrad. Around the outside edge of the medallion is the inscription: **"Captain Robert Dexter Conrad Award - for Scientific Achievement."**

Reverse. An anchor with a plaque for the recipient's name; at top the inscription: **"Department of the Navy."**

Ribbon. Dark blue center stripe flanked by a thin stripe of gold, a thin stripe of dark blue, a wide stripe of white, edged in dark blue.

116.

Distinguished Achievement in Science Medal

Established January 1961; awarded for breakthroughs in science.

Obverse. A gold medallion on which is centered a sextant superimposed on an anchor with a microscope at right and a retort (vessel used in chemistry) at left looking at it. Inscribed around the outside edge of the medallion starting at top: **"Department of the Navy - Distinguished Achievement in Science."**

Reverse. Blank.

Ribbon. Blue overall with three thin gold stripes toward each edge.

Note: Very rare.

117.

Air Force Civilian Medal for Valor

Established in 1965; awarded by the Secretary of the Air Force to civilians serving in a capacity in the Air Force, who demonstrate unusual competence or courage while on duty.

Obverse. A gold medallion portraying an eagle of the Air Force seal superimposed on an equilateral triangle perched on a scroll inscribed **"Valor"**. The triangle is then superimposed on an olive wreath.

Reverse. Around the outside edge of the medallion the inscription: **"Civilian Award for Valor - United States Air Force"** at center top in straight line **"Awarded to."**

Ribbon. Red stripe in center flanked by a thin stripe of yellow, a narrow stripe of dark blue, a thin stripe of yellow, edged in a wide stripe of light blue.

118.

Air Force Command Civilian Medal for Valor

Established in 1965; awarded to civilians who demonstrate unusual courage. This award must be approved by the Chief of Staff, U.S.A.F. or a major commander.

Obverse. A silver medallion portraying an eagle of the Air Force seal superimposed on an equilateral triangle perched on a scroll inscribed **"Valor"**. The triangle is then superimposed on an olive wreath.

Reverse. Around the outside edge of the medallion the inscription: **"Civilian Award for Valor - United States Air Force."** At center in two straight lines **"Awarded to."**

Ribbon. Red stripe in center flanked by a thin stripe of yellow, a narrow stripe of light blue, a thin stripe of yellow, edged in a wide stripe of light blue.

119.

Air Force Exceptional Civilian Service Medal

Established August 30, 1948; awarded for exceptional service rendered to the Department of the Air Force by civilian employees. This award may also be given for an act of heroism involving voluntary risk of life.

Obverse. A gold medallion encircled on its outside edge by a laurel wreath. Centered is the Air Force coat of arms, above this is the American eagle with its wings outstretched, perched on a baton. Behind the eagle is a cloud.

Reverse. Engraved: **"To** (recipient's name) **for Exceptional Service – to the Department of the Air Force."**

Ribbon. Dark blue with three dotted orange stripes in the center.

Note: This decoration may also be awarded to any U.S. civilian or foreign national not employed by the U.S. government.

120.

Air Force Meritorious Civilian Service Medal

Established August 30, 1948; awarded for services so outstandingly performed by civilian employees of the Department of the Air Force that recognition by the Chief of Staff, U.S.A.F., is merited.

Obverse. A silver medallion encircled on its outside edge by a laurel wreath. Centered is the Air Force Coat of Arms, above this is the American eagle with its wings outstretched, perched on a baton. Behind the eagle is a cloud.

Reverse. Engraved: **"To** (recipient's name) **for Meritorious Service to the Department of the Air Force."**

Ribbon. A thin center stripe of dark blue, flanked by a narrow stripe of gold, a thin stripe of dark blue, a narrow stripe of gold, edged in a wide stripe of light blue.

121.

U.S. Coast Guard Distinguished Public Service Medal

I have no information on what this medal is awarded for.

Obverse. A gold medal portraying the crossed anchors and shield of the U.S. Coast Guard, inside a rope circle. These are then superimposed over an eight-pointed star.

Reverse. In a circle the inscription, **"Distinguished Public Service – U.S. Coast Guard."**

Ribbon. I have no information on this.

122.

U.S. Coast Guard Meritorious Public Service Medal

I have no information on what this medal is awarded for.

Obverse. A silver medal portraying the crossed anchors and shield of the U.S. Coast Guard, inside a rope circle. These are then superimposed over an eight-pointed star.

Reverse. In a circle the inscription, **"Meritorious Public Service – U.S. Coast Guard."**

Ribbon. I have no information on this.

123.

Vietnam Civilian Service Medal

Established January 15, 1968, retroactive to January 1, 1962; awarded to all U.S. government employees who completed one full calendar year in Vietnam. Employees who were injured or had suffered other disabilities and were forced to leave Vietnam before their completion of the one year requirement were also eligible.

Obverse. A 1 1/4 inch bronze medallion. The center portrays a torch of liberty, at slight angle, surrounded by an oriental dragon. At the top the inscription: **"Vietnam"** and at the bottom **"Service."**

Reverse. Has the shield of the United States centered, flanked by a branch of laurel. Around the outside edge of the medallion the words: (starting with a tiny star) **"Government of** (tiny star) **the United States."**

Ribbon. Thin red stripe centered, flanked by a thin gold stripe, a wide blue stripe, a thin gold, thin red, thin gold, and edged with a narrow blue.

124.

Navy Good Conduct Medal
(New Design Old Ribbon Drape)

In 1884 a new design was adopted with a further provision as follows: the Good Conduct Medals are special distinctions for fidelity, zeal, and obedience, and will not be granted for the first term of enlistment under continuous service. At the expiation of subsequent re-enlistments, men who hold honorable discharges and Continuous Service Certificates, will be entitled to receive the medal.

Obverse. A bronze medallion, 1 and 1/2 inches in diameter. In the center, encircled by a rope, a fully rigged sailing ship, below it the word **"Constitution."** This is then superimposed over an anchor. The stock of which appears above and the flukes below. Attached to the anchor is a chain which forms a circle around the outside edge. On the left side of the medallion, looking at it, between the rope and chain the word **"United."** On the right side, same area, the word **"States."** At bottom, on the lower part of the anchor, the word **"Navy."**

Reverse. Plain field with the inscription around the outside edge facing out **"Fidelity - Zeal - Obedience."** The medal is attached to a plain open clasp.

Ribbon. Maroon-red.

Designer. U.S. Mint in Philadelphia.

125.

Navy Good Conduct - Current

The medal awarded today is the same as above with two minor changes; the medallion was reduced from 1 and 1/2 inches to 1 and 1/4 inches; the medal was then suspended from a ring instead of an open clasp.

Note: This was the first Good Conduct Medal authorized in any of the services and has retained its present pendent design since July 13, 1892.

U.

Good Conduct Medal, Navy 1869 - 1884

Awarded to any seaman holding a Continuous Service Certificate who is distinguished for obedience, sobriety, and cleanliness, and is proficient in seamanship and gunnery; received upon the expiration of his enlistment.

Obverse. A Maltese Cross of nickel, bearing a circular medallion with the inscription **"Fidelity - Zeal - Obedience"** around the edge, with the letters U.S.N. in the center.

Reverse. Plain - The cross is attached to the ribbon by a plain, open clasp.

Ribbon. Equal stripes of red, white, and blue 1/2 half inch in width.

126.

Marine Corps Good Conduct Medal - First Type

Established July 20, 1896, by the Secretary of the Navy, for award to any man holding an Excellent Discharge who shall reenlist. Only those men who are distinguished for obedience, sobriety, industry, courage, neatness, and proficiency shall be recommended for Good Conduct Medals.

Obverse. A bronze medallion 1 and 5/16 inches in diameter. In the center encircled by a rope, a gunner standing behind a gun, below, a scroll bearing the inscription **"Semper Fidelis"** (always faithful). This is then superimposed over an anchor, the stock of which appears above, and slightly to the left, and the flukes below, and slightly to the right looking at it. Attached to the anchor is a chain forming a circle around the edge. On the left side looking at it between the rope and chain the words **"United States"**; on the right side, same area, the words **"Marine Corps."**

Reverse. Encircling a plain field around the outside edge the inscription facing out **"Fidelity - Zeal - Obedience."** The medal is then attached to a clasp in the shape of a carbine.

Ribbon. Navy blue stripe centered flanked by red.

Designer. Major General Charles Heywood, U.S.M.C.

127.

127.

Marine Corps Good Conduct - Current Type

The medal awarded today is the same as above but with one change; the carbine was replaced by a simple ring through which the ribbon is passed.

128.

Army Good Conduct Medal

Established by Executive Order June 28, 1941; conditions for award to read: enlisted personnel **"Who on or after August 27, 1940, had or shall have honorably completed three years of active federal military service, or who after December 7, 1941, have or shall have honorably served one year of federal military service while the United States is at war.**

Obverse. A 1 and 1/4 inch bronze medallion, at center portraying an eagle with wings raised up, tips down, perched on a sword, which is laid across a closed book. Around the outside edge the words: **"Efficiency, Honor, Fidelity."**

Reverse. At center is a five-pointed star above a scroll, for the recipient's name. Above the star the words: **"For Good."** At bottom, below the scroll, the word: **"Conduct."** All this then is encircled by an oak and laurel wreath.

Ribbon. Red overall with three thin white stripes towards each edge. Ribbon design by Arthur E. DuBus.

Designer. Joseph Kiselewski.

129.

Air Force Good Conduct Medal

Air Force personnel were previously awarded the Army Good Conduct Medal; then in June 1963 the Air Force authorized its own Good Conduct Medal based on executive order April 10, 1953. Those Air Force personnel who previously were awarded the Army Good Conduct Medal will continue to wear the Army medal. Any person qualifying for a Good Conduct Medal after June 1, 1963, will be awarded the Air Force Good Conduct Medal; so it is quite common to see Air Force personnel wearing both the Army and Air Force Good Conduct Medals.

Obverse. A 1 and 1/4 inch bronze medallion, at center portraying an eagle with wings raised up, tips down, perched on a sword, which is laid across a closed book. Around the outside edge the words **"Efficiency, Honor, Fidelity."**

Reverse. At center is a five-pointed star above a scroll, for the recipient's name. Above the star the words, **"For Good."**, at bottom, below the scroll, the word, **"Conduct."** All this then is encircled by an oak and laurel wreath.

Ribbon. A wide light blue stripe flanked by a thin stripe of blue, thin stripe of white, thin stripe of red, edged by a narrow stripe of light blue. Ribbon designed by the Institute of Heraldry, U.S. Army.

Designer. Joseph Kiselewski.

130.

Coast Guard Good Conduct Medal
First Type

Originally authorized on December 12, 1923, and made retroactive to May 17, 1920. The medal is awarded to enlisted personnel for three-year periods of demonstrated proficiency and good conduct.

Obverse. A bronze medallion, 1 and 1/2 inches in diameter. Centered is a ship within a rope circle, surrounded by the motto **Semper Paratus"** (always ready). Around the outside edge of the medal is a chain. At bottom between the end of the chain, are crossed oars. At the top of the suspension ribbon is a bar inscribed **"U.S. Coast Guard."**

Reverse. Around the edge of the medal facing in the inscription **"Fidelity - Zeal - Obedience".** Just inside this is a circle formed by a rope, with ends crossing at bottom. The medal is attached to a plain open clasp.

Ribbon. Maroon-red with a white center stripe.

131.

Coast Guard Good Conduct Medal
Current

The current Coast Guard Good Conduct Medal is similar to the first but with three changes; first, centered on the obverse is the Coast Guard Seal of crossed anchors and shield, instead of the ship; second, the plain open clasp is replaced by a simple ring through which the ribbon is replaced by a simple ring through which the ribbon is passed; third, the inscribed bar at top has been eliminated.

132. and 133.

Civil War Campaign Medal - Army

Established by the War Department January 11, 1905, for those persons who served in the Union forces during the Civil War.

Obverse. A bronze medallion 1 1/4 inches in diameter; centered is a bust of President Lincoln facing three-quarters to the right looking at it. Around the outside edge the inscription - **"With Malice Toward None With Charity For All."**

Reverse. Around the outside edge an oak and laurel wreath. Inside the wreath the words, **"The Civil War"**, below this separated by a bar the dates **"1861 - 1865."**

Ribbon #132. The first ribbon design was a thin white stripe centered, flanked by a wide blue stripe, a white stripe, edged in red.

Ribbon #133. The ribbon was changed to match the Navy and Marine Corps Civil War Medal which was, left side blue, right side gray looking at it.

Designer. Francis D. Millet.

134.and 135.

Civil War Campaign Medal - Navy and Marine Corps

Established by the Department of the Navy June 27, 1908, to be awarded to those persons who served in the Union forces during the Civil War.

Obverse. A bronze medallion 1 and 1/4 inches in diameter, center portrays the battle between the Monitor and Merrimac. At top along the edge the words **"The Civil War,"** at bottom the dates **"1861 - 1865."**

Reverse. At center is an eagle with wings outstretched looking to the left, perched on an anchor. At top along the outside edge the words **"United States Navy"** #134 or **"United States Marine Corps"** #135. Below the anchor the words, **"For Service"**, and below this around the outside edge, a branch of oak to the left, a branch of laurel to the right, looking at the medal. The two branches are then tied together at bottom center.

Ribbon. Left side blue, right side gray looking at it.

Designer. Bailey, Banks, and Biddle.

Note: The Navy and Marine Corps Medals are identical except on the reverse, #134 is inscribed **"Navy"** and #135 is inscribed **"Marine Corps."**

136. and 137.

Indian Wars Campaign Medal - Army

Authorized January 11, 1905, and awarded for service against hostile Indians from 1865 to 1891. This medal commemorates over 30 years of campaigns and battles fought against the American Indians in the southwest and far west of the United States. Names and dates of the Indian Wars are as follows:

1865–1868	In southern Oregon and Idaho and northern parts of California and Nevada.
1867–1869	Against Cheyennes, Arapahoes, Kiowas, and Commanches in Kansas, Colorado, and Oklahoma Indian Territory.
1872–1873	Modoc War.
1873	Against the Apaches in Arizona.
1874–1875	Against Kiowas, Commanches, and Cheyennes in Kansas, Colorado, Texas, Oklahoma, and New Mexico.
1876–1877	Against Northern Cheyennes and Sioux.
1877	Nez Perce War.
1878	Bannock War.
1878–1879	Against Northern Cheyennes.
1879–1880	Against Utes in Colorado.
1885–1886	Against Apaches in Arizona.
1890–1891	Against Sioux.

Obverse. A bronze medallion 1 and 1/4 inches in diameter; centered is an Indian mounted on a horse. The Indian is wearing a war headdress and carrying a spear. The Indian and horse are both facing right looking at the medal. At top around the outside edge the inscription, **"Indian Wars."** At bottom center is a buffalo skull, on either side of the skull are arrowheads going two-thirds the way up outside edge of the medal.

Reverse. In the center is an eagle facing right perched on a cannon supported by crossed flags, rifles, Indian shield, spear, and a quiver of arrows; below this the inscription, **"For Service."** Along the outside edge at top the inscription **"United States Army,"** at bottom edge, thirteen stars.

Ribbon #136. The first ribbon for this medal was red with a thin dark red stripe at each edge.

Ribbon #137. In 1917 the ribbon was changed to a wide red stripe, centered, flanked by a black stripe, edged with red.

Designer. Francis D. Millet.

138.

Sampson Medal, Navy and Marine Corps

Authorized by Congress on March 3, 1901, to be awarded to the officers and men of the Navy and Marine Corps who participated in the engagements in the West Indies.

Obverse. Admiral Sampson in uniform facing left. Around the top outside edge is the inscription, **"U.S. Naval Campaign – West Indies 1898."** At bottom left the inscription, **"William Sampson"**, bottom right **"Commander in Chief."**

Reverse. Officer, gunner, and Marine on deck of battleship in action, below is a tablet bearing name of engagement, followed by date.

Ribbon. A wide navy blue center stripe flanked by red.

Designer.
Obverse. Charles E. Barber.
Reverse. George T. Morgan.

139.

Spanish War Service Medal – Army

Authorized by Congress July 9, 1918, for service between April 20, 1898, and April 11, 1899, in the War with Spain; awarded to those men not eligible to receive the Spanish Campaign Medal.

Obverse. A bronze medallion 1 and 1/4 inches in diameter portraying a Roman sword hanging in its sheath from a tablet on which appears the words, **"For Service in the Spanish War."** The sword is sheathed to indicate National Guard Service in the Continental United States, not in normal combat.

Reverse. Centered over a scroll is the United States Coat of Arms surrounded by a laurel wreath over which is superimposed the insignia of the Infantry at left, Artillery at the bottom, and Cavalry at right.

Ribbon. A wide green center stripe flanked by a yellow stripe, and edged by a green stripe.

Designer.
Obverse. Col. J.R.M. Taylor.
Reverse. Bailey, Banks, and Biddle.

140. and 141.

West Indies Campaign
Navy and Marine Corps

Awarded to Navy and Marine Corps personnel for service aboard ships in the West Indies, but since most of the personnel had also qualified for the **"Sampson Medal"** there was little need for the West Indies Campaign Medal, and it was quickly discontinued.

Obverse. A bronze medallion 1 and 1/4 inches in diameter. In the center an excellent relief of Morro Castle in Cuba. In the foreground is a stack of cannon balls. Around the outside edge at top the inscription, **"West Indies Campaign"** at bottom the date **"1898"**.

Reverse. An eagle with wings outstretched looking to the left, perched on an anchor. At top along the outside edge the words **"United States Navy"** #140 or **"United States Marine Corps"** #141. Below the anchor the words **"United Service"** and below this around the outside edge a branch of oak to the left, a branch of laurel to the right, looking at the medal, the two branches are then tied together at bottom center.

Ribbon. Same for both medals, a wide yellow stripe at center, flanked by a wide blue stripe, edged by a yellow stripe.

Designer. Bailey, Banks, and Biddle.

Note: There was an earlier version of the ribbon. The first type was yellow overall with a narrow red stripe toward each edge.

142.

Dewey Medal - Navy and Marine Corps

Authorized by Congress June 3, 1898, commemorating the Battle of Manila Bay. The medal was awarded to the officers and men who were with Commodore Dewey at Manila.

Obverse. A bronze medallion 1 and 7/8 inches in diameter. Centered is a relief of Commodore Dewey in uniform facing right. At bottom right is an anchor on laurel wreath with star below. Starting at top coming down and around the relief of Dewey the inscription, **"The Gift of the people of the United States to the officers and men of the Asiatic Squadron under the command of Commodore George Dewey."**

Holding Bar. Centered is an eagle resting on waves. To the right of the eagle the hilt of a cross-handled sword; to the left, an olive branch. Half a helmsman's wheel is on each end.

Reverse. Centered is a half nude gunner seated upon the barrel of a gun, holding a flag horizontally across his lap; at bottom a plaque to be stamped with the name of the recipient's ship. Around the outside edge of the medal is the inscription **"In Memory of the Victory of Manila Bay, May 1, 1898."**

Ribbon. A wide gold stripe at center, edged in blue. This medal is unusual due to the fact that the ribbon is draped from the holding bar down behind the medal pendant.

Designer. Daniel Chester French.

Note: This medal is also known as the Manila Bay Medal.

143. and 144.

War with Spain Campaign Medal - Army

Established January 11, 1905, for service ashore in Cuba, Puerto Rico, or the Philippine Islands or enroute thereto on the high seas, during 1898.

Obverse. A bronze medallion 1 and 1/4 inches in diameter. In center is a castle with two small round towers at corners, said to be a modification of the castle that appears on the Royal Arms of Spain, the round towers possibly referring to the two Morro Castles, at Havana and Santiago de Cuba. At top around the outside edge of the medal is the inscription **"War with Spain."** At bottom the date **"1898"** to the left of the date is a branch of tobacco plant, and to the right a stalk of sugar cane.

Reverse. In the center is an eagle facing right perched on a cannon supported by crossed flags, rifles, Indian shield, spear, and a quiver of arrows; below this the inscription, **"For Service."** Along the outside edge at top the inscription **"United States Army"**, at bottom edge, thirteen stars.

Ribbon #143. The first ribbon design had a wide center stripe of gold, flanked by a narrow stripe of red, edged with a thin stripe of blue.

Ribbon. #144. The second ribbon design has a wide stripe of yellow flanked by a wide stripe of blue, edged in yellow.

Designer. Francis D. Millet.

145. and 146.

Spanish Campaign Medal – Navy and Marine Corps

Established June 27, 1908, for service afloat or on shore in Cuba, Puerto Rico, the Philippines, or Guam. The medal was awarded to Navy and Marine Corps personnel who had served in these areas between May 1 and August 16, 1898.

Obverse. A bronze medallion 1 and 1/4 inches in diameter. In the center an excellent relief of Morro Castle of Cuba. In the foreground is a stack of cannon balls. Around the outside edge at top the inscription **"Spanish Campaign."** At bottom the date **"1898."**

Reverse. An eagle with wings outstretched looking to the left, perched on an anchor. At top along the outside edge the words **"United States Navy"** #145 or **"United States Marine Corps"** #146. Below the anchor the words **"For Service"** and below this around the outside edge, a branch of oak to the left, a branch of laurel to the right, looking at the medal; the two branches are then tied together at bottom center.

Ribbon. Same for both medals, a wide yellow stripe at center, flanked by a wide blue stripe edge by a yellow stripe.

Designer. Bailey, Banks, and Biddle.

147.

Philippine Congressional Medal

Established June 29, 1906, for those who served beyond the date on which they were entitled to discharge, during the War with Spain, to help suppress Philippine Insurrection.

Obverse. A bronze medallion 1 and 1/4 inches in diameter. At center is a color guard consisting of a color bearer holding a United States Flag, flanked by two soldiers shouldering rifles. Around the outside edge the words, **"Philippine Insurrection"** at bottom the date **"1899."**

Reverse. The inscription **"For Patriotism Fortitude and Loyalty;"** surrounding this is a wreath made up of a pine branch to the left, and palm branch to the right. The two branches are then tied together at bottom center with a bow.

Ribbon. Dark blue center flanked on each side by a white stripe, a red stripe, a white stripe and edged in dark blue.

Designer. Francis D. Millet.

148.

Philippine Campaign - Army

Authorized January 11, 1905, and issued to Army personnel who served in the Philippine Islands against hostile natives between February 4, 1899, and December 31, 1913.

Obverse. A bronze medallion 1 and 1/4 inches in diameter. Centered is a coconut-palm tree. To the left, looking at the medal is the lamp of knowledge, to the right the scales of justice. Around the outside edge, facing in, the inscription **"Philippine Insurrection."** At bottom the date **"1899."**

Reverse. In the center is an eagle facing right perched on a cannon supported by crossed flags, rifles, Indian shield, spear, and a quiver of arrows; below this the inscription **"For Service."** Along the outside edge at top the inscription **"United States Army",** at bottom edge, thirteen stars.

Ribbon. A wide blue stripe at center flanked by a red stripe, edged in a thin blue stripe.

Designer. Francis D. Millet.

149. and 150.

Philippine Campaign Medal Navy and Marine Corps

Authorized June 27, 1908, and issued to Navy and Marine Corps personnel who served in and around the Philippine Islands against hostile natives between February 4, 1899, and July 4, 1902, or between February 4, 1899, and December 31, 1904.

Obverse. A bronze medallion 1 and 1/4 inches in diameter. Centered is an old gateway in the Ancient Barrio of Manila. At the top around the outside edge of the medal is the inscription, **"Philippine Campaign"** at bottom the dates **"1899-1903";** flanked the dates is a branch of laurel.

Reverse. At center is an eagle with wings outstretched looking to the left, perched on an anchor. At top along the outside edge the words **"United States Navy"** #149 or **"United States Marine Corps"** #150. Below the anchor the words **"For Service"** and below this around the outside edge, a branch of oak to the left, looking at the medal, and a branch of laurel to the right. The two branches are then tied together at bottom center.

Ribbon. A wide blue stripe at center flanked by a red stripe, edged in a thin blue stripe.

Note: The ribbon is the same for both the Navy and Marine Corps medals.

Designer. Bailey, Banks, and Biddle.

151.

China Relief Expedition Campaign Medal - Army

Authorized for award January 11, 1905, for service ashore with the Peking Relief Expedition during the Boxer Rebellion, between June 20, 1900, and May 27, 1901.

Obverse. A bronze medallion 1 and 1/4 inches in diameter. At center the Imperial Chinese five-toed Dragon. Around the upper outside edge the inscription **"China Relief Expedition"** and at bottom the dates **"1900 - 1901."**

Reverse. In the center is an eagle facing right with wings stretched out, perched on a cannon supported by crossed flags, rifles, Indian shield, spear, and a quiver of arrows; below this the inscription, **"For Service."** Along the upper outside edge the inscription, **"United States Army,"** along the bottom edge are thirteen stars.

Ribbon. Yellow with a narrow navy blue stripe at each edge.

Designer. Francis D. Millet.

152., 153., and 154.

China Relief Expedition Campaign Medal Navy and Marine Corps

Authorized for award August 13, 1909, to Navy and Marine Corps personnel for service ashore with the Peking Relief Expedition or service ashore with the Peking Relief Expedition or service on a naval vessel in that area during the Boxer Rebellion between May 24, 1900, and May 27, 1901.

Obverse. A bronze medallion 1 and 1/4 inches in diameter. At center, the main gate to the walled city of Peking, below this is the Imperial Chinese Dragon. Around the upper outside edge the words, **"China Relief Expedition"** at bottom edge center is the date **"1900."**

Reverse. At center is an eagle with wings outstretched looking to the left, perched on an anchor. At top along the outside edge the words, **"United States Navy"**, #153 or, **"United States Marine Corps"**, #154. Below the anchor the words **"For Service"**, and below this around the outside edge, a branch of oak, looking at the medal, to the right a branch of laurel. The two branches are then tied together at bottom center.

Ribbon. #152 was the first ribbon design for these medals - yellow overall with a narrow black stripe toward each edge.

Ribbon. The new ribbon Navy #153 and Marine Corps #154 are the same - yellow with a narrow navy blue stripe at each edge (same as the Army Campaign Medal).

Designer. Bailey, Banks, and Biddle.

155.

Cuban Pacification Campaign Medal - Army

Authorization for award May 11, 1909, for service in Cuba between October 6, 1906, and April 1, 1909.

Obverse. A bronze medallion 1 and 1/4 inches in diameter. At center is the shield from the Cuban Coat of Arms, superimposed over a fasces, flanked by an oak branch to the left, looking at the medal, and a laurel branch to the right. Flanking all of this are two American soldiers with rifles, one to each side of the shield. At top written in straight lines the words, **"Cuban Pacification."** At bottom the dates, **"1906 - 1909."**

Reverse. In the center is an eagle facing right with wings outstretched, perched on a cannon supported by crossed flags, rifles, Indian shield, spear, and a quiver of arrows; below this the inscription, **"For Service."** Along the upper outside edge the inscription, **"United States Army,"** and along the bottom edge are thirteen stars.

Ribbon. At center a wide stripe of olive-drab flanked by a narrow blue stripe, a narrow white stripe, and edged with a narrow red stripe.

Designer. By the Institute of Heraldry, U.S. Army.

156. and 157.

Cuban Pacification Campaign Medal Navy and Marine Corps

Authorized for award August 13, 1909, for service in Cuba between September 12, 1906, and April 1, 1909, by Navy and Marine Corps personnel in expeditionary forces.

Obverse. A bronze medallion 1 and 1/4 inches in diameter. At center right is a female figure, Columbia, representing America wearing a sword in scabbard from her girdle; she is holding the staff of a flag in her left hand and offering a Cuban an olive branch with her right. Before her is a Cuban kneeling.

Reverse. At center is an eagle with wings outstretched looking to the left, perched on anchor. At top along the outside edge the words, **"United States Navy"**, #156 or **"United States Marine Corps"**, #157. Below the anchor the words, **"For Service"**, and below this, around the outside edge, a branch of oak, looking at the medal, to the right a branch of laurel. The two branches are then tied together at bottom center.

Ribbon. The ribbon is the same for both the Navy and Marine Corps medals. At center a wide stripe of olive-drab flanked by a narrow blue stripe, a narrow white stripe, and edged with a narrow red stripe. Same as the Army Campaign Medal.

Designer. Bailey, Banks, and Biddle.

158.

War with Mexico Campaign Medal - Army

Authorized for award December 12, 1917, to Army personnel who served against hostile Mexicans between April 12, 1911, and June 16, 1919.

Obverse. A bronze medallion 1 and 1/4 inches in diameter. At center is a Yucca plant in bloom, with mountains in the background. Around the outside edge at top is the inscription, **"Mexican Service"**, at the bottom are the dates, **"1911 - 1917"**.

Reverse. In the center is an eagle facing right with wings outstretched, perched on a cannon supported by crossed flags, rifles, Indian shield, spear, and a quiver of arrows; below this the inscription **"For Service"**. Along the upper outside edge the inscription, **"United States Army,"** and along the bottom edge are thirteen stars.

Ribbon. A center is a wide blue stripe, flanked by a wide yellow stripe, edged with a narrow green stripe.

Designer. Col. J.R.M. Taylor.

159. and 160.

War with Mexico Campaign Medal
Navy and Marine Corps

Authorized for award December 12, 1917, to Navy and Marine Corps personnel who served against hostile Mexicans between April 12, 1911, and February 7, 1917.

Obverse. A bronze medallion 1 and 1/4 inches in diameter at center, the old castle of San Juan Ulloa looking across the water of Veracruz Harbor. To the right and left of this in an outside ring are branches of cactus. At top in the same ring the inscription, **"Mexico"**, and at bottom the dates, **"1911 - 1917."**

Obverse. At center is an eagle with wings outstretched looking to the left, perched on an anchor. At top along the outside edge the words, **"United States Navy,"** #150 or **"United States Marine Corps"**, #160. Below the anchor the words, **"For Service,"** and below this, around the outside edge, a branch of oak, looking at the medal, to the right a branch of laurel. The two branches are then tied together at bottom center.

Ribbon. The ribbon is the same for both the Navy and Marine Corps. At center is a wide blue stripe, flanked by a wide yellow stripe, edged with a narrow green stripe.

Designer. Bailey, Banks, and Biddle.

161. and 162.

Nicaraguan Campaign Medal
Navy and Marine Corps

Authorized for award, December 22, 1913, to personnel of the Navy and Marine Corps who served in Nicaragua, or on board certain ships in that area between July 29, 1912, and November 14, 1912.

Obverse. A bronze medallion 1 and 1/4 inches in diameter. At center is the volcano Mt. Momotombo; in front of this is a rain forest flanking Lake Managua. Along the upper outside edge is the inscription, **"Nicaraguan Campaign"**, at the bottom edge the date **"1912"**. To the right of the date is an oak branch, to the left a laurel branch.

Reverse. At center is an eagle with wings outstretched looking to the left, perched on an anchor. At top along the outside edge the words, **"United States Navy"**, #161 or, **"United States Marine Corps"**, #162. Below the anchor the words, **"For Service"**, and below this, around the outside edge, a branch of oak looking at the medal to the right a branch of laurel. The two branches are then tied together at bottom center.

Ribbon. The ribbon is the same for both branches. Red overall with a wide blue stripe toward each edge.

Designer. Bailey, Banks, and Biddle.

163. and 164.

Haitian Campaign Medal 1915
Navy and Marine Corps

Authorized for award, June 22, 1917, to Navy and Marine Corps personnel who participated in joint expedition to Haiti between July 9, 1915, and December 6, 1915.

Obverse. A bronze medallion 1 and 1/4 inches in diameter. At left foreground is a tropical palm. Behind this in the background are waves, a shoreline, and mountains. Around the upper edge the inscription, **"Haitian Campaign"**, and at bottom center the date, **"1915."**

Reverse. At center is an eagle with wings outstretched looking to the left, perched on an anchor. At top along the outside edge the words, **"United States Navy"**, #163 or, **"United States Marine Corps,"** #164. Below the anchor the words, **"For Service"**, and below this, around the outside edge, a branch of oak, looking at the medal, to the right a branch of laurel. The two branches are then tied together at bottom center.

Ribbon. The ribbon is the same for both branches. At center a thin blue stripe flanked by a narrow stripe of red, edged with blue.

Designer. Bailey, Banks, and Biddle.

165.

Mexican Border Service Medal - Army

Authorized for award July 9, 1918, for service in the Mexican Border Patrol by the National Guard from May 9, 1916, to March 24, 1917, and by the Regular Army from January 1, 1916, to April 6, 1917.

Obverse. A bronze medallion 1 and 1/4 inches in diameter portraying a Roman sword hanging in its sheath from a tablet on which appears the words, **"For Service On - The Mexican Border."** The sword is sheathed to indicate National Guard Service, not in normal combat.

Reverse. Centered over a scroll is the United States Coat of Arms surrounded by a laurel wreath over which is superimposed the insignia of the Infantry at left, Artillery at the bottom, and Cavalry at right.

Ribbon. Divided in three equal stripes with gold at center flanked by green.

Designer.
Obverse. Col. J.R.M. Taylor.
Reverse. Bailey, Banks, and Biddle.

166. and 167.

Dominican Campaign Medal Navy and Marine Corps

Authorized for award December 19, 1921, to commemorate services by Naval and Marine Corps who served in operations in Santo Domingo from May 5, 1916, to December 4, 1916.

Obverse. A bronze medallion 1 and 1/4 inches in diameter. At center is the **"Tower of Homage"** at Ciudad Trujillo; in the foreground, breaking waves and a seawall. Around the upper outside edge is the inscription, **"Dominican Campaign"**. At bottom center the date **"1916"**.

Reverse. At center is an eagle perched on shank of an anchor laid horizontally. Behind this is a branch of laurel entwined about the anchor. To the left of the eagle just above the laurel is the word, **"For"**, to the right side, same area, the word **"Service"**. Around the top outside edge the inscription, **"United States Navy"**, #166 or, **"United States Marine Corps"**, #167.

Ribbon. The ribbon is the same for both branches. At center is a thin red stripe, flanked by a narrow blue stripe. Edged with a wide red stripe.

Designer.
Obverse. A.A. Weinman.

168. and 169.

Haitian Campaign Medal 1919–1920
Navy and Marine Corps

Authorized for award to Navy and Marine Corps personnel who participated in joint expedition to Haiti between April 1, 1919, and June 15, 1920.

Obverse. A bronze medallion 1 and 1/4 inches in diameter. At left foreground is a tropical palm, behind this in the background are waves, a shoreline, and mountains. Around the upper edge the inscription, **"Haitian Campaign"**, and at bottom center the date, **"1919 - 1920"**.

Reverse. At center is an eagle with wings outstretched looking to the left, perched on an anchor. At top along the outside edge the words, **"United States Navy"**, #168 or, **"United States Marine Corps"**, #169. Below the anchor the words, **"For Service"**, and below this, around the outside edge, a branch of oak, looking at the medal, to the right a branch of laurel. The two branches are then tied together at bottom center.

Ribbon. The same for both branches, at center a thin blue stripe flanked by a narrow stripe of red edged with blue, same as the 1915 medal.

Designer. Bailey, Banks, and Biddle.

Note: For individuals who had already received the 1915 Haitian Campaign medal, a clasp inscribed with the dates 1919 - 1920 was given in lieu of the medal.

170. and 171.

Second Nicaraguan Campaign Medal
Navy and Marine Corps

Authorized for award November 8, 1929, and awarded to personnel of the Navy and Marine Corps who participated in operations in Nicaragua from August 27, 1926, to January 2, 1933.

Obverse. A bronze medallion 1 and 1/4 inches in diameter. At center the poetic feminine symbol of the United States, Columbia. She is shown ready with sword drawn, shielding a male and female figure behind her cape. Around the upper outside edge the inscription, **"Second Nicaraguan Campaign."**

Reverse. At center is an eagle perched on the shank of an anchor laid horizontally. Behind this is a branch of laurel entwined about the anchor. To the left of the eagle just above the laurel is the word, **"For"**, to the right side, same area, the word, **"Service"**. Around the top outside edge the inscription, **"United States Navy,"** #170 or **"United States Marine Corps"**, #171.

Ribbon. Same for both branches. At center is a thin red stripe, flanked by a narrow white stripe, a wide red, narrow white, thin red, narrow white, wide red, narrow white, edged in a narrow red.

Designer.
Obverse. Albert Stewart.
Reverse. A.A. Weinman.

Note: Army personnel who participated in the Nicaraguan Campaigns were also awarded the medal.

172. and 173.

Yangtze Service Campaign Medal
Navy and Marine Corps

Authorized for award April 28, 1930, for personnel of the Navy and Marine Corps who participated in operations in the Yangtze River Valley, China, or at Shanghai, between September 3, 1926, and October 21, 1927, or from March 1, 1930, to December 31, 1932.

Obverse. A bronze medallion 1 and 1/4 inches in diameter, at center a Chinese junk at sea with bow facing left looking at the medal. Around the upper outside edge the inscription, **"Yangtze Service."**

Reverse. At center is an eagle perched on the shank of an anchor laid horizontally. Behind this is a branch of laurel entwined about the anchor. To the left of the eagle just above the laurel is the word, **"For"**, to the right side, same area, the word, **"Service"**. Around the top outside edge the inscription, **"United States Navy"**, #172 or, **"United States Marine Corps"**, #173.

Ribbon. Same for both branches. At center a wide blue stripe flanked by a red stripe, a yellow stripe, edged with a blue stripe.

Designer.
Obverse. John R. Sinnock.
Reverse. A.A. Weinman.

174. and 175.

China Service Campaign Medal
Navy and Marine Corps

Authorized for award August 23, 1940. For participation during operations in China, Taiwan, and the Matsu Straits by Navy and Marine Corps personnel between the dates July 7, 1937, and September 7, 1939, or September 2, 1945, through April 1, 1957.

Obverse. A bronze medallion 1 and 1/4 inches in diameter. At center a Chinese junk resting on waves with bow facing right, looking at the medal. Around this along the outside edge in lettering intended to appear similar to Chinese calligraphic word symbols the inscription, **"China Service."**

Reverse. At center is an eagle perched on the shank of an anchor laid horizontally. Behind this is a branch of laurel entwined about the anchor. To the left of the eagle just above the laurel is the word, **"For"**, to the right side, same area, the word, **"Service"**. Around the top outside edge the inscription, **"United States Navy"**, #174 or, **"United States Marine Corps,"** #175.

Ribbon. Same for both branches - yellow with a thin red stripe toward each edge.

Designer.
Obverse. George H. Snowden.
Reverse. A.A. Wienman.

Note: Personnel who earned the China Service Medal between 1937 and 1939 and then earned the medal again from 1945 to 1957, may wear a bronze star on the ribbon drape of the medal, and ribbon bar. Personnel of the Army and Air Force who participated in the operations were also eligible for the medal.

176

Navy Expeditionary Campaign Medal

Awarded to Navy personnel who have landed on foreign territory and engaged armed enemy opposition under circumstances for which no special medal has been awarded.

Officers and men who served in defense of Wake Island from December 7, to December 22, 1941, wear a silver **"W"** on their ribbon bar, and a Wake Island clasp on the ribbon drape of the medal. This is the only case in which the expeditionary medal was issued for service for which a campaign or service medal is also authorized.

Obverse. A bronze medallion 1 and 5/16 inches in diameter. At center, in water to his knees, is a sailor laboring, at bow, to bring a landing boat around. The boat containing an officer, Marines, and flag of the United States. In the background on the horizon is a large ship. At top the inscription, **"Expeditions."**

Reverse. At center is an eagle perched on the shank of an anchor laid horizontally. Behind this is a branch of laurel entwined about the anchor. To the left of the eagle just above the laurel is the word, **"For"**, to the right side, same area, the word, **"Service."** Around the top outside edge the inscription, **"United States Navy."**

Ribbon. At center a wide stripe of blue, flanked by a wide stripe of yellow, edged with a narrow stripe of blue.

Designer. A.A. Wienman.

177.

Marine Corps Expeditionary Campaign Medal

Awarded to Marine Corps personnel who have landed on foreign territory and engaged armed enemy opposition under circumstances for which no special medal has been awarded.

Obverse. A bronze medallion 1 5/16 inches in diameter. At center, a Marine, facing left, charging with fixed bayonet, wearing full pack and gear. At bottom are waves to indicate the Naval phase of the Marines' duty. Around the top outside edge the inscription, **"Expeditions."**

Reverse. At center is an eagle perched on the shank of an anchor laid horizontally. Behind this is a branch of laurel entwined about the anchor. To the left of the eagle just above the laurel is the word, **"For"**, to the right side, same area, the word, **"Service"**. Around the top outside edge the inscription, **"United States Marine Corps."**

Ribbon. At center a wide stripe of red, flanked by a wide stripe of gold, edged with a thin stripe of red.

Designer.
Obverse. Walker Hancock.
Reverse. A.A. Weinman.

178.

Asiatic-Pacific Campaign Medal

Awarded for service in the United States Armed Forces in the Asiatic-Pacific Campaign Theater from December 7, 1941, to March 2, 1946.

Obverse. A bronze medallion 1 and 1/4 inches in diameter. In foreground are two GI's with carbines; behind them is a landing craft unloading men, and palm trees. In the background is the ocean having on its horizon a battleship, aircraft carrier, and submarine. Above them are aircraft. Around the upper outside edge is the inscription, **"Asiatic-Pacific Campaign."**

Reverse. An American Bald Eagle, facing left, perched on a slab of rock. To the left of the eagle are the dates, **"1941 – 1945,"** to the eagles back the inscription, **"United States of America."**

Ribbon. At center a thin white stripe to the right of this is a thin red stripe, and to the left a thin blue stripe. Flanking these three stripes is a wide orange stripe, a narrow white stripe, narrow red, narrow white, edged in orange.

Note: The colors of the ribbon have a significant meaning. The red, white, and blue stripes in the center represent the United States. The red stripe is worn to the left of the wearer. The red and white stripes toward the edge at each end of the ribbon represent the colors of Japan. To the best of my knowledge the yellow-orange color has no meaning.

Designer. Institute of Heraldry, U.S. Army.

179.

American Campaign Medal

Awarded for service in the Armed Forces within the American Theater from December 7, 1941, to March 2, 1946.

Obverse. A bronze medallion 1 and 1/4 inches in diameter. At center foreground is a sinking enemy submarine, behind this is a Navy cruiser, and in the background are some buildings representing the arsenal of democracy. Flying overhead is a B-24 Bomber. Around the outside upper edge the inscription, **"American Campaign."**

Reverse. An American Bald Eagle, facing left, perched on a slab of rock. To the left of the eagle the dates, **"1941 - 1945"**, to the eagle's back the inscription, **"United States of America."**

Ribbon. At center is a thin white stripe, to the right of this is a thin red stripe, and to the left a thin blue stripe. Flanking these three stripes is a wide blue stripe, a thin white, thin red, thin black, a thin white, edged in a wide blue stripe.

Note: The colors of the ribbon have a significant meaning. The red, white, and blue stripes in the center represent the United States. The red stripe is worn to the left of the wearer. The black and white stripes toward the outside edge, at each end of the ribbon, represent the colors of Germany; Next to these, toward the inside, on each side is a red stripe and a white stripe which represent the colors of Japan. The medium blue color represents the United States.

Designer. Institute of Heraldry, U.S. Army.

180.

European - African - Middle Eastern Campaign Medal

Awarded to personnel of the United States Armed Forces for service in the European - African - Middle Eastern Theater from December 7, 1941, to November 8, 1945.

Obverse. A bronze medallion 1 and 1/4 inches in diameter. At center are troops unloading, while under fire, from LST landing craft. In the background is an aircraft in flight.

Reverse. An American Bald Eagle, facing left, perched on a slab of rock. To the left of the eagle the dates, **"1941 - 1945,"** to the eagle's back the inscription, **"United States of America."**

Ribbon. At center is a thin stripe, to the right of this is a thin red stripe, and to the left a thin blue stripe. At right of these three stripes is a wide green, narrow white, narrow black, narrow white, edged in brown. To the left of the three center stripes is a wide green stripe, a narrow red, narrow white, narrow green, edged in brown.

Note: The colors of the ribbon have a significant meaning. The red, white, and blue stripes in the center represent the United States. The red stripe is worn to the left of the wearer. The wide green stripes flanking the center stripes represent the green fields of Europe. The thin green, white, and red stripes on the wearer's right represent Italy. The thin black and white stripes to the wearer's left represent Germany. The brown stripes that edge each end of the ribbon represent the sands of the African desert.

Designer. Institute of Heraldry, U.S. Army.

181.

Korean Service Campaign Medal

Awarded to personnel of the United States Armed Forces for service in the Korean Theater from June 27, 1950, to July 27, 1954.

Obverse. A bronze medallion 1 and 1/4 inches in diameter. At center is a Korean gateway. Around the upper outside edge is the inscription, **"Korean Service."**

Reverse. The Korean Tah Gook taken from the center of the Korean National Flag, which is a circle divided by an S shaped line, representing the essential unit of all. Around the upper outside edge is the inscription, **"United States of America."** At bottom is a spray of laurel and oak tied together at center.

Ribbon. A narrow stripe of white flanked by light blue, at each side is a very thin white stripe.

Designer. Institute of Heraldry, U.S. Army.

182.

Armed Forces Expeditionary Campaign Medal

Awarded to any member of the United States Armed Forces who has participated in military operations for which no other service or campaign medal has been authorized.

Operations for which the Armed Forces Expeditionary Service Medal has been awarded:

Berlin ----------- August 14, 1961, to June 1, 1963
Lebanon --------- July 1, 1958, to November 1, 1958
Quemoy and--
Matsu Islands---- August 23, 1958, to June 1, 1963
Taiwan Straits -- August 23, 1958, to January 11, 1959
Cuba ------------ October 24, 1962, to June 1, 1963
Congo------------ November 23 through 27, 1964
Dominican
Republic --------- April 28, 1965, to September 21, 1966
Congo ----------- July 14, 1960, to September 1, 1962
Korea ------------ October 1, 1966, to date to be determined
Laos-------------- April 19, 1961, to October 7, 1962
Vietnam --------- July 1, 1958, to July 3, 1965
Thailand, in
support of
Vietnam War ----- July 1, 1958, to July 3, 1965

Note: Personnel who earned the Armed Forces Expeditionary Medal for services in Vietnam prior to July 4, 1965, may exchange it for the Vietnam Service Medal, but will not be permitted to revert back to wearing the Armed Forces Expeditionary Medal for Vietnam service.

Obverse. A bronze medallion 1 and 1/4 inches in diameter. At center is an eagle with wings inverted, facing left, perched on a sword loosened in its scabbard, superimposed over a radiant compass rose of eight points. Around the outside edge the inscription, **"Armed Forces"** separating this on both sides from the word, **"Expeditionary,"** is a spray of laurel.

Reverse. At center is the shield from the Coat of Arms of the United States. Along the upper outside edge is the inscription, **"United States of America."** At bottom flanking a bullet is a branch of laurel.

Ribbon. At center is a thin white stripe, to the right of this is a thin red stripe, and to the left is a thin blue stripe. Flanking these stripes is a wide light blue stripe, a narrow black, narrow brown, narrow yellow, edged in a narrow green.

Designer. Institute of Heraldry, U.S. Army.

183.

Vietnam Campaign Service Medal

Awarded for service in the Republic of Vietnam, the waters off Vietnam, and in Thailand. Personnel in Thailand were eligible only only if engaged in direct support of operations in Vietnam.

Obverse. A bronze medallion 1 and 1/4 inches in diameter. At center is a dragon behind a grove of bamboo trees. At bottom is the inscription, **"Republic of Vietnam Service."**

Reverse. At center is a cross-bow, mounted vertically, surmounted by a lighted torch. Along the bottom edge is the inscription, **"United States of America."**

Ribbon. A thin red stripe flanked by a narrow yellow stripe, a thin red, a wide yellow, edged with a narrow green stripe.

Designer. Thomas H. Jones.

184.

Air Force Combat Readiness Service Medal

The combat readiness medal is awarded to members of the Air Force who are combat-ready aircraft crew members for a four year period. The term **"Combat Ready"** is defined as being professionally or technically qualified in an aircraft crew position in an aircraft which can be used in combat.

When first established, the Combat Readiness Medal was classified as a decoration, ranking over the Service Commendation Medals, the Lifesaving Medals, and the Purple Heart. This was quite unique in that persons who qualified for the award were not required to distinguish themselves by the usual standards of achievement, meritorious service, or heroism, becoming the first decoration of its kind in United States history. Recipients merely met training and professional standards in their particular skills and maintained them for a four year period.

In September 1967, after recommendations from highly placed officials throughout the Air Force, the awards branch of the Air Force realigned the medal to its present position as the top-ranking service medal.

Obverse. This 1 1/2 inch bronze medal, its rim concave between 12 points has a border of concentric rays, charged with six arrowheads, alternating with the points of two triangular flight symbols. One is pointed south and overlaps the other which is pointed nòrth with the apex extending beyond the rim, becoming the point of suspension of the medal.

Reverse. Has the inscription around the upper edge **"For Combat Readiness"** and around the bottom **"Air Force."**

Ribbon. Predominently Old Glory red, is banded near edge on both sides with stripes of light blue with thin stripes of dark blue in center of the light blue.

Rank. Just under the Air Force Commendation or Achievement Medal and just over the Air Force Good Conduct Medal.

Designer. Institute of Heraldry, U.S. Army.

Note: Members of missile-launch crews are also eligible. Serving in combat is not required. Authorized by a directive of the Secretary of the Air Force on March 9, 1964, with effective date of August 1, 1964, and amended on August 28, 1967.

185.

NC-4 Service Medal

Authorized by Congress February 9, 1929, gold medals were presented by the President in the name of Congress to Commander John H. Powers for conceiving, organizing, and commanding the first successful transAtlantic flight in May 1919, and to officers and crew members of the Navy Flying Boat NC-4 who crossed the Atlantic with him.

Originally struck as a large gold table medal, not designed for wear, Congress authorized, April 25, 1935, a bronze miniature, as large as a usual full-sized medal, to be issued to the men.

Obverse. A bronze medallion 1 and 1/4 inches in diameter. At center is a gull flying over waves. Around the outside edge is the inscription, **"First TransAtlantic Flight United States Navy May 1919."**

Reverse. At center is a circle inscribed with large letters, **"NC-4"** above this the word **"Newfoundland"** and below the word **"Portugal"**. Outside this circle around the upper half is inscribed the names of the recipients. Listed in the inner ring **"H.C. Rood, J.L. Breese, F. Rhodes."** Around the outer ring upper half the names, **"J.H. Towers, A.C. Read, E.F. Stone, W. Hinton."** In the lower part of the medal is the inscription, **"Presented by the President of the United States in the name of Congress."**

Ribbon. In five equal stripes starting at left, red, white, blue, green, then again red.

Designer. Catherine G. Barton.

186.

American Defense Service Medal

Established by executive order June 28, 1941. Awarded to personnel of the United States Armed Forces, who had one year of service during the limited emergency proclaimed by the President on September 8, 1939, or during the unlimited emergency proclaimed by the President on May 27, 1941. The one year of service must have been between September 8, 1939, and December 7, 1941.

Obverse. A bronze medallion 1 and 1/4 inches in diameter. In the center is a female figure representing Liberty. She is standing, facing right, on a live oak branch, holding with her left arm a shield, holding up in her left hand, in attitude of defense, a sword. The oak branch she is standing on is terminating in four leaves, behind her.

Reverse. The inscription in straight lines, **"For service during the limited emergency proclaimed by the President on September 8, 1939, or during the unlimited emergency proclaimed by the President on May 27, 1941."** At bottom below this is a spray of laurel.

Reverse. A very wide stripe of yellow, flanked by a thin stripe of red, thin white, thin blue edged in a wide stripe of yellow. Designer of the ribbon is Arthur E. DuBois.

Designer and And Sculptor. Lee Lawrie.

187.

Women's Army Corps Service Medal

Awarded to women who served in the Women's Auxiliary Corps from July 20, 1942, to August 31, 1943, and to those who served in the Women's Army Corps from September 1, 1943, to September 2, 1945.

Obverse. A bronze medallion 1 and 1/4 inches in diameter. At center the head of Pallas Athene, wearing a helmet with plume of feathers, at top center, flowing down the band of her head. She is then superimposed over a sheathed sword crossed with oak leaves and palm branches. At top around the outside edge the word, **"Women's"** at bottom the words **"Army Corps."**

Reverse. At center is a scroll, inscribed on this in faint large letters, **"U.S."**; superimposed over this the inscription, **"For Service in the Women's Army Auxiliary Corps".** At the top of the scroll is perched an eagle with wings outstretched. Under each wing is a five-pointed star. At the left of the scroll along the outside edge of the medal are four, five-pointed stars. To the right side, same area, are four more stars. Just under the scroll at bottom are three, five-pointed stars. There are thirteen stars total. At bottom along the outside edge are inscribed the dates, **"1942 - 1943."**

Ribbon. Moss-green edged with a narrow stripe of old gold.

Designer. Institute of Heraldry, U.S. Army.

188.

Medal for Humane Action
Berlin Air Lift

Awarded to personnel assigned to the Berlin Air Lift, or assigned to units that directly supported the Air Lift, for 120 days or more from June 26, 1948, to September 30, 1949.

Obverse. A bronze medallion 1 and 1/4 inches in diameter. At center, at an angle pointing down, is a C-54 aircraft. Along the bottom half, outside edge, a wreath of wheat. At bottom center, superimposed over the wheat, is the coat of arms of the city of Berlin.

Reverse. At center is an eagle, with wings outstretched, perched on three crossed war arrows. In the center of the eagle's chest is the shield of the U.S. Around the upper half, outside edge, is the inscription, **"For Humane Action."** In the bottom half, inscribed in straight lines, the inscription, **"To supply necessities of life to the people of Berlin, Germany."**

Ribbon. At center is a thin red stripe, flanked by a narrow stripe of white, a wide stripe of marine blue, narrow stripe of white, edged with a wide stripe of black.

Designer. Institute of Heraldry, U.S. Army.

189.

National Defense Service Medal

Awarded to personnel of the United States Armed Forces who served between June 27, 1950, and July 27, 1954, or from January 1, 1961 to January 1, 1974. Reserve personnel were not eligible for the medal unless their unit was activated or the individual was recalled to extended active duty. Also, service as a cadet or midshipman at any of the Armed Forces Academies during either of the periods entitles these individuals to the award.

Obverse. A bronze medallion 1 and 1/4 inches in diameter. At center is an eagle with wings raised with tips down, perched on a sword overlayed with a palm branch. A top around the outside edge of the medal is the inscription **"National Defense."**

Reverse. At center is the shield taken from the U.S. Coat of Arms. At bottom is an open wreath composed of an oak branch at right and a laurel branch at left, tied together at bottom center.

Ribbon. At center is a wide yellow stripe, flanked by a thin red stripe, thin white, thin blue, thin white, edged in a very wide stripe of red.

Designer. Institute of Heraldry, U.S. Army.

190.

Medal for Humanitarian Service

This medal was established to honor personnel of the Armed Forces who have rendered service to mankind.
See page 290 for list of operations for which this medal issued.

Obverse. A bronze medallion 1 and 1/4 inches in diameter. At center is a right hand, at an angle pointing upward, to symbolize a giving or helping hand. This is then inside a ring 1/8 of an inch from the outside edge of the medal.

Reverse. At top in a straight line is the inscription, **"For Humanitarian Service."** Below this is an oak branch with three leaves and three acorns. Below this, around the outside edge of the medal, is the inscription, **"United States Armed Forces."**

Ribbon. At center is a wide navy blue stripe, a thin white stripe, edged in purple-maroon.

191.

Multinational Force Medal

This medal is awarded to personnel of the Marine Corps stationed in Lebanon in 1982 (and still there as of this date) as part of the Multinational Peacekeeping Force.

Obverse. A bronze medallion 1 and 3/8 inches in diameter. At center is a stylized dove and olive branch, inside an inner ring. Between the inner ring and the outside edge of the medal is the inscription, at top, **"Multinational Force"**, and at bottom **"& Observers."** All this then is superimposed over a grid pattern.

Reverse. The inscription in straight lines, **"United in Service for Peace."** Each word is in a different line.

Ribbon. At center is a wide white stripe, flanked by a thin olive green stripe, edged in a wide orange stripe.

192.

Perry Polar Expedition Medal 1908 - 1909

Established January 28, 1944, to commemorate members of the Perry Polar Expedition during the years 1908-1909 for the cause of Polar exploration and for their service in the field of science by aiding Admiral Robert E. Perry in the discovery of the North Pole.

Obverse. A silver medallion 1 and 1/4 inches in diameter. At center is Admiral Perry wearing a fur parka, holding in his right hand the end of a ski pole. Just below this in three horizontal lines in bold type is the inscription, **"Perry Polar - Expedition 1908-1909."** Around all of this on the inner rim of the medal are the fifteen points of a compass rose, which has the top center point replaced by a fleur-de-lis.

Reverse. On the top third, centered, is a United States flag with 46 stars flanked by Eskimo dogs, one on each side. In the middle third is the inscription, **"Presented in the name of Congress in recognition of his efforts and services as a member of the Perry Polar Expedition of 1908-1909 in the field of science and for the cause of Polar exploration by aiding in the discovery of the North Pole by Admiral Perry."** The bottom third is blank except for a pair of miniature snow shoes at the very bottom center.

Design. Was approved by the Secretary of the Navy November 30, 1944.

Ribbon. At center is a wide ivory stripe, flanked by a 1/4 inch turquoise stripe, edged in a narrow stripe of ivory.

Designer. John R. Sinnock.

193

First Byrd Antarctic Expedition Medal 1928 - 1930

Established by Act of Congress May 23, 1930, and awarded to express the high admiration that Congress and the American people held for the members of the First Byrd Antarctic Expedition 1928–30.

Obverse. This medal was issued to Admiral Byrd in gold, to his officers in silver, and to all other personnel in bronze. The medallion is 1 and 1/4 inches in diameter. At center is Admiral Byrd in Arctic clothing holding a ski pole in right hand. Encircled around the outside edge of the medal is the inscription **"Byrd Antarctic Expedition 1928–1930."**

Reverse. In the top third is a full-rigged sailing ship. Underneath the ship in ten horizontal lines the inscription, **"Presented to the Officers and Men of the Byrd Antarctic Expedition to Express the High Admiration in which the Congress and American People hold their Heroic and Undaunted Service in Connection with the Scientific Investigations and Extraordinary Aerial Exploration of the Antarctic Continent."** At bottom just under the inscription is a head on view of a Ford Trimotor Aircraft used in the Antarctic flights.

Ribbon. At center is a very wide stripe of ice-blue, flanked by silver-white.

Designer. Francis H. Packer.

194.

Second Byrd Antarctic Expedition Medal 1933-1935

Established by Act of Congress June 2, 1936, and awarded to personnel of the Second Byrd Antarctic Expedition who either commanded one of the expedition ships throughout the expedition or who spent the winter night at Little America.

Obverse. A silver medallion 1 and 1/4 inches in diameter. At center is Admiral Byrd in Arctic clothing. To the right and wrapping behind the Admiral is an Eskimo dog. The Admiral also has a ski pole in his left hand. The background behind the Admiral represents the Arctic terrain. Around the upper outside edge the inscription, **"Byrd Antarctic Expedition."** In a section at lower right are the dates, **"1933"**, and below this **"1935."**

Reverse. At center is a plaque with the inscription, **"Presented to the officers and men of the second Byrd Antarctic Expedition to express the very high admiration in which the Congress and the American People hold their Heroic and Undaunted accomplishments for Science unequaled in the history of Polar Exploration."** Above the plaque is a Ford Tri-motor, to the left, looking at the medal, are Little America's radio towers, to the right a fully-rigged sailing ship, and at bottom a dog sled and team.

Ribbon. Silver-white overall.

Designer. Heinz Warnicke.

195.

U.S. Antarctic Expedition Medal
1939 - 41

Authorized by Act of Congress September 24, 1945, and awarded to personnel of the United States Antarctic Expedition of 1939-1941 to recognize their valuable services to the nation in Polar Exploration and science.

Obverse. Awarded in gold to command rank, silver to officers, and bronze to all other personnel. Around the outside edge of the medal is the inscription, **"The United States Antarctic Expedition 1939-1941."** Just inside the inscription is an inner circle which at its top is a scroll in three tiers bearing a word on each, **"Science", "Pioneering",** and **"Expedition".** Below this is a map marked off in grid lines of longitude and latitude of the Polar region inscribed in tiny letters **"South Pacific Ocean - Little America - Palmerland - Antarctic and South Pole."**

Reverse. At top inscribed in four lines the words **"By Act of - The Congress of the - United States of America - to,"** a blank space for the recipient's name, in the bottom half of the medal in very fine print the inscription, **"In recognition of invaluable service to this nation by courageous pioneering in Polar Expedition which resulted in important geographical and scientific discoveries."**

Ribbon. At center is a wide silver-white stripe, flanked by thin red stripes, thin silver-white, edged in a wide stripe of ice-blue.

Designer. John R. Sinnock.

196.

Antarctic Service Medal

Authorized July 7, 1960, by Act of Congress and awarded to recognize service performed after January 1, 1946, on the Antarctic Continent or in support of U.S. operations there. Persons eligible for this award are as follows:

1. U.S. Armed Forces or civilians, who participate in scientific direct support, or exploratory operations on the Antarctic Continent.
2. U.S. Armed Forces aircraft crews flying to and from the Continent.
3. U.S. Armed Forces ship crews operating south of latitude 60 degrees south in support of U.S. operations in Antarctica.

Obverse. A medallion green-gold in color 1 and 1/4 inches in diameter. At center, superimposed over a Polar landscape, is a figure of a man standing in Antarctic clothing, facing front. Below the right hand to the outside edge of the medal is the word **"Antarctica"**, to his left, same area, but just a little lower, is the word **"Service"**.

Reverse. At center is a map of the Antarctic Continent with geodesic lines of longitude and latitude. Superimposed over this in three separate lines, **"Courage"** - **"Sacrifice"** - and **"Devotion"**. Around the outside edge of the medal is a decorative border of penguins and fish.

Ribbon. At center is a narrow stripe of white which is blended into the flanking stripes of pale-blue, which is blended into greenish-blue, a narrow stripe of medium blue, edged in a narrow stripe of black.

Designer. U.S. Mint.

197.

Arctic Service Medal
Coast Guard

Awarded for - I have no information on this.

Obverse. A bronze medallion 1 and 1/4 inches in diameter. At center is a Polar Bear facing left. Below the bear is stylized ice and water. Above the bear is an eight-pointed star. At top around the outside edge are the words, **"Arctic Service."**

Reverse. At center is the shield and crossed anchors of the U.S. Coast Guard. Above the shield the word, **"Semper."** Below it the word **"Paratus."** Around the shield in a ring is the inscription **"United States Coast Guard - 1970".**

Ribbon. At center is a narrow black stripe flanked by a narrow medium blue stripe, a narrow greenish-blue stripe, a narrow light blue stripe, a narrow pale blue stripe, edged in white.

198.

Army of Occupation of Puerto Rico 1898

Awarded to personnel who served in Puerto Rico from August 14, 1898, to December 10, 1898.

Obverse. A bronze medallion 1 and 1/4 inches in diameter. Centered is a castle with two small round towers at its corners, said to be a modification of the castle which appears on the Royal Arms of Spain. At top around the outside edge of the medal is the inscription **"Army of Occupation of Puerto Rico".** At bottom the date **"1898."** To the left of the date is a branch of tobacco plant, and to the right a stalk of sugar cane.

Reverse. In the center is an eagle facing right perched on a cannon supported by crossed flags, rifles, Indian shield, spear and a quiver of arrows; below this the inscription, **"For Service".** Along the outside edge at top the inscription **"United States Army",** at bottom edge, thirteen stars.

Ribbon. At center is a wide stripe of red, flanked by a thin stripe of yellow, a wide stripe of blue, edged with a thin stripe of red.

Designer. Francis D. Millet.

199.

Army of Occupation of Cuba 1898-1902

Awarded to Army personnel who served with the occupation fcrces in Cuba from July 18, 1898, to May 20, 1902.

Obverse. At center is the shield from the Coat of Arms of the Republic of Cuba. Behind the shield is a fasces and flanking the shield to the left, looking at the medal, is a branch of oak, to the right a branch of laurel. Above the shield to the left is the date **"1898"**, to the right the date **"1902"**. Around the outside edge is the inscription, **"Army of Occupation Military Government of Cuba."** At bottom center is a dot with arrow heads pointing both directions.

Reverse. In the center is an eagle facing right, perched on a cannon supported by crossed flags, rifles, Indian shield, spear, and a quiver of arrows; below this the inscription, **"For Service"**. Along the outside edge at top the inscription **"United States Army"**, at bottom edge, thirteen stars.

Ribbon. A center is a wide blue stripe, flanked by a narrow yellow stripe, a wide red stripe, edged by a narrow blue stripe.

Designer. Francis D. Millet.

200. and 201.

Army of Occupation of Germany WWI

Awarded to personnel of the United States Army, or Navy and Marine Corps with shore duties, for service with the occupation forces in Germany and Austria from November 12, 1918, to July 11, 1923.

Obverse. A bronze medallion 1 and 1/4 inches in diameter. At center is a profile, looking left, the chin at lower left the inscription, **"General John J. Pershing."** At right center is an unsheathed sword, with point up, laid over a laurel wreath; superimposed over this are the dates, **"1918–1923"**. Around the upper edge of the medal are four five-pointed stars.

Reverse. At center is an eagle, wings spread out with tips down, and facing left. The eagle is then perched on a representation of castle Ehrenbreitstein. Around the outside edge of the medal is the inscription, **"U.S. Army of Occupation of Germany"**. At bottom center are three five-pointed stars.

Ribbon. #200. The first ribbon had a very wide black stripe center, flanked by a narrow white, narrow red, edged in blue. The border between the red and blue was wavy. This was changed shortly after authorization due to cost.

Ribbon #201. The second ribbon has a very wide black stripe at center, flanked by a narrow white stripe, a thin red stripe, and edged in a thin stripe of blue.

Designer. Trygue A. Rovelstad.

202.

Army of Occupation of Germany and Japan WWII - Army

Awarded to Army and Air Force personnel for 30 days or more consecutive service in the occupation forces subsequent to World War II. Listed below are the time limits of the occupation zones:

1. Austria - May 9, 1945, to July 2, 1955
2. Berlin - May 9, 1945, to date to be announced
3. Italy - May 9, 1945, to September 15, 1947
4. Japan - September 3, 1945, to April 27, 1952
5. Korea - September 3, 1945, to June 29, 1949

Obverse. A bronze medallion 1 and 1/4 inches in diameter. At center the medal portrays the Remagen Bridge Abutments; above this in straight lines the inscription, **"Army of Occupation."**

Reverse. At bottom center the date **"1945;"** above this the representation of water, two Japanese sailing vessels, and in the background, Mt. Fuji.

Ribbon. Starting at far left, a narrow stripe of white, wide stripe of black, wide stripe of red, narrow stripe of white.

Designer. Institute of Heraldry, U.S. Army.

203. and 204.

Army of Occupation of Germany and Japan WW II - Navy and Marine Corps

Awarded to Navy and Marine Corps personnel for 30 days or more consecutive service in the occupation forces subsequent to World War II. Listed below are the time limits of the occupation zones:

1. Austria - May 9, 1945, to July 2, 1955
2. Berlin - May 9, 1945, to date to be announced
3. Italy - May 9, 1945, to September 15, 1947
4. Japan - September 3, 1945, to April 27, 1952
5. Korea - September 3, 1945, to June 29, 1949

Obverse. A bronze medallion 1 and 1/4 inches in diameter. At bottom center is the inscription, **"Occupation Service."** Above this is a representation of Neptune, God of the Sea in Roman mythology holding a trident in his right hand. the Roman God is then mounted on a composite creature of a charging horse and a sea serpent. Separating this representation and the inscriptions are wave scrolls that represent the sea.

Reverse. At center is an eagle perched on the shank of an anchor laid horizontally. Behind this is a branch of laurel entwined about the anchor. To the left of the eagle just above the laurel is the word, **"For"**, to the right side, same area, the word, **"Service"**. Around the top outside edge the inscription, **"United States Navy,"** #203 or **"United States Marine Corps"**, #204.

Ribbon. Right half starting at center, a wide stripe of red, edged in a narrow stripe of white. Left half starting at center, a wide stripe of black, edged in a narrow stripe of white.

Designer. A.A. Weinman.

205.

Victory Medal World War I

Established by Act of Congress 1919 and awarded to personnel of the U.S. Army, Navy, and Marine Corps for service between April 6, 1917, and November 11, 1918, or for later service from November 12, 1918, to August 5, 1919, with the American Expeditionary Forces in European Russia; also awarded for service in Siberia from November 12, 1918, to April 1, 1920.

Before World War I, it was the custom for nations to bestow medals on personnel of their allies' armed forces. The massive sizes of the 14 Allied Armies made such an exchange impossible. It was then decided that the Allies should have a similar medal. All 14 Allied Nations decided on a single ribbon. The pendant portrayed winged Victory with each country selecting its own artist.

Obverse. A bronze medallion 1 and 3/8 inches in diameter, at center is a female figure with wings outstretched wearing a crown similar to the Statue of Liberty. She has a sword drawn in right hand, carrying a shield in her left.

Reverse. At center is a double-bladed fasces superimposed over a U.S. shield. At top, around the outside edge, is the inscription, **"The Great War for Civilization."** To the left of the shield are the names of these seven countries, **"France, Italy, Serbia, Japan, Montenegro, Russia, and Greece."** To the right of the shield, six more countries, **"Great Britain, Belgium, Brazil, Portugal, Rumania, and China."** At the bottom of the medal are six, five-pointed stars.

Ribbon. Called the double rainbow having red center, edged in purple.

Designer. James E. Fraser.

206.

Victory Medal World War II

Established by Act of Congress July 9, 1945, and awarded to personnel of 'the United States Armed Forces who served between December 7, 1941, to December 31, 1946.

Obverse. A bronze medallion 1 and 3/8 inches in diameter. At center is a female figure with right foot resting on a war god's helmet. Behind the helmet is a multi-rayed sun. Looking as though she has just broken a sword over her right knee, she holds the hilt of a broken sword in her right hand, and the broken blade in her left hand. Below the right hand the word, **"World"**, and below the left hand the inscription, **"War II."**

Reverse. Around the outside edge of the medal is the inscription, **"United States of America 1941 - 1945."** At center is a palm branch above which is the inscription, **"Freedom from Fear and Want"**, and below the words, **"Freedom of Speech and Religion."**

Ribbon. At center is a wide red stripe flanked by a thin white stripe. The ribbon is then edged with the double rainbow of the World War I Victory Medal having a red center and butting up to the thin white stripe and both outside edges of the ribbon with purple.

Designer. Institute of Heraldry, U.S. Army.

207.

Victory Medal World War II Merchant Marines

Authorized of Act of Congress August 8, 1946, and awarded to personnel of the Merchant Marines who served between December 7, 1941, and September 3, 1945.

Obverse. A bronze medallion 1 and 3/8 inches in diameter; at center is a female figure facing right, holding in her right hand, a trident, and in her left hand a laurel branch. Laying over her left arm and going back behind her is the drape of the back of her gown. Next to her right knee to the left of the medal is the word, **"World"**; to the right of the medal, just under the laurel branch is the inscription, **"War II"**. She is standing on waves, and in the background is a conning tower of an enemy sub.

Reverse. I have no information on this.

Ribbon. At center is a narrow red stripe, flanked by a thin stripe of white, a thin stripe of green, a narrow stripe of blue, a thin white, edged with a wide stripe of red.

Designer. John R. Sinnock.

208.

Armed Forces Reserve Medal - Air Force

Authorized by Congress September 25, 1950, and awarded to personnel of the reserve components of the United States Air Force who have completed ten years of honorable and satisfactory service within a twelve year period.

Obverse. A bronze medallion 1 and 1/4 inches in diameter. At center is a flaming torch superimposed over a crossed powder horn and bugle. Around the outside edge of the medal are thirteen five-pointed stars.

Reverse. At center symbolizing the air power of the United States, is an American eagle, with wings outstretched, superimposed over clouds. This is surrounded by a small circle leaving the eagle's wing tips to the outside. Around the outside edge of the medal is the inscription, **"Armed Forces Reserve."**

Ribbon. At center is a narrow stripe of light-blue, flanked by a wide stripe of buff, a thin stripe of light-blue, a thinner stripe of buff, a thin stripe of light-blue, a thinner stripe of buff, edged in a thin stripe of light-blue.

Designer. Institute of Heraldry, U.S. Army.

209.

Armed Forces Reserve - National Guard

Authorized by Congress September 25, 1950, and awarded to personnel of the Reserve Components of the Air National Guard, National Guard in service to the United States, and National Guard of the United States who have completed ten years of honorable and satisfactory service within a twelve year period.

Obverse. A bronze medallion 1 and 1/4 inches in diameter. At center is a flaming torch superimposed over a crossed powder horn and bugle. Around the outside edge of the medal are thirteen. five-pointed stars.

Reverse. At center is the National Guard insignia, which is an eagle, with wings outstretched and wing tips pointing down. Across the eagle's chest are crossed fasces. Around the outside edge of the medal is the inscription, **"Armed Forces Reserve".**

Ribbon. At center is a narrow stripe of light-blue, flanked by a wide stripe of buff, a thin stripe of light-blue, a thinner stripe of buff, a thin stripe of light-blue, a thinner stripe of buff, edged in a thin stripe of light-blue.

Designer. Institute of Heraldry, U.S. Army.

210.

Armed Forces Reserve Medal - Navy

Authorized by Congress September 25, 1950, and awarded to personnel of the Reserve Components of the United States Naval Reserve, Naval Militia, and National Naval Volunteers who have completed ten years of honorable and satisfactory service within a twelve year period.

Obverse. A bronze medal 1 and 1/4 inches in diameter. At center is a flaming torch superimposed over a crossed powder horn and bugle. Around the outside of the medal are thirteen, five-pointed, stars.

Reverse. At center is an eagle with wings outstretched perched on the flukes of a standard anchor behind which is a fully-rigged sailing ship with bow to the left. Around the outside edge of the medallion is the inscription, **"Armed Forces Reserve."**

Ribbon. At center is a narrow stripe of light-blue, flanked by a wide stripe of buff, a thin stripe of light-blue, a thinner stripe of buff, a thin stripe of light-blue, a thinner stripe of buff, edged in a thin stripe of light-blue.

Designer. Institute of Heraldry, U.S. Army.

211.

Armed Forces Reserve Medal - Coast Guard

Authorized by Congress September 25, 1950, and awarded to personnel of the Reserve Components of the United States Coast Guard who have completed ten years of honorable and satisfactory service within a twelve year period.

Obverse. A bronze medallion 1 and 1/4 inches in diameter. At center is a flaming torch superimposed over a crossed powder horn and bugle. Around the outside edge of the medal are thirteen, five-pointed stars.

Reverse. At center is the Coast Guard insignia, which is a U.S. shield inside a ring superimposed over crossed anchors. Around the outside edge of the medal are the words, **"Armed Forces Reserve."**

Ribbon. At center is a narrow stripe of light-blue, flanked by a wide stripe of buff, a thin stripe of light-blue, a thinner stripe of buff, a thin stripe of light-blue, a thinner stripe of buff, edged in a thin stripe of light-blue.

Designer. Institute of Heraldry, U.S. Army.

212.

Armed Forces Reserve Medal - Army

Authorized by Congress September 25, 1950, and awarded to personnel of the Reserve Components of the United States Organized Reserve Corps, Army of the United States, and Officers Reserve Corps who have completed ten years of honorable and satisfactory service within a twelve year period.

Obverse. A bronze medal 1 and 1/4 inches in diameter. At center is a flaming torch superimposed over a crossed powder horn and bugle. Around the outside edge of the medallion are thirteen five-pointed stars.

Reverse. At center is the Minute Man, from the crest of the Organized Reserves, encircled by thirteen five-pointed, stars. Around the outside edge of the medal are the words, **"Armed Forces Reserve."**

Ribbon. At center is a narrow stripe of light-blue, flanked by a wide stripe of buff, a thin stripe of light-blue, a thinner stripe of buff, a thin stripe of light-blue, a thinner stripe of buff, edged in a thin stripe of light-blue.

Designer. Institute of Heraldry, U.S. Army.

213.

Armed Forces Reserve Medal - Marine Corps

Authorized by Congress September 25, 1950, and awarded to personnel of the Reserve Components of the United States Marine Corps who have completed ten years of service within a twelve year period.

Obverse. A bronze medallion 1 and 1/4 inches in diameter. At center is a flaming torch superimposed over a crossed powder horn and bugle. Around the outside edge of the medal are thirteen, five-pointed stars.

Reverse. At center is the insignia of the Marine Corps, which is an American eagle perched on a globe of the earth and superimposed over a fouled anchor in a 45 degree angle with stock at top right. Around the outside edge of the medal is the inscription, **"Armed Forces Reserve."**

Ribbon. At center is a narrow stripe of light-blue, flanked by a wide stripe of buff, a thin stripe of light-blue, a thinner stripe of buff, a thin stripe of light-blue, a thinner stripe of buff, edged in a thin stripe of light-blue.

Designer. Institute of Heraldry, U.S. Army.

214.

Marine Corps Organized Reserve Medal

Authorized by the Secretary of the Navy on February 19, 1939, and awarded to personnel of the Organized Marine Corps Reserve for four years of service after the date July 1, 1925. To qualify personnel had to attend four annual 14 day field training periods; attend at least eighty percent of all scheduled drills with an organized unit of the Reserve over a period of four years; having received no unsatisfactory fitness reports, for officers, and a service record marking of 4.5 for enlisted men.

Obverse. A bronze medallion 1 and 5/16 inches in diameter. At center two male figures, one in an old style Marine uniform, and a civilian reservist striding together. Below them are the words, **"For Service."** Along the top outside edge is the inscription, **"Marine Corps Reserve."** The first medal pendant had the inscription, **"Organized Marine Corps Reserve."**

Reverse. At top center is a blank shield. Around the outside edge are the words facing out **"Fidelity"**, at left, **"Zeal,"** at bottom, **"Obedience"**, at right.

Ribbon. At center a wide stripe of red, flanked by a wide stripe of old yellow, a narrow stripe of blue, narrow white, edged in a narrow stripe of red.

Designer. John R. Sinnock.

215.

Naval Reserve Meritorious Service Medal

Authorized by the Secretary of the Navy September 12, 1958, and awarded to those Naval reservists who performed at a higher level than that normally expected of a reservist, over a period of four years.

Obverse. A bronze medallion 1 and 3/8 inches in diameter. At center is a fouled anchor in a vertical position. The anchor is wrapped with a ribbon having the words, **"Meritorious - Service,"** inscribed upon it. Around the outside edge of the medal the inscription, **"United States Naval Reserve"**.

Reverse. Blank.

Ribbon. At center is a narrow stripe of blue, flanked by a wide stripe of red, a very thin stripe of gold, edged in a thin stripe of blue.

216.

Naval Reserve Medal - Obsolete Since 1958

Authorized by the Secretary of the Navy September 12, 1938, and awarded to personnel of the Naval Reserve who had completed ten years of satisfactory service. This medal was discontinued September 12, 1958, and any service terminating after this date can be credited only for the Armed Forces Reserve Medal.

Obverse. A bronze medallion 1 and 5/16 inches in diameter. At center is an American eagle, facing left, with wings arched. The eagle on a huge rock grasping a traditional Naval anchor in his talons. In the background is the sea, and clouds with sunrays coming from behind them.

Reverse. At center in straight lines the words, **"Faithful - Service"**; below this at bottom center is a five-pointed star. Around the outside edge of the medal is the inscription, **"United States Naval Reserve."**

Ribbon. Red, edged in a thin stripe of gold and thin stripe of blue.

Designer. U.S. Mint.

217a

Army National Guard Achievement Medal

Awarded for satisfactory service above that expected of a guardsman in an Army National Guard Troop Program unit for a period of four years.

Obverse. A bronze medallion 1 and 1/4 inches in diameter. At center is a flaming torch between two crossed swords with a five-pointed star to the right and left; surrounding this is a laurel wreath, superimposed over a twelve-pointed star, which is superimposed over a larger twelve-pointed star. In between the points of the larger star are laurel leaves and a berry.

Reverse. At upper center is a miniature breast plate; above this along the outside edge of the medal is the inscription, **"Army National Guard"**; along the bottom in smaller letters the words, **"For Achievement."**

Ribbon. At center is a wide red stripe flanked by a thin stripe of white, a narrow stripe of blue, edged in a wide stripe of old yellow.

217b

United States Army Reserve Achievement Medal

Awarded for satisfactory service above that expected of a reservist in an Army Reserve Troop Program unit for a period of four years.

Obverse. A bronze medallion 1 and 1/4 inches in diameter. At center is a flaming torch between two crossed swords with a five-pointed star to the right and left, surrounding this a laurel wreath, superimposed over a twelve-pointed star, which is superimposed over a larger twelve-pointed star. In between the points of the larger star are laurel leaves and a berry.

Reverse. At upper center is a miniature breast plate; above this along the outside edge of the medal is the inscription, **"United States Army Reserve"**; along the bottom in smaller letters the words, **"For Achievement"**.

Ribbon. At center is a wide red stripe flanked by a thin stripe of white, a narrow stripe of blue, edged in a wide stripe of old yellow.

218.

Department of the Army Commander's Award for Civilian Service

I have no information on what this medal is awarded for.

Obverse. A gold medallion 1 and 1/4 inches in diameter which has, centered, a five-pointed star; surrounding the star are three triangles, one above, one bottom left, and one bottom right.

Reverse. In straight lines the inscription, **"Department of the Army"** in small letters **"Commanders Award for Civilian Service"** in large letters.

Ribbon. A wide medium green stripe flanked by a thin white stripe, a wide medium green stripe, a narrow white stripe, edged in medium green.

219.

Air Reserve Meritorious Service Medal

Authorized by the Secretary of the Air Force April 7, 1964. Basically an Air Force Reserve Good Conduct Award for four years of exemplary behavior, efficiency, and fidelity. Service as a commissioned officer is not creditable toward qualifying for this award, nor is service in the Reserve Components of the Army, Navy, Marine Corps, or Coast Guard. The first awards of the medal were made after April 1, 1965, based on the four continuous years of service immediately preceding the award.

Obverse. A bronze medallion 1 and 3/8 inches in diameter. At center is an American eagle, with wings outstretched, perched on a wide ring containing a five-pointed star within which is a circle. Between the points of the eagle's wing tips is a banner with the words, **"Meritorious - Service".** To the left of the eagle around the outside edge of the medal are the words, **"Air Reserve."** To the right side, same area, the word, **"Forces,"** with arrow heads or wing shapes on either side of the word. All this then is superimposed over lines dividing the medal in thirteen equal pieces.

Reverse. At center is a circle made to look like a cloud having at top the wings and thunderbolts of the Air Force Coat of Arms, below this is the word, **"To"**. Around the outside edge of the medal is the inscription, **"Exemplary Behavior - Efficiency - Fidelity."**

Ribbon. At center is a very wide light-blue stripe, flanked by a narrow blue stripe, a thin gold stripe, a narrow blue stripe, a wide white stripe, edged with a very thin stripe of light-blue.

Designer. Institute of Heraldry, U.S. Army.

220.

Reserve Officers Association Medal

I have no information on what this medal is awarded for.

Obverse. A bronze octagon medallion having at center the Minute Man, facing left, inside a circle. Around the upper outside edge of the medal the inscription **"Reserve Officers Ass'n".** At bottom, below the circle in smaller letters, the inscription, **"Of the United States".**

Reverse. Blank.

Ribbon. At center is a thin stripe of blue having to the right of it a thin white stripe and to the left a thin red stripe. The ribbon is then edged in a wide light-blue stripe.

221.

United Nations Service Medal

Authorized by the United Nations General Assembly December 12, 1950, and awarded to personnel of the United States Armed Forces for service in the Korean Theater on behalf of the United Nations Command from June 27, 1950, to July 27, 1954.

This medal was made up and issued in the different languages of the U.N. participants in the Korean War. While the obverse of the pendent remained the same, the spelling of **"Korea"** on the fixed clasp differed and the words on the reverse were lettered in the language of the various participating countries.

Obverse. Suspended by a fixed bar is a bronze medallion 1 and 3/8 inches in diameter. At center is the emblem of the United Nations, being that of a globe surrounded by a laurel wreath.

Reverse. At center, in five separate lines, the inscription **"For Service in – Defence of the – Principles of the – Charter of the – United Nations."**

Ribbon. Divided in seventeen equal thin stripes, eight white, and nine light-blue.

Designer. By the staff of the United Nations.

222.

United Nations Medal

Authorized by the Secretary General of the United Nations July 30, 1959, and awarded to personnel of the United States Armed Forces for service, not less than six months, with one of the following United Nations units: U.N. observers group in Lebanon, U.N. truce supervision organization in Palestine; U.N. Military observers group in India and Pakistan.

Obverse. A bronze medallion 1 and 3/8 inches in diameter. At center is the emblem of the United Nations, being that of a globe surrounded by a laurel wreath. Above this are the letters **"U.N."**

Reverse. The inscription **"In the Service of Peace."**

Ribbon. Light-blue overall with a thin white stripe towards each edge.

223.

United Nations Emergency Force Medal

I have no information on what this medal is awarded for.

Obverse. A bronze medallion 1 and 3/8 inches in diameter. At center is the emblem of the United Nations, being that of a globe surrounded by a laurel wreath. Above this are the letters **"U.N.E.F."** This is the only U.N. medal with this inscription; all the others have "U.N." only.

Reverse. Inscribed in two straight lines are the words, **"In The Service - Of Peace."**

Ribbon. At center is a wide light-blue stripe, flanked by a wide stripe of buff, a thin stripe of green, a narrow stripe of buff, a thin stripe of dark blue, edged by a narrow stripe of buff.

224.

Philippine Liberation Medal

Established by the Philippine Commonwealth government, Army Headquarters, 1944. This medal is awarded to personnel of the United States Armed Forces for service in the liberation of the Philippines from October 17, 1944, to September 3, 1945.

Obverse. A bronze medallion 1 and 3/8 inches across. At center is an Asian sword superimposed over a shield. At the top of this shield are three gold stars on white enamel, below this in a gold band is the word **"Liberty"**; below this gold band are equal vertical stripes of blue, white, and red starting at left; these three stripes are separated by gold borders. The sword is mounted vertically in the white stripe. The bottom of the shield is white enamel. This shield is then superimposed over a pair of arched wings, starting at top flowing down each side.

Reverse. Has the inscription in four separate lines, **"For The – Liberation – Of The – Philippines."**

Ribbon. Red overall having at center equal stripes of narrow blue, and white. The blue is to the left looking at the medal.

225.

Philippine Defense Medal

Established by the Philippine Commonwealth government, Army Headquarters, 1944. Awarded to personnel of the United States Armed Forces for service in defense of the Philippines from December 8, 1941, to June 15, 1942.

Obverse. A bronze medallion 1 and 1/2 inches in diameter. The outside edge of the medal is circular with ten scallops. At center is a female with sword and shield. Above her head are three stars, surrounding her is a stylized, green enameled, wreath. Just inside the wreath, at bottom right, is a map of Corregidor and Bataan. To the left of the female figure is a flower of some kind.

Reverse. In four straight lines the inscription, **"For The – Defense – Of The – Philippines."**

Ribbon. At center is a wide red stripe, in the center of the stripe are three white stars forming a triangle with one at top. Flanking this red stripe is a narrow white stripe edge with a slightly wider red stripe.

226.

Philippine Independence Medal

Established by the Philippine Commonwealth government, Army Headquarters, 1946. Awarded to personnel of the United States Armed Forces who have been awarded either, or both, Philippine Liberation and Defense Medals.

Obverse. A bronze medallion 1 and 1/2 inches in diameter. At center is a female figure, facing front, holding the staff of a Philippine flag. She is flanked by other flags in prospective view. The female figure is centered in a circle 1 and 1/8 inches in diameter, between this circle and the outside edge of the medal is the inscription, **"Philippine Independence"** separated by two five-pointed stars from the date **"July 4, 1946."**

Reverse. In six separate lines the inscription, **"Granted – Philippine – Independence – By The – United States – Of America."**

Ribbon. At center is a narrow white stripe, flanked by a narrow red stripe, a wide blue stripe, edged with a narrow yellow stripe.

227.

Republic of Vietnam Campaign Medal

This medal was authorized by the Department of Defense June 20, 1966, thus clearing the way for U.S. military personnel to accept and wear a service medal tendered by a foreign government. The requirements for this award to U.S. servicemen are that they first earn the U.S. Vietnam Service Medal and serve six months in direct support of military operations in Vietnam. If a person is wounded and evacuated before serving a full six months, they also are eligible. Posthumous awards were also made. Personnel wishing to have this medal must produce it from a commercial source.

Obverse. A gold colored medal, 1 and 3/4 of an inch across. At center is a green enameled circle 3/4 of an inch in diameter, with a thin gold border. At the center of this circle is a gold representation of the country of Vietnam; at the center of this dividing the country is a red enamel flame with a gold border; this circle is then superimposed over a white enamel, six-pointed star. Emitting from the apex between the six points are gold rays as though the white star is shining; these rays form another six-pointed star backing up the first.

Reverse. At center are two circles one inside the other. Between these two circles is the inscription, **"Chien-Dich"** at top, and **"Boi-Thinh"**, at bottom. In the middle of the center circle is the inscription, **"Viet-Nam"**. A horizontal line design fills the circle between the words.

Ribbon. At center is a narrow white stripe, flanked by a narrow green stripe, a narrow white stripe, edged by a thin green stripe. In the center of the suspension ribbon of the award medal is a small silver plated banner device with the date inscribed, **"1960-"** to denote the period of war. On the service ribbon and miniature medal is a small silver plated banner device with the last two digits of the date **"60-"** to denote the period of war.

228.

U.S. Navy Expert Pistol Shot Medal

Awarded for qualification under rigidly prescribed marksmanship requirements established by the Navy for the automatic pistol.

Obverse. A 1 and 1/4 inch bronze medallion with a 3/4 inch smaller disk superimposed at the top to which the pendent is hooked to the ribbon. The larger disk has a bull's eye target in raised relief in the center and on the lower edge in the inscription: **"United States Navy"** above the target **"Expert Pistol Shot."** Around the bigger medallion a rope edge. The smaller disk has a U.S. stylized eagle with wings outspread, grasping in its talons the traditional Navy anchor. Surrounding the eagle are thin lines or rays going out in a circle.

Reverse. Blank.

Ribbon. Navy-blue with two thin green stripes, one towards each edge.

Rank. Worn under all other U.S. and foreign medals.

Designer. U.S. Mint.

229.

U.S. Navy Expert Rifleman's Medal

Awarded for qualification under rigidly prescribed marksmanship requirements established by the Navy for either rifle or carbine.

Obverse. A 1 and 1/4 inch bronze medallion with a 3/4 inch smaller disk superimposed at the top which is hooked to the ribbon. The larger disk has a bull's eye target in raised relief in the center and on the lower edge is the inscription: **"United States Navy"** above the target **"Expert Rifleman."** Around the bigger medallion a rope edge. The smaller disk has a U.S. styled eagle with wings outspread, grasping in its talons the traditional Navy anchor. Surrounding the eagle are thin lines or rays going out in a circle.

Reverse. Blank.

Ribbon. Navy-blue with three thin stripes of green, one centered, and one toward each edge.

Rank. Worn under all other U.S. and foreign medals.

Designer. U.S. Mint.

230.

Coast Guard Expert
Pistol Shot Medal

Awarded for qualification under rigidly prescribed marksmanhip requirements established by the Commandant, U.S. Coast Guard. Authorized by the Secretary of Transportation.

Obverse. A bronze shield 1 and 5/16 inches high. Centered are crossed automatic pistols over a raised relief bullseye target lower center. In the upper part of the shield separated by a line or bar is the inscription: **"U.S. Coast Guard"** and below that the word: **"Expert."**

Reverse. Blank.

Ribbon. Navy-blue with a thin white stripe toward each edge.

Rank. Worn under all other U.S. and foreign medals.

231.

Coast Guard Expert
Rifleman's Medal

Awarded for qualification under rigidly prescribed marksmanship requirements established by the Commandant, U.S. Coast Guard. Authorized by the Secretary of Transportation.

Obverse. A bronze shield 1 and 5/16 of an inch high. Centered are crossed rifles over a raised relief bullseye target lower center. In the upper part of the shield separated by a line or bar is the inscription: **"U.S. Coast Guard"** and below that the word: **"Expert."**

Reverse. Blank.

Ribbon. A narrow Navy-blue stripe centered flanked by a thin white stripe, a wide Navy-blue stripe, a thin white, edged in a narrow Navy-blue stripe.

Rank. Worn under all other U.S. and foreign medals.

232.

Coast Guard Auxiliary Plaque of Merit Medal "A" Award

I have no information on what this medal is awarded for.

Obverse. A bronze medallion; at center is the Coast Guard crossed anchors and shield; this is superimposed over an eight-pointed star, having four large points with a smaller point in between each. This star is then superimposed over, and superimposed by, a double circle with eight indentures to represent coastal waves.

Reverse. Plain, with a rope circle around the outside edge.

Ribbon. At center is a narrow red stripe, a thin silver stripe, edged with a very thin red stripe.

Note: This medal is also referred to as the Coast Guard Auxiliary Life Saving Medal with Risk of Life.

233.

Coast Guard Auxiliary Certificate of Operational Merit "B" Award

I have no information on what this medal is awarded for.

Obverse. A bronze medallion having at its center the Coast Guard crossed anchors and shield. This is superimposed over an eight-pointed star, having four large points with a smaller point in between each. This star is then superimposed over, and superimposed by, a double circle with eight indentures to represent coastal waves.

Reverse. Plain, with a rope circle around the outside edge.

Ribbon. At center is a narrow stripe of silver, flanked by a thin stripe of red, a narrow stripe of silver, a thin stripe of red, a very thin stripe of silver.

Note: This medal is also referred to as the Coast Guard Auxiliary Life Saving Medal without Risk of Life.

234.

Coast Guard Auxiliary Certificate of Administrative Merit "C" Award

I have no information on what this medal is awarded for.

Obverse. A bronze medallion having at its center the Coast Guard crossed anchors and shield. This is superimposed over an eight-pointed star, having four large points with a smaller point in between each. This star is then superimposed over, and superimposed by, a double circle with eight indentures to represent coastal waves.

Reverse. Plain, with a rope circle around the outside edge.

Ribbon. Silver overall having a narrow red stripe toward each edge.

235.

Coast Guard Auxiliary Specialty Training Ribbon Bar

No medal awarded.

Ribbon. At center is a narrow silver stripe, flanked by a thin blue stripe, a narrow silver stripe, a thin blue stripe, edged with a very thin silver stripe.

236.

Coast Guard Auxiliary Courtesy Examiner Medal

I have no information on what this medal is awarded for.

Obverse. A bronze medallion having at its center the Coast Guard crossed anchors and shield inside a small circle. This is then superimposed over a stylized five-pointed star similar to the Legion of Merit; inside each point are two rays, or lines, starting from the small circle at center going outward, to almost the outside edge of the point. This five-pointed star is then superimposed over a two ring, stylized pentagon.

Reverse. Plain, with a rope circle around the outside edge.

Ribbon. At center is a wide blue stripe, edged by a wide silver stripe.

237.

Coast Guard Auxiliary Instructor Medal

I have no information on what this medal is awarded for.

Obverse. A bronze medallion having at its center the Coast Guard crossed anchors and shield inside a small circle. This is then superimposed over a stylized five-pointed star similar to the Legion of Merit; inside each point are two rays, or lines, starting from the small circle at center going outward to almost the outside edge of the point. This five-pointed star is then superimposed over a two ring, stylized pentagon.

Reverse. Plain, with a rope circle around the outside edge.

Ribbon. At center is a thin silver stripe flanked by a narrow blue stripe, edged with a wide silver stripe.

238.

Coast Guard Auxiliary Operational Service Medal

I have no information on what this medal is awarded for.

Obverse. A bronze medallion having at its center the Coast Guard crossed anchors and shield inside a small circle. This is then superimposed over a stylized five-pointed star similar to the Legion of Merit; inside each point are two rays, or lines, starting from the small circle at center going outward to almost the outside edge of the point. This five-pointed star is then superimposed over a two ring, stylized pentagon.

Reverse. Plain, with a rope circle around the outside edge.

Ribbon. At center is a narrow blue stripe, flanked by a narrow silver stripe, a narrow blue stripe, edged with a narrow silver stripe.

239.

Coast Guard Auxiliary Five Year Membership Medal

I have no information on what this medal is awarded for.

Obverse. A bronze medallion having at its center the Coast Guard crossed anchors and shield inside a small circle. This is then superimposed over a stylized five-pointed star similar to the Legion of Merit; inside each point are two rays, or lines, starting from the small circle at center going outward to almost the outside edge of the point. This five-pointed star is then superimposed over a two ring, stylized pentagon.

Reverse. Plain, with a rope circle around the outside edge.

Ribbon. At center is a wide silver stripe, flanked by a wide blue stripe, edged with a wide silver stripe.

240.

Coast Guard Auxiliary District Awards Ribbon Bar

No medal awarded.

Ribbon. At center is a thin white stripe, flanked by a wide stripe of turquoise, a thin stripe of white, a narrow stripe of silver-gray, a thin stripe of white, a thin stripe of green, a thin stripe of white, edged in a thin stripe of light-green.

241.

Coast Guard Flotilla Meritorious Achievement Medal

I have no information on what this medal is awarded for.

Obverse. A bronze medallion having at its center the Coast Guard crossed anchors and shield inside a small circle. This is then superimposed over a stylized five-pointed star similar to the Legion of Merit; inside each point are two rays, or lines, starting from the small circle at center going outward to almost the outside edge of the point. This five-pointed star is then superimposed over a two ring, stylized pentagon.

Reverse. Plain, with a rope circle around the outside edge.

Ribbon. At center is a very wide green stripe, edged with a narrow stripe of silver.

242.

Coast Guard Flotilla CME
Achievement Medal

I have no information on what this medal is awarded for.

Obverse. A bronze medallion having at its center the Coast Guard crossed anchors and shield inside a small circle. This is then superimposed over a stylized five-pointed star similar to the Legion of Merit; inside each point are two rays, or lines, starting from the small circle at center going outward to almost the outside edge of the point. This five-pointed star is then superimposed over a two ring, stylized pentagon.

Reverse. Plain, with a rope circle around the outside edge.

Ribbon. Silver overall having a wide stripe of green at center.

243.

Coast Guard Flotilla PEC
Achievement Medal

I have no information on what this medal is awarded for.

Obverse. A bronze medallion having at its center the Coast Guard crossed anchors and shield inside a small circle. This is then superimposed over a stylized five-pointed star similar to the Legion of Merit; inside each point are two rays, or lines, starting from the small circle at center going outward to almost the outside edge of the point. This five-pointed star is then superimposed over a two ring, stylized pentagon.

Reverse. Plain, with a rope circle around the outside edge.

Ribbon. At center is a wide silver stripe, flanked by a wide stripe of green, edged in a wide stripe of silver.

244.

Coast Guard Flotilla Operations Achievement Medal

I have no information on what this medal is awarded for.

Obverse. A bronze medallion having at its center the Coast Guard crossed anchors and shield inside a small circle. This is then superimposed over a stylized five-pointed star similar to the Legion of Merit; inside each point are two rays, or lines, starting from the small circle at center going outward to almost the outside edge of the point. This five-pointed star is then superimposed over a two ring stylized pentagon.

Reverse. Plain, with a rope circle around the outside edge.

Ribbon. At center is a wide stripe of green, flanked by a narrow stripe of green, edged with a narrow stripe of silver.

245.

Coast Guard Flotilla Training Achievement Medal

I have no information on what this medal is awarded for.

Obverse. A bronze medallion having at its center the Coast Guard crossed anchors and shield inside a small circle. This is then superimposed over a stylized five-pointed star similar to the Legion of Merit; inside each point are two rays, or lines, starting from the small circle at center going outward to almost the outside edge of the point. This five-pointed star is then superimposed over a two ring stylized pentagon.

Reverse. Plain, with a rope circle around the outside edge.

Ribbon. Green overall, having at center a wide silver stripe.

246.

Coast Guard Flotilla Growth and Retention Achievement Medal

I have no information on what this medal is awarded for.

Obverse. A bronze medallion having at its center the Coast Guard crossed anchors and shield inside a small circle. This is then superimposed over a stylized five-pointed star similar to the Legion of Merit; inside each point are two rays, or lines, starting from the small circle at center going outward to almost the outside edge of the point. This five-pointed star is then superimposed over a two ring stylized pentagon.

Reverse. Plain, with a rope circle around the outside edge.

Ribbon. At center is a wide green stripe, flanked by a wide silver stripe, edged with a wide green stripe.

247.

Coast Guard Flotilla Public Relations Achievement Medal

I have no information on what this medal is awarded for.

Obverse. A bronze medallion having at its center the Coast Guard crossed anchors and shield inside a small circle. This is then superimposed over a stylized five-pointed star similar to the Legion of Merit; inside each point are two rays, or lines, starting from the small circle at center going outward to almost the outside edge of the point. This five-pointed star is then superimposed over a two ring stylized pentagon.

Reverse. Plain, with a rope circle around the outside edge.

Ribbon. At center is a wide silver stripe, flanked by a narrow green stripe, a wide silver stripe, edged with a narrow green stripe.

248.

Navy "E" Award

I have no information on what this ribbon is awarded for.

Ribbon. At center is a wide navy-blue stripe, flanked by a narrow white stripe, edged with a thin gold stripe.

Note: Succeeding awards are denoted by a gold **"E"** device.

249.

Navy Sea Service Ribbon Bar

I have no information on what this ribbon is awarded for.

Ribbon. At center is a wide light-blue stripe, flanked by a narrow stripe of medium-blue, a wide stripe of gold, wide stripe of red, edged with a wide stripe of navy-blue.

250.

Presidential Unit Citation – Army and Air Force

Authorized by executive order February 26, 1942, and awarded for service in a unit cited in the name of the President, for extraordinary heroism in action occurring on or after December 7, 1941.

Ribbon. The Army emblem is a blue ribbon 1 and 3/8 inches wide and 3/8 of an inch high behind a gold-colored 1/16 inch wide metal frame with laurel leaves; worn on the right breast over the pocket.

The Air Force emblem is basically the same; however, the frame is narrower so that it will fit in alignment with other ribbons on the left breast.

Designer. Arthur E. Dubois

Note: Succeeding awards are denoted by bronze oak leaf clusters.

251.

Presidential Unit Citation - Navy and Marine Corps

Established by executive order January 10, 1957, and awarded for service in a unit cited in the name of the President for outstanding performance in action.

Ribbon. Three horizontal stripes, top stripe blue, middle stripe gold, and bottom stripe red.

Note: Succeeding awards are denoted by bronze stars.

252.

Valorous Unit Award - Army

Awarded by the Army to units of the United States Armed Forces for extraordinary heroism, against an armed enemy in actions on or after August 3, 1963. It is awarded for a lesser degree of gallantry than that required for the Presidential Unit Citation.

Ribbon. At center is a narrow stripe of red, flanked by a narrow white stripe, a narrow blue stripe, a thin white stripe, a narrow blue stripe, edged with a wide red stripe. The ribbon is behind a gold-colored 1/16 inch wide metal frame with laurel leaves.

Worn on the right breast by Army personnel, on the left breast by all other branches.

Designer. By the Institute of Heraldry, U.S. Army.

Note: Succeeding awards are denoted by bronze oak-leaf clusters.

253.

Meritorious Unit Citation – Army

Awarded to a unit for at least six months of outstanding service during a period of combat on or after January 1, 1944. The Army Meritorious Unit Commendation was originally awarded to only Army units and was not authorized for wear by the other services. However, since March 1, 1961, the award can be made to any of the units of the United States Armed Forces or its Allies.

Ribbon. Scarlet behind a gold colored 1/16 inch frame with laurel leaves. Worn on the right breast by Army personnel, on the left breast by all other branches.

Designer. Institute of Heraldry, U.S. Army.

Note: Succeeding awards are denoted by Bronze oak-leaf clusters.

254.

Meritorious Unit Citation – Navy and Marine Corps

Authorized by the Secretary of the Navy December 8, 1944; awarded to units which distinguished themselves or by outstanding heroism in action against the enemy, or for valorous or meritorious achievement or service not involving combat which renders the units outstanding compared to other other units performing the same service.

Ribbon. At center is a narrow red stripe, flanked by a thin stripe of gold, a narrow stripe of blue, a thin stripe of gold, edged with a wide stripe of green.

Note: Succeeding awards are denoted by bronze stars.

255.

Philippine Republic Presidential Unit Citation

This emblem was awarded to members of the United States Armed Forces for services culminating in the liberation of the Philippine Islands during World War II. The conditions of the award were the same as would have been required for award of the United States Presidential Unit Citation. The award was made in the name of the President of the Republic of the Philippines. The Army wears the emblem in the large size on the right breast. All other branches wear a smaller size on the left breast.

Ribbon. Starting at left looking at the award, a wide blue stripe, a wide white stripe, a wide red stripe. The ribbon is behind a gold-colored 1/16 inch gold frame with laurel leaves.

Note: There are no devices authorized for succeeding awards.

256.

Republic of Korea Presidential Unit Citation

This award was made in the name of the President of the Republic of Korea. This unit emblem was first awarded to units of the United Nations Command for service in Korea under the same conditions as would be required for an award of the U.S. Presidential Unit Citation. The Army wears the emblem in the large size on the right breast. All other branches wear the smaller size over the left breast.

Ribbon. At center is a very wide stripe of white, flanked by a very thin stripe of green, very thin white, very thin red, very thin white, very thin red, very thin white, edged in a wide green stripe. In the center of the very wide stripe of white is a red and blue tah gook with the red portion worn uppermost. The ribbon is behind a gold-colored 1/16 inch frame with laurel leaves.

Note: There are no devices authorized to denote succeeding awards.

257.

Viet-Nam Presidential Unit Citation Or Friendship Ribbon

The emblem was tendered to the United States Military Assistance Advisory Group in Indo-China for services rendered during August and September 1954. The Army wears a large version of the emblem on the right breast. The other branches wear a smaller size over the left breast.

Ribbon. At center is a narrow red stripe, flanked by a thin gold stripe, a narrow red stripe, edged with a wide gold stripe. The ribbon is behind a gold-colored 1/16 inch frame with laurel leaves.

Designer. Heraldic Section, Ministry of Armed Forces, Republic of Vietnam.

258.

Republic of Vietnam Civil Actions Unit Citation

Awarded by the Republic of Vietnam to units of the United States Armed Forces in recognition of meritorious civil action service.

Ribbon. At center is a narrow dark green stripe, flanked by a very thin red stripe, a very wide dark green stripe, a wide red stripe, edged with a narrow dark green stripe. The ribbon is behind a 1/16 inch, gold-colored, frame with laurel leaves. At the center of the ribbon is a bronze palm branch.

Note: The Army wears the larger size over the right breast; all other branches wear the smaller size over the left breast.

259.

Republic of Vietnam Cross
Of Gallantry Unit Citation

Awarded by the Republic of Vietnam to units of the United States Armed Forces in recognition for valorous combat achievement.

Ribbon. At center is a narrow gold stripe, flanked by a very thin red, thin gold, very thin red, narrow gold, very thin red, thin gold, very thin red, narrow gold, very thin red, thin gold, very thin red, narrow gold, very thin red, thin gold, very thin red, narrow gold stripes edged with a wide red stripe. This ribbon is behind a 1/16 inch gold-colored frame with laurel leaves. At the center of the ribbon is a bronze palm branch.

Note: The Army wears the larger size over the right breast; all other branches wear the smaller size over the left breast.

260.

Merchant Marine Pacific War
Zone Ribbon Bar

Authorized by Act of Congress May 10, 1943, and awarded to crew members of the ships operated by or for the War Shipping Administration who served in the Pacific War Zone which included the North Pacific, South Pacific, and the Indian Ocean east of 80 degrees east longitude, during the period December 7, 1941, to March 2, 1946.

Ribbon. At center is a wide red stripe, flanked by a narrow white stripe, a narrow blue stripe, a wide stripe of red and lavender, edged with a wide stripe of yellow.

Designer. Headquarters Staff, Maritime Administration.

261.

Merchant Marine Atlantic War Zone Ribbon Bar

Authorized by Act of Congress May 10, 1943, and awarded to crew members of ships operated by or for the War Shipping Administration who saw service in the Atlantic War Zone, including the North Atlantic, South Atlantic, Gulf of Mexico, Carribbean, Barents Sea, and the Greenland Sea, during the period from December 7, 1941, to November 8, 1945.

Ribbon. At center is a wide stripe of maroon, flanked by a wide stripe of blended white, lavender, a thin stripe of burgundy, a thin stripe of lavender edged with a narrow stripe of maroon.

Designer. Headquarters Staff, Maritime Administration.

262.

Merchant Marine Mediterranean, Middle East War Zone Ribbon Bar

Authorized by Act of Congress May 10, 1943, and awarded to crew members of ships operated by or for the War Shipping Administration who served in the zone including the Mediterranean Sea, Red Sea, Arabian Sea, and Indian Ocean West of 80 degrees east longitude, during the period from December 7, 1941, to November 8, 1945.

Ribbon. At center is a narrow stripe of white, flanked by a narrow stripe of green, a wide stripe of yellow, a narrow stripe of red, narrow stripe of white, edged with a narrow stripe of blue.

Designer. Headquarters Staff, Maritime Administration.

263.

Merchant Marine Gallant Ship Citation

Authorized by Act of Congress May 10, 1943, and awarded to officers and seamen who served on a ship which, at the time of such service, between December 7, 1941, and July 25, 1947, was cited for gallantry by the Administrator of the War Shipping Administration. In the center of the citation ribbon is a tiny silver sea horse; reactivated by Act of the 84th Congress, effective July 24, 1956.

Ribbon. Aqua-green edged with a tiny white stripe.

Designer. Headquarters Staff, Maritime Administration.

264.

Merchant Marine Defense Ribbon Bar

Authorized by Act of Congress May 10, 1943, and awarded for service in the U.S. Merchant Marine prior to Pearl Harbor. It may be worn by all Merchant Seamen who served as members of the crews of U.S. merchant ships between September 8, 1939, and December 7, 1941.

Ribbon. At center is a wide black stripe blended into dark red, which is blended into red, which is blended into light red, which is blended into buff, which is blended into white, edged with a narrow stripe of green.

Designer. Headquarters Staff, Maritime Administration.

265.

Merchant Marine Combat Ribbon Bar

Authorized by Act of Congress May 10, 1943, and awarded to Merchant Seamen who served on a ship which at the time of such service was attacked or damaged by an instrumentality of war between December 7, 1941, and July 25, 1947.

Ribbon. In horizontal stripes starting at top is a wide stripe of light-blue, a thin stripe of white, a narrow stripe of red, a thin stripe of white and having at bottom a wide stripe of dark-blue.

Note: A silver star is attached if the seaman was forced to abandon ship. For each additional abandonment a star is added.

Designer. Headquarters Staff, Maritime Administration.

266.

Merchant Marine Korean Service Ribbon Bar

Awarded for service between June 30, 1950, and September 30, 1953, in waters adjacent to Korea.

Ribbon. At center is a wide blue stripe blended into white, which is blended into red, which is blended into and edged with white.

Designer. Headquarters Staff, Maritime Administration.

267.

Merchant Marine Vietnam Service Ribbon Bar

Awarded to personnel for service on U.S. ships serving in waters in and adjacent to Vietnam.

Ribbon. At center is a thin red stripe, flanked by a thin yellow stripe, a thin red stripe, a wide yellow stripe, and edged with a narrow blue stripe.

Designer. R.A. Chandler, Maritime Administration.

268.

Combat Action - Navy, Marine Corps and Coast Guard Ribbon Bar

For active participation in ground or surface combat subsequent to March 1, 1961, while in the grade of captain, colonel or junior thereto.

Ribbon. Starting at left looking at the ribbon, a wide blue stripe, a wide yellow stripe, a thin red stripe, thin white, thin blue, a wide yellow, and a wide red stripe.

269.

NATO Ribbon Bar

I have no information on what this ribbon is awarded for.

Ribbon. At center is a very wide black stripe, flanked by a narrow light-blue stripe, a narrow white stripe, a narrow red stripe, edged with a narrow white stripe.

270.

Air Force Longevity Ribbon Bar

Awarded for four years of active service in any branch.

Ribbon. At center is a wide dark-blue stripe, flanked by a narrow light-blue stripe, a narrow dark-blue stripe, a narrow light-blue stripe, edged with a narrow stripe of dark-blue.

Note: Bronze oak leaves denote succeeding awards.

271.

Air Force Training Ribbon Bar

I have no information on what this ribbon is awarded for.

Ribbon. At center is a wide red stripe, flanked by a wide stripe of blue, a narrow yellow stripe, edged by a narrow blue stripe.

272.

Air Force Overseas Short Service Ribbon Bar

I have no information on what this ribbon is awarded for.

Ribbon. At center is wide blue stripe, flanked by a thin white, thin light-blue, thin white, thin light-blue, thin white stripes, edged with a narrow light-blue stripe.

273.

Air Force Overseas Long Service Ribbon Bar

I have no information on what this ribbon is awarded for.

Ribbon. At center is a wide blue stripe, within it are three evenly spaced vertical dotted stripes; flanking this blue stripe are thin stripes of white, light-blue, white, light-blue, white, edged with a narrow stripe of light-blue.

274.

Air Force Outstanding Airman Of the Year Ribbon Bar

Awarded to Airman selected as outstanding Airman of the year or Distinguished First Term Reenlistee of the Air Force.

Ribbon. At center is a wide white stripe, flanked by a narrow blue stripe, a narrow orange stripe, edged with a very wide light-blue stripe.

275.

Air Force Outstanding Unit Award Ribbon Bar

In recognition of achievement of a unit whether in peacetime or wartime.

Ribbon. At center is a narrow red stripe, flanked by a thin white stripe, a wide blue stripe, a thin white stripe, edged with a narrow red stripe.

Note: A bronze "V" device is worn to denote award for combat or direct combat support actions.

276.

Air Force Organizational Excellence Award Ribbon Bar

In recognition of achievement of an organization or activity whether in peacetime or wartime.

Ribbon. At center is a narrow blue stripe, flanked by a thin white, a wide red, a thin white, edged with a narrow blue stripe.

Note: A bronze "V" device is worn to denote award for combat or direct combat support action.

277.

Air Force Non-Commissioned Officer Academy Graduate Ribbon Bar

For graduation from an accredited Air Force Non-Commissioned Officer Academy.

Ribbon. At center is a narrow red stripe, flanked by a slightly thinner blue stripe, a wide red stripe, a thin white stripe, edged with a narrow red stripe.

278.

Air Force Recognition Ribbon Bar

I have no information on what this ribbon is awarded for.

Ribbon. At center is a wide red stripe, flanked by a very wide light-blue stripe, a thin white stripe, edged with a thin red stripe.

279.

Air Force Small Arms Expert Marksman Ribbon Bar

Awarded to Air Force personnel who qualify as **"Expert"** in small arms marksmanship.

Ribbon. At center is a very wide green stripe, flanked by a thin yellow stripe, edged with a wide light-blue stripe.

280.

Army Non-Commissioned Officer Ribbon Bar

For graduation from an accredited Army NCO Academy.

Ribbon. At center is a wide black stripe, flanked by a thin gold stripe, a wide green stripe, a narrow gold stripe, edged with a wide green stripe.

281.

Army Service Ribbon Bar

I have no information on what this ribbon is awarded for.

Ribbon. At center is a wide blue stripe, flanked by a narrow green, narrow yellow, wide orange stripes, edged with a wide red stripe.

282.

Army Overseas Ribbon Bar

I have no information on what this ribbon is awarded for.

Ribbon. At center is a wide maroon stripe, flanked by a thin yellow, a very wide light-blue stripes, edged with a narrow dark blue stripe.

283.

Navy Unit Commendation Ribbon Bar

Awarded to Navy or Marine Corps personnel for outstanding heroism in action or extremely meritorious service, other than combat, in support of military operations.

Ribbon. At center is a wide green stripe, flanked by a narrow red, narrow yellow stripes, edged with a narrow blue stripe.

Note: Bronze stars denote succeeding awards.

284.

Coast Guard Unit Commendation Ribbon Bar

Awarded to a unit for meritorious service rendering it outstanding, compared to others providing similar services.

Ribbon. At center is a thin white stripe, flanked by a wide green, a narrow red, narrow yellow stripes, edged with a narrow stripe of blue.

Note: A silver "O" device for operational distinguished service denotes an award for operational performance.

285.

Navy Reserve Special Commendation Ribbon Bar

Authorized by the Secretary of the Navy April 16, 1946, for award to those officers of the organized reserve who officially commanded in a meritorious manner for a period of four years between January 1, 1930, and December 7, 1941, in an organized battalion, squadron, or separate division of the Naval or Marine Corps Reserves and had a total service in the Reserve of at least 10 years. Four years of commanding such units were required for award of the ribbon but they need not have been continuous.

Ribbon. At center is a wide green stripe, flanked by a wide red stripe, a narrow gold stripe, edged by a thin blue stripe.

286.

Coast Guard Reserve Meritorious Service Ribbon Bar

Awarded for four consecutive years of meritorious enlisted service in the Coast Guard Reserve.

Ribbon. At center is a narrow white stripe, flanked by a narrow blue stripe, a wide red stripe, a thin gold stripe, edged with a narrow blue stripe.

287.

Marine Corps Reserve Ribbon Bar

Awarded by the Commandant of the Marine Corps to personnel of the Marine Corps Reserve who had completed ten years of honorable service in the Reserve between December 17, 1945, and December 17, 1964.

Ribbon. A tarnished gold color overall, edged with a thin stripe of scarlet.

Note: Succeeding awards of the ribbon are shown by bronze stars.

288.

Navy Distinguished Marksman Distinguished Pistol Shot Ribbon Bar

Awarded to individuals who have won three medals in either or both National Rifle Matches, or who have won two medals in National Rifle Matches and a place medal in either Force or Fleet Rifle Matches.

Ribbon. At center is a wide blue stripe, flanked by a thin green stripe, a wide blue stripe, a thin green stripe, edged with a narrow blue stripe.

289.

Navy Distinguished Marksman Ribbon Bar

I have no information on what this ribbon is awarded for.

Ribbon. At center is a thin gold stripe, flanked by a wide blue stripe, a thin gold stripe, edged with a narrow blue stripe.

290.

Navy Distinguished Pistol Shot Ribbon Bar

I have no information on what this ribbon is awarded for.

Ribbon. Blue overall with a thin gold stripe toward each edge.

291.

National Matches Marksmanship Medals

The National Matches Marksmanship Medals are awarded by the National Board for the Promotion of rifle practice, under the Department of Defense. Many of these matches are open to all branches of the Armed Forces and to civilians. I have no information on how many different National Marksmanship Medals there are but to my knowledge all of these medals are authorized for wear upon military uniforms on specified occasions.

Ribbon. To the best of my knowledge all of these medals have the same ribbon; being that of equal stripes of red, white, and blue.

292.

Organization of American States Medal

In 1965 the United States sent troops into the Dominican Republic. All troops who were involved were to receive this medal but for some reason President Johnson blocked the issuing of this medal, and the medal was never issued.

Obverse. A bronze medallion 1 and 1/4 inches in diameter. At center is a map of North and South America. Around the outside edge of the medal is the inscription, **"Fuzrea InterAmericana de Paz"**; at bottom are crossed olive branches.

Reverse. At center is the inscription, **"Al Merito"** surrounded by a fancy line design.

Ribbon. Starting at the left, looking at the medal is a narrow stripe of white, a thin stripe of blue, a thin stripe of black, a thin stripe of red, a thin stripe of white, a thin stripe of yellow, a thin stripe of light green, a thin stripe of black, edged again with a narrow stripe of white.

293.

United States Coast Guard Reserve Unit Citation

Awarded to personnel of the United States Coast Guard Reserve for outstanding heroism in action or extremely meritorious service, other than combat, in support of military operations. This award is a ribbon bar only at this time.

Ribbon. At center is a narrow stripe of light blue, flanked by a narrow stripe of white, a wide stripe of green, a narrow stripe of white, edged with a narrow stripe of purple.

190. HUMANITARIAN SERVICE MEDAL

This medal was authorized April 1, 1975. The following are some of the operations.

Eagle Pull
Frequent Wind
Baby Lift
Evacuation of Laos
New Life?New Arrival
Typhoon Olga
Lion Assist
Typhoon Pamela
Teton Dam Disaster
Guatemalian Relief
NMCB 40
NMCB 1
Evacuation Operations Lebanon
Big Thompson Flood Disaster
Bolivian Commercial Disaster
Turkey Earthquake Operation
Snow Go
Canary Islands (Comm. Aircraft Disaster
Port au Prince Relief Operation
Appalachian Flood Relief
Johnstown, Penn. Flood
Flood Releif of Texas
N. Carolina Flood Relief
Washington State Flood Relief
Operation Snow Blow & Snow Blow II
Jonestown Guyana Disaster
Sn. Lanka Disaster Relief
Louisana Tornado Operation
Northern Ill. Snow Relief
Evacuation of US Pers. Iran
Texas Tornado Operation
No Dakata Relief Operation
Red RiverNo. Operation
Zaire Airlift Operation
Jackson MS. Flood Operation
Cheyenne Wyo. Tornado Operation
Nicaragua Noncombatants Evacuation
Panama Canal Company

Dominican Republic Disaster Relief Operation
Dominican Disaster Relief Operation
Jamaica Disaster Relief Operation
Majuro Atoll Disaster Relief Operation
Azores Disaster Relief Operation
Hurricane Fredrick Disaster
Nicaragua Disaster Relief Operation
San Bernardino Flood/Mud Slide
Enewetak Radiological Cleanup Operation
Gallup Indian Medical Center Relief Operation
Indochinese Refugee Relief Operation
Rescue of Hostages in Iran
Cuban Refugee Resettlement Operation Costa Rica
Liberia Evacuation
Grand Island Neb. Tornado Disaster Relief
Haiti Hurricane Relief Operation
Saint Lucia Hurricane Relief Operation
Sigeria Earthquake Disaster Relief Operation
Italy Disaster Relief Operation
Saipan Disaster (Typhoon Dinah)
Operation Boat People
USS Reasoner
USS Flasher
USS Francis Hammond
USS Shipple
USS Downes
USS Robert E Perry
USS McCormick
USS Safeguard
USS Chicago
USS Jouett
USS Rathbourne
USS Badge
Cuban Refugee Resettlement in CONUS
Mt. St Helens Rescue & Recovery Operation
Haitian Refugee Resettlement Operation
Strike by Civilian Air Traffic Controllers
Air Florida Crash Recovery Operation

This is up to Jan. 1982